CUTTING EDGE ADVERTISING

HOW TO CREATE THE WORLD'S BEST PRINT FOR BRANDS IN THE 21ST CENTURY

Jim Aitchison

PRENTICE HALL

Singapore   New York   London   Toronto   Sydney   Mexico City

Published in 1999 by
Prentice Hall
317 Alexandra Road
#04-01 IKEA Building
Singapore 159965

Prentice Hall offices in Asia: *Bangkok, Beijing, Hong Kong, Jakarta, Kuala Lumpur, Manila, New Delhi, Seoul, Singapore, Taipei, Tokyo*

Printed in Singapore

5   4   3   2   1
03   02   01   00   99

ISBN 0-13-012897-X

Prentice-Hall (Singapore) Pte Ltd, *Singapore*
Prentice Hall, Inc., *Upper Saddle River, New Jersey*
Prentice Hall Europe, *London*
Prentice Hall Canada Inc., *Toronto*
Prentice Hall of Australia Pty Limited, *Sydney*
Prentice Hall Hispanoamericana, S.A., *Mexico*

CONTENTS

The Cast
(In order of appearance)

Indra Sinha	Bob Barrie
Roy Grace	Ron Mather
Lionel Hunt	Saint Augustine
Hugh Mackay	Bruce Bildsten
David Abbott	Bertrand Russell
Tim Delaney	Carl Jung
Neil Godfrey	Steve Browning
Mary Stow	Bill Bernbach
Neil French	Ezra Pound
John Hegarty	Rod Wright
Nick Cohen	Will Self
John Salmon	Jean-Marie Dru
Bill Oberlander	Fiona Clancy
Jeff Goodby	Antony Redman
Howard Gossage	Rick Scott-Blackhall
Kirk Souder	Mike Skelton
Gary Goldsmith	Jay Pond-Jones
Siimon Reynolds	Charles Liddall
David Droga	David Mattingly
Ed McCabe	Patrick Low
Ian Batey	Dorothy Parker
Graham Fink	Dean Buckhorn
Leon Festinger	Robin Wight
Dr Herbert Krugman	Rowan Chanen
Andrew Ehrenberg	Ted Royer
Oscar Wilde	Malcolm Pryce
Simon Sherwood	Marc Schattner
Bob Isherwood	Frank Lowe
Garry Abbott	Steve Elrick
Steve Henry	Dean Hanson
Guido Heffels	Phil Marchington
Richard Kirshenbaum	Danny Higgins
Jonathan Bond	Peter Soh
Jim Mountjoy	John Messum
William Shakespeare	Bill Gallacher

Mike Lescarbeau	Theseus Chan
John Bevins	David Chin
Tony Brignull	Kim Thorp
Jarl Olsen	Ken Double
Rick Dublin	Steve Cooper
George Lois	Evan Purdie
Andrew Clarke	Alexandra Taylor
Simon Mainwaring	Carl Ally
Dean Mortenson	Oakley Hall
Norman Alcuri	Jorge Luis Borges
Ben Hunt	Ernest Hemingway
John Clang	John Hersey
Francis Tan	William Wordsworth
Steve Dunn	Eric Lomax
Scott Sheinberg	Raymond Chandler
Heintje Moo	Rudyard Kipling
Gordon Tan	Dylan Thomas
Yue Chee Guan	Jack Kerouac
Linda Leong	Richard Foster
Paul Ruta	Peter Souter
Len Cheeseman	Malcolm Duffy
Chris Bleakley	Charles Dickens
Maggie Mouat	Daphne du Maurier
Helmut Krone	Mike Boles
Paul Arden	Samuel Goldwyn
Chet Baker	Jay Furby
Tom Lichtenheld	Linda Locke
Daniel Lim	Andrew Bell
Edmund Choe	David Guerrero
Jagdish Ramakrishnan	Robert Gibralter
David Fowler	Michael Ball
Andrew Bruck	Judy Wald
Eric De Vries	Sir Alec Guinness
Gerard Huerta	Ron Brown
Daniel Pelavin	Anthony Vagnoni
Tham Khai Meng	Gee Thomson
Michael Lui	Michael Lynch
Janet Woolley	Ken McKenzie
Robin Heighway-Bury	Lee Strasberg

FOREWORD

"You will, Oscar; you will."

I wish *I'd* said that.

I'm a sucker for quotation anthologies, aren't you? I've got dozens of them, and most are exactly the same.

But still I browse for an original thought, usually while on the bog, and the sense of achievement in finding *exactly* the phrase you're looking for is a pleasure that transcends the most spectacular of dumps.

Sorry, I was away there, for a moment. Happy days, happy days. Where were we? Right. Book review.

You know, when you consider how many excellent writers have spent at least a *little* time in ad agencies, it's rather odd that there are so few good books on the subject.

The first I read, when I was still grovelling for unpaid rents, in Birmingham's red-light district, was Vance Packard's *Hidden Persuaders*. It sounded like being a sort of spy, and I fancied the idea mightily, at the time. (It would sure beat being thumped by pimps on a daily basis, anyway.)

Then, too late, after I joined up, and my job consisted of scrabbling about in a damp cellar, looking for printing blocks, came *Those Wonderful People Who Gave You Pearl Harbour* by Jerry Della Femina.

OK, then! We weren't James Bonds. We were jolly, rollicking, devil-may-care iconoclasts, with a witty rejoinder for the dullest client. Even if we had names like a brand of sanitary napkins. *Much* better.

(I wonder if Jerry ever had to kill a rat with a printing block, to stop it making a nest in the media files. Just a thought.)

It was only *much* later, after I'd graduated to waisted suits with Jason Queen cuffs, that I read David Ogilvy's brilliantly disguised, direct-selling piece for his agency, *Confessions of an Advertising Man*. Even the *title* was a con. You *had* to love the old bugger, for his sheer audacity.

But that's about the lot. There have been others, too many others, but they've all been close relatives of these three. Or deadly dull, and utterly misleading, 'How To' tomes that must have been the cause of umpteen failed careers.

But Aitchison has cracked it, I reckon.

Look how thick this book is; Jim actually wrote about a quarter of it, at most. Money for jam!

His annoyingly simple idea was to allow *other* people to write the damn thing for him.

(Note, children, how the writer is finally bringing the piece round to the point where it has some vague relevance to the otherwise baffling 'headline'. You'll find this tip on ... whatever page it's on. Can't be bothered to look it up. I'm doing this for free, you know.)

Hang on. I've lost the thread again.

OK. Got it. The snag about David Ogilvy's books are that they're the firmly-held opinions of a single mind. However brilliant, that's limiting, by its own definition.

Aitchison has persuaded anyone who's anyone in this racket to turn over the tricks of their trade to him. In fact, if you look at the list of 'contributors' and find any glaring absentees, Jim probably asked them stuff, and they didn't bother to respond. Their loss, I tend to think.

This is destined to be essential reading for anyone in the business or thinking of getting into it. The book would be inestimably useful to any client who wondered how his money was spent, and wanted to get more bang for his buck. (Mind you, in the latter case, he'd have to concede that he didn't already know all there was to know, so perhaps not, after all.)

Finally, the *fun* thing about reading this is that Jim has quoted each contributor verbatim. As he put it to me, "letting the individual vocabularies and rhythms of the actual voices delineate the speakers". (Sorry, what's that in English, James?)

But it works. Only Indra Sinha burbles and booms *quite* like Indra, and you can hear him in these pages. Only Hegarty has *quite* such an icy mastery of clipped syntax, and the studied pause and throwaway; listen while you read.

And apparently only *I* sound like a rambling, babbling, incoherent twat.

Thanks a bundle, Jim.

I hope yer book rots on the remainder shelves.

Neil French
Worldwide Creative Director
Ogilvy & Mather

WITH SPECIAL THANKS

To Andrew Clarke, Saatchi & Saatchi, London, for designing the covers; to Jenny Wee, who typed everything between them; to Michael Larsen, literary agent and author, for invaluable advice; to Shutter Bug Photography Services and ProColor, Singapore, for all their professional help; and to everyone who generously contributed their time and talent in my quest for information.

Cover artwork: Paul Clarke

ACKNOWLEDGEMENTS

Extract from *The Confessions of Saint Augustine* by E. M. Blaiklock, Copyright © 1983 by E. M. Blaiklock, reproduced by permission of Hodder and Stoughton Limited and William Neill-Hall Ltd.

Extracts from *Why Don't People Listen?*, republished as *The Good Listener*, by Hugh Mackay, Copyright © Mackay Research Pty Limited 1994, published by Pan Macmillan Publishers Australia, permission granted by the copyright owner care of Curtis Brown (Aust) Pty Ltd.

Extracts from *The Art & Craft of Novel Writing* by Oakley Hall, Copyright © 1989 by Oakley Hall, used by permission of Story Press, an imprint of F&W Publications, Inc.

Extracts from interview with Will Self in *Publishers Weekly*, 8 September 1997, reprinted with permission of Publishers Weekly.

Extract from *Rebecca* by Daphne du Maurier reproduced with permission of Curtis Brown Ltd., London, on behalf of the Estate of Daphne du Maurier. Copyright © Daphne du Maurier.

Extract from *A Tale of Two Cities* by Charles Dickens, published by Penguin Books USA Inc., by courtesy of Penguin Putnam Inc.

Extracts from *Under Milk Wood* by Dylan Thomas, Copyright © 1952 by Dylan Thomas, published by J. M. Dent & Sons Ltd., reprinted by permission of the Trustees for the Copyrights of Dylan Thomas and New Directions Publishing Corporation.

Extracts from *The Railway Man* by Eric Lomax, Copyright © Eric Lomax 1995, reprinted by permission of the publishers, Random House UK Limited and W. W. Norton & Company, Inc.

Extract from *Strasberg at The Actors Studio* by Lee Strasberg, edited by Robert H. Hethmon, Copyright © 1965 by Lee Strasberg and Robert H. Hethmon, reprinted by permission of Theatre Communications Group, Inc.

1

UNCONVENTIONAL WISDOM

"The written word is the deepest dagger you can drive into a man's soul."

British writer Indra Sinha should know. His print campaign for Amnesty International punctured public apathy and raised a fighting fund against oppression.

Ironically, print advertising itself has become a victim, burdened with more outdated rules and creative conventions than any other medium. The evidence of intellectual oppression is alarming. Hall of Fame art director Roy Grace calls it "a high level of mediocrity". Others are less kind.

But while print is the oldest advertising medium, it is also the most resilient. In the post-war years, it witnessed the transition from one type of advertising to another. It will again become the front line in the battle between the prevailing wisdom of one century, and the unconventional wisdom of the next.

Print exercises an irresistible charisma. It is the permanence of the page, the romance of paper and ink, the presses thundering at midnight. No television channel would dare call itself a *Tribune* or a *Chronicle* or a *Guardian*, nor claim to speak for the *Times* in which we live. Only the economy of print can *Telegraph* a message. Only the power of print can *Post* an image in the mind's eye. Only the pages of *Time, Newsweek, Fortune* and *The Economist* can report world events while shaping them at the same time. There could never be a *Viewer's Digest*, only a *Reader's Digest*. If television reduces us, print enlarges us.

"It's interesting that nothing has killed off the printed word," muses Lionel Hunt of Australia's Lowe Hunt & Partners. "Not radio, not cinema, not television, not even the Internet, which is still largely a print medium anyway. Whenever there's a new medium invented, there are always these dire predictions about the demise of the earlier ones, but it just doesn't happen. OK, so silent movies aren't that big at the moment, but Marcel Marceau still makes a living."

Print creativity is not the result of mystical inspiration. It is an art and, like every art, is the result of conscious effort and preparation. Developing a conscious understanding of the medium and its possibilities is the first step; individual ability and fickle inspiration will remain unconscious factors in this equation. At least for the time being.

DIMENSION

A cynic once called television a medium because it is neither rare nor well done. Yet, in comparison, print is often regarded as a passive, one-dimensional medium.

"It's a cretinous thing to say," asserts Sinha. "How much depth is there in one page of the *King James Bible*? How much depth is there in the opening line of *Lolita*?" Sinha believes the printed word has a greater capacity to free the imagination than television does. "Television imposes a visual on the viewer. It doesn't allow him the choice of imagining the world to be the way he wants it to be. Print can actually liberate the mind and create far more intense illusions, far deeper experiences, than any television or film ever will."

Australia's foremost social researcher, Hugh Mackay, agrees. "The words are asking *me* to make up the pictures, so they're *my* pictures. There's a creative act within the reader. On television, the work's all done. I only receive; I don't construct and create the way I do with print."

Britain's David Abbott of Abbott Mead Vickers regards print's effect as an all-encompassing stimulus. "It's because of what words do. They engage the *whole* mind, and you don't think or feel in one dimension. Generally in advertising, I think it's the words you remember."

At Leagas Delaney, London, Tim Delaney argues that print's strength lies in its involvement with the reader. "Print is different from television and radio in that it's slower, more rational, in a number of areas. If you're trying to create a personality, or sustain a personality, print takes longer because of its rationality, because you need to engage the reader in more than just an assertive, image-based discussion. You've got to give them something which makes them stop, look, and respond. The whole process seems to be slightly *tougher* on the recipient. Because it's tougher, it's also *deeper*. If you do care to stop, if you do want to read, if you do get into an ad, even if you just look at an image and there are no words on it, just a logo, it's somehow deeper and more rewarding than something that lasts a few seconds on television or radio."

Perhaps the silence of print reinforces its depth. The reader's mind can concentrate on what is written, and on what is written between the lines. Print permits more subtlety, more verbal and visual nuances; what Britain's most highly awarded art director Neil Godfrey describes as "an elbow touching you".

"A print ad is a journey," says Mary Stow, head of planning at London's Howell Henry Chaldecott Lury & Partners. "You can read through it, flow with the logic. In print, things are written down in black and white. It means that people are much harder on print. You've got the evidence in front of you. With television advertising, people quite willingly accept what's being done to them. They collude with it. But if you're sitting reading a newspaper, the context all around the ad is pretty hard. Real life stories, facts. Therefore, the advertising has to acknowledge people are in that state of mind. They're not reading in the same way they watch TV."

Passive or Active? Public or Private?

Print is the only medium we can hold and touch. Communication is one-to-one. The only barriers are those erected by advertisers, art directors and writers.

The physical reading experience, admits Neil French, worldwide creative director of Ogilvy & Mather, has coloured the way he creates for the medium. "Reading is governed by the length of your arms. Old blokes like me have either got their nose pressed up against the print, or they're holding their heads back and their arms out straight like they're driving a racing car." As a result, French believes these intimate, individualistic traits make print a very private medium. "The relationship between your eye and the page is a personal one. That's why people get stroppy when you read over their shoulders. It destroys the privacy of the moment."

Describing print as a private, exclusive channel, Mackay cites research on the levels of involvement with advertising. "With the Internet, and with print, the message is very close to you. You're only about twelve inches away from the page or the screen. Both are very active communication experiences. You're reading what is on the screen, manipulating the mouse or the keyboard, or you're turning the pages, a very active relationship with the medium. Whereas with television, most of the time you're just sitting there, you're not even sitting forward, and the audio-visual waterfall just flows over you. Sometimes you're alert, sometimes you're quite soporific."

The intimacy of the relationship between the reader and the page does not exist between the viewer and the television screen. According to Mackay, another reason why readers love reading is their control of the process. "It's all on their terms. They're utterly in control. If I don't like you, I'll just turn the page and you're gone."

CONTROL

If the reader has control, so too do creatives. Each time a page is turned, a curtain rises to reveal a fresh scene. Print is a stage, a personal stage, where creativity can be stamped with individuality and soul. Creatives are alone and naked on that stage. Pretentious creativity is exposed. Superficiality becomes transparent. The inept cannot escape their fate.

There is *nowhere* to hide in a print ad, stresses Hunt, who is deeply suspicious of creative teams that only want to do television. "When I am interviewing writers or art directors, particularly art directors, I always ask to see their print work first. When you see a good TV spot, it's difficult to be sure who's responsible. It can be the writer, the art director, or both, or the director, or the talent. It doesn't matter for the end result, but it does matter if you're thinking of hiring someone on the strength of it."

"Although I like TV, I'm always drawn back to print," confesses Godfrey. "I think it's the control one has. Inevitably, a TV commercial is never quite like what you'd imagined. In print, I'm in control. It's my baby. All the decisions are mine."

In print, creative shortcomings cannot be ascribed to the director, the casting department, or even the catering company. "If there are flaws in your concept," cautions Sinha, "they're your flaws, your faults. If you take the client out of the equation, there's no one to blame but yourself. Everything is under your control and therefore can be changed and adjusted if you wish it to be so."

Being armed with absolute control over infinite possibilities is a tantalising prospect. Words can be words, words can be visuals. But the toy shop is not all it appears. If print creativity offers such freedom and depth, how does that explain the plethora of mediocrity and incest?

The next stage of conscious preparation should be to draw some parameters; to identify what constitutes great, cutting edge print.

GREAT PRINT: WHAT IS IT?

Bartle Bogle Hegarty's John Hegarty is convinced that print has to do more, to work harder, to get noticed. "You could argue that it has to be more provocative. So if being more provocative means being more creative, then you've to be more creative in print."

Delaney looks for stopping power in either the headline or visual. "Not something gratuitously wacky, but something strong and relevant. And it isn't always that the strength of a line or image solves a problem. Life is more complex than that. Sometimes it's about the sixth ad in a series that stops you and clicks in."

For Abbott, the greatest print ideas are those which contain a human insight; an insight into human behaviour, for example, with which a reader can relate. "A spark of recognition is there at the root of most good communication," Abbott explains. "It's true of a painting or a novel. It's true of great advertising, too."

Nick Cohen of New York's Mad Dogs & Englishmen defines a great print ad as one that connects with people. "It's not about one that's simple, or one that's got a clever twist in it. It's one that people look at, that starts a relationship." In fact, Cohen sees connecting people with brands as the essence of all great advertising. "People have more choice than they ever did, but in the end, they vote with their dollar. They pick brands that they relate to, and that relate to them."

Insightful, impactful, provocative, connective: deceptively simple words, and any number of workmanlike ads could be rationalised to comply with them. Even the author of a headline reading "Save 50%" could argue it was provocative. But such debates are becoming increasingly academic. Print creativity is redefining itself.

A new generation of advertisers, radical new marketing paradigms, the advent of planning, and a new wave of cutting edge agencies and creatives are challenging and changing the old, established order of things.

Godfrey, whose career spanned over forty years at the cutting edge of British advertising, provides a perspective: "When I started, we were turning a corner from one type of advertising, mainly slogans and illustrations, to another. We needed to move away from the 1950s' dry brush illustrated feel where everything was a slogan that was shouted, to something much more modern. When I worked at Doyle Dane Bernbach (DDB), we did the very first full page ad. Until then, the biggest ads people had bought were half pages; mostly the ads were things like twelve-inch double columns, tiny ads. I remember doing the first double page spread in a newspaper, in colour, for Lufthansa. As the dimension of the ads grew bigger, we had to design a more angular, impactful way of doing them, no longer based on prissiness but said in a really strong way. We came into a period where we had something to say, not just showing the product."

Many of Godfrey's campaigns have become icons for the industry, slavishly imitated to this day. Yet Godfrey himself admits that if he was doing them now, they would probably look different. "I'd have to think in a completely different way, according to the style and mentality of life today. It's really quite different. There's a much broader, younger market. Things are sold directly to teenagers and younger children which, in the old days, were aimed at mothers and fathers."

John Salmon, creative director at London's Collett Dickenson Pearce, presided over that agency's golden years of creativity. His department was the legendary domain of Britain's reigning creative elite. "The advertising business is subject to fashion, there's no question about it, and a lot of the products that advertising sells have to do with fashion," he observes. "However, there are certain sorts of agencies who inch products into this arena of fashion, *regardless*. Cars, for example, are now sold on their visual appearance alone. The performance characteristics of the car, the price of the car, what the car will do for you, these things have been subordinated to the salesman." The implication is that advertising creativity in many categories will be led by external forces like the fashion industry. In certain categories, though, Salmon foresees no change. "If you're selling plates with rabbits on them, and selling them off the page, there'll be a lot of copy and the ads will look pretty much the same now as they looked ten years ago, and ten years on I'm sure they'll still look very much the same."

"I think print advertising changes *superficially*," reflects Abbott. "We go through fashions: borders, typography, coloured type, or whatever. Techniques change, but I don't think the enduring principles of good communication will change that much. I haven't noticed them change that much in all the years I've been doing it. I don't see why they should change because it's about human behaviour and reaction."

If Abbott is right, and human behaviour *is* immutable, will the fundamentals of print creativity remain the same?

Delaney sheds further light: "It's not that there's one way of doing something that's right, and another one that's wrong. *It's what's appropriate at the time.* There are some learnings, and some things that people say. You still like Volkswagen ads because they're intelligent, and they show how simple a thought can be, and yet how compelling it can be. It isn't a rule, but it's certainly something you want to try and emulate. The writing on Avis was fresh and interesting, intelligent and accessible, and all kinds of other things that most ads still aren't today. They stand as campaigns that mean something to people because they've done what everyone else has done, but they've done it in a simple way."

Appropriate at the time. If Volkswagen and Avis were appropriate in Bill Bernbach's time, what is appropriate now?

NEW RULES?

There are no rules. Sooner or later, everything must become institutionalised and formulaic. At that point, creativity must move on. Fundamentals do not change; the way we address them does. Therein lies the problem.

Advertising has existed for centuries. As Sinha reminds us: "Advertising is the second oldest profession and it arose directly out of the needs of the oldest."

Hegarty traces print advertising's lineage to identify the accumulation of conventions: "One can argue that the first poster was a food ad. It was a cave painting of a bison. Since that time, print has gathered around it a series of rules and attitudes that can be quite limiting to its development. As much as some people deplore the Apple Mac, it broke down the conventional layout that we'd all been paying homage to, the great Volkswagen layout done by Helmut Krone, the big picture, the small headline, the three columns of copy and the logo in the bottom right-hand corner. The versatility of the Mac broke that down. Things could be done in a different way."

Hegarty includes books and pamphlets in print's lineage. "Print is burdened by writing in a very profound way. There's a methodology about it which doesn't necessarily relate to the way the modern consumer approaches and touches advertising."

Hegarty argues that the art of advertising is about *reduction*: the ability to write less and say more.

"As an industry, we occupy the margins, the bits in between the editorial content, the bits in between the programmes. Therefore, our creativity is a kind of *guerilla* creativity. It comes in, makes a hit, and goes out again. It strikes me as odd that so often we make our work longer, rather than making it shorter. The French philosopher Pascal once wrote: *My apologies for this letter being so long; had I more time, it would have been shorter.* The fact is, it's harder to write less than it is to write more. Yet in our industry there's an idea that, somehow, length has a value. What we should be doing is reducing, because when you do that, you create an idea that is actually more powerful."

Hegarty's logic is that the only space he is trying to buy is inside the consumer's head. "The access point to it might be a print ad. If you take an idea down to its essentials, it has a chance of going in *faster*. The faster I can get my idea to go in there, the more likely it is to open out in there, like a seed. That's the place I want an idea to open out, *not* on the page. When I see ads where it's all written out, it's all long and complex. Sometimes, that's very much the case of what you need to do. But when you see awards for copywriting in the annuals, they always give it to a piece of long copy. They never actually give it to a very short piece of copy. If you believe Pascal, who is probably a more profound thinker than most people in advertising, it's the opposite of what it should be."

Sinha also questions current industry conventions. "We're talking to ourselves. We tend to be writing for award juries. After twenty years' experience of British advertising, anyone who says it isn't so is a liar. What you see is innovation often happening in fringe media, like compact disc sleeves, then it becomes trendy, then advertising picks it up. The distressed typefaces that punky publications put together with chewing gum and string ten years ago, which were picked up by art directors in trendy agencies five years ago, are now being picked up by art directors in mainstream agencies. It gets so boring. If we stopped being so self-regarding, so inward-looking, and looked at what the *consumer* is about, we will find new ways. If we set ourselves impossible tasks, if we tried to communicate things we might have thought were impossible to communicate, if we tried to achieve a level of impact we might have always considered to be impossible to achieve, if we made those our goals, we'd find that traditional methods are inadequate to cope with them. Therefore, by definition, we'd have to find some new ways to do it, like water running around an obstacle."

What, in fact, we are witnessing now is not so much a superficial, stylistic period of change in creative terms, but a revolution against self-imposed conventions and self-inflicted handicaps. It is advertising methodology which is being challenged, not merely its creative manifestation.

At New York's Kirshenbaum Bond & Partners, Bill Oberlander sums it up: "The Harvard Business School-Procter & Gamble matrix of how to do advertising that sells brands is *broken*. A lot of people are realising that books like Ogilvy's, and Leo Burnett's rules, even Doyle Dane Bernbach's rules, are *obsolete*. They're antiquated. There are sets of new paradigms about how to speak to consumers. You have to look at the entrepreneurs, the brands like Coke. These guys are the SWAT teams, the stealth bombers, of how to speak to consumers."

There is an ugliness about advertising, too, a crassness, which not only consumers reject.

"I'd call our philosophy *environmentalist*," says Jeff Goodby, chairman of Goodby, Silverstein & Partners, San Francisco. "I believe that advertising, like architecture or urban planning, is an unavoidable part of our environment. Thus, we want to create advertising that's intelligent, humorous, beautiful and moving. In general, a welcome and *respected* part of what we all have to walk through each day." Implicit in that belief is a rejection of the simplistic and banal. "It begins with a determination to find the *highest* common denominators, rather than the lowest, as most advertising unerringly does. We try to approach people with respect, out of a belief that if we expect a certain intelligence, attention and sense of humour on their part, we'll get it. There's a part of the circle we always leave for them to complete, which involves them in the advertising and makes it a more memorable experience." Goodby's philosophy opposes another pillar of formulaic advertising: mind-numbing repetition. "Our approach results in a kind of advertising that works, we think, without lots of repetition or exposure. As the infamous San Francisco copywriter Howard Gossage said, how many times do we have to read a book or see a movie? Once, maybe twice, even in the best cases. *Why* do we suppose that advertising must be seen over and over again to have an effect?"

Goodby's point is valid. We cannot divorce ourselves from what we inflict upon society. We should aspire to create and approve advertising of which we are not ashamed.

If we agree, then it is not an option; it becomes a responsibility.

For advertisers, agencies and creatives, the game is indeed changing. Long-held tenets and industry dogma distort our perspective, cobwebbing our view of what might be and what should be. All very well, but what is going to replace them? Anarchy?

In the search for cutting edge wisdom, it seems the new rule-book has yet to be written. There is more scope for intuitive thinking, for experimentation, for innovation. The fact that advertisers themselves are very often leading the charge has accelerated the revolution.

As Kirk Souder of Santa Monica agency Ground Zero observes: "If you ask people to create advertising, that's exactly what they'll create. If you ask people to do something more, then they'll do something more."

The question is, what are we consciously asking ourselves to do and be?

WHY BE CREATIVE?

Hegarty views creativity as the essence of humanity. "Humanity's leapt forward because it was creative; it could think, and it could put different thoughts together and come to different conclusions. It's part of what makes us what we are. It's always odd when people say to me, oh, you're creative, as though you're a different species." In Hegarty's book, everybody is creative. "You're creative when you put your clothes on in the morning, when you comb your hair, when you decide what car you're going to buy, what drink you're going to drink. It's all part of our creative persona."

Souder contends the reason for being creative has absolutely nothing to do with creating great advertising. "Being creative is about why we're here. The primary directive of existence must be growth. The moment that stops, we die. Either physically, intellectually, or spiritually." Souder draws an analogy with water. "Running water promotes life, stagnant water suffocates it. We can continue to grow by being like running water, through the experience and assimilation of new things. *By going where we haven't gone before.* That could be the execution of an ad, finding a new way home from work, or selling everything you have to live with an isolated tribe on a remote tributary of the Amazon for three years. Because the more things we *see*, the more things we *taste*, the more things we *try*, the more accurate our personal model of the universe is, and the closer we get to ultimate truth."

If Hegarty and Souder are right, and creativity is at our core, why is it that so many creative people seem prepared to accept a lesser standard?

Creativity is subjective. Some believe that writers and art directors are motivated by ego and awards. Others argue that achieving creative breakthroughs is a responsibility to their clients; the awards will follow, as French once said, like end-of-term prizes.

Cohen does not think people are happy to achieve mediocrity. "It's a very hard industry. You deal with a lot of rejection and therefore your optimism gets sucked out of you. You start second-guessing your clients, second-guessing what's possible. It grinds you down. I think they give up a little bit; they lose their optimism about why they got into the business in the first place."

Gary Goldsmith of Lowe & Partners, New York, pinpoints unrealistic expectations and pain. "Young people coming in assume that there are great clients and bad clients, and if you happen to get a great one you'll do great work. They're really all the same; you just have to make something of it. It's very hard to do good work. There's a certain amount of pain involved. You've got to force yourself into a discomfort zone of working on something, day after day, and not having it. We all want to relieve that pain, so we come up with something and we convince ourselves it's pretty good and we move on to the next. You also tend to rationalise; you tend to look up and down a hallway and say, 'Well, my work's better than the guy's in the room next to me', or 'My work's better than some other agency's work', or 'That client will never buy anything good'. So you take the pressure off yourself and put it on anything around you, instead of forcing yourself to confront the fact that if it's not good, it's *your* fault."

"There is a kind of predisposition towards the acceptable rather than the remarkable," considers Salmon. "The emphasis of a lot of clients is not harnessed to the content of their advertising so much as to the economy of it. The emphasis is on buying media economically, on ads that are not going to be controversial, and on ads that will research well. Very few clients now have the ability to say, I know a good ad when I see one. Consequently, this has an effect on creative people who say, well, they'll never buy that, and on account people who say the same, without giving the client a chance to say whether he'll buy it or not." One result of this, Salmon believes, is the stress placed on visual techniques. "If an ad has a very uninteresting content, they hope it can be overcome by visual impact."

A month before starting legendary Australian agency OMON, Siimon Reynolds said that the two most popular words in his country's advertising industry were *"That's nice"*. "You show someone an okay job and you get 'that's nice'. Ten times a week I hear it, that's nice, did a nice idea yesterday, that's nice! Nice, nice, nice, that's nice. And in a funny way, That's Nice says everything about what *isn't* nice about our industry. There isn't enough 'Is it Great?' being said. That's Nice has become the criteria at which we can stop work, satisfied."

David Droga, executive creative director, Saatchi & Saatchi, London, warns that mediocrity is contagious. "It's easy to get opinions, it's hard to get great opinions. You've got to surround yourself with people you respect. If you surround yourself with morons who say everything you do is brilliant, you'll end up being just like the morons."

Roy Grace is a veteran of the Bill Bernbach-Volkswagen era at DDB. His stance is uncompromising. "A lot of creative people are capable only of mediocrity. They take perfect aim at it and hit it right between the eyes. Mediocrity is easy. Mediocrity means being easy on yourself, taking the easy way out, not suffering, not being obsessively and compulsively focused on excellence." Grace equates cutting edge work with basic talent, drive and intelligence. "I always wanted to be the best. In my mind I said I've got to be the best, I *need* to be the best."

The choice is clear. Creative people can leave behind landmarks in their industry, or spend a lifetime in bland obscurity. There are no ifs and buts; no shades of grey.

Beyond individual aspirations is a bigger picture. Creativity is the external face of the advertising agency. Creativity is the external manifestation of the agency's culture. Every piece of creative work builds the agency's brand as well as the client's brand. Therefore, it is an inescapable fact that every lesser ad lessens the agency's brand in the market as well as the client's brand. The results of agency brand building can be measured in five ways: by the number of clients who stay or leave; by the number of pitches to which the agency is invited; by the calibre of people the agency can attract; by what the agency's competitors say about it; and by the awards the agency wins.

It is no coincidence that those new agencies which registered meteoric growth in the past three decades have all been creatively driven: America's Chiat/Day, Fallon McElligott and Wieden & Kennedy; Britain's Saatchi & Saatchi, Abbott Mead Vickers and Bartle Bogle Hegarty; France's BDDP; Australia's Campaign Palace; South Africa's Hunt Lascaris. They, and dozens more, have cut through the ranks of the establishment with unconventional campaigns for blue chip advertisers.

Their voices will be heard in the next chapter.

WHY BUY CREATIVE?

Ed McCabe said: "To produce great advertising, you need three things in an agency. The management that wants it. The creative people who can produce it. And most important of all, the clients who will buy it."

What *are* clients buying?

Rather than view creativity as dangerous, many advertisers now deem it mandatory. Apple, Nike, Benetton and Absolut have become household names as the result of breakthrough advertising ideas. The Virgin brand has defied conventional industry logic to become a record company, an airline, a megastore and a cola. Coca-Cola, meanwhile, took control of its own advertising destiny. America's cutting edge agencies are now on its roster.

"It's great clients who makes agencies great, *not* the reverse," points out Ian Batey, group chairman of Batey Ads, Singapore. "*They've* got to take the risk, *they've* got to buy the stuff and run with it. If you look around over the last twenty years, and look behind the great advertising, you'll find a great company. And behind the great company will be a great man. If you can find those guys early on, you've struck gold," says Batey. "A lot of clients treat advertising as a necessary evil. You could go through life as an advertising agency, having all those grey, boring accounts, but you've got to earn a living, so you do a decent job, the stuff works. Sometimes, in fifty or sixty accounts, there might be only ten that are really dancing, but those ten keep you electrified. Those guys knocked on your door, as much as you knocked on theirs. You connected with each other, you can relate. They've got to have trust in you, and vice versa. The entrepreneur who wants to lift his game also stimulates you. It *can't* be a one-way thing."

"At a lot of agencies," Goodby muses, "the clients are invariably treated as Neanderthal adversaries. Not only is life too short for that, but I've found that clients often have very good ideas that you can listen to, appropriate, and ultimately get credit for."

Abbott believes agencies cannot expect their clients to be courageous. "You must interest them in being effective, and educate them with evidence by the way you work with them. They are not in business to be brave."

Abbott sees a duality of interests in the agency-client relationship. "The clients you get in the early days are clients who come to you because you're small and you've got a reputation. They know that they need great work to compete, to make their pound or their dollar go further. I think the hard phase is when clients come to you who have got enough money to *blast* their way to recognition. Nevertheless, you want to use that budget, because you're the agency you are, to further your own creative reputation. You still believe that if you can make forty million look like eighty million, it's just as good as making two million look like four million."

Persuading a client to run cutting edge advertising, in Abbott's view, centres on trust. "It's about winning their confidence; it's about maybe proving yourself on some small things; it's about trying to think in terms of campaigns and not just ads, so that they understand this isn't just a one-shot piece of brilliance. It's also being careful about what clients you take; it's being honest about what you're good at, and what you're not good at. I always try and view new business in that light. 'Could we do a good job on it?' is one of the questions I think you should ask yourself, and you should be honest enough, if you say it's not really your bag, not to go for it."

THE CUTTING EDGE.
SOMETIMES, IT CAN HURT.

Life at the cutting edge is a heady mix of sacrilege and sacrifice.

The sacrilege first. Creativity is a destructive process, tearing down what has gone before and rebuilding afresh. We have to shift gears, from logic to intuition, and adjust perspectives in line with new realities. The fundamentals of human behaviour have not changed; simply the environment in which we find them, and the creative means by which we access them. To quote Delaney, it is what is appropriate at the time.

And so to the sacrifice. To create cutting edge work, to make a difference, you must first make a difference within yourself. As Oberlander puts it, "Being different is synonymous with being creative." You will need a strong, intense base for your advertising ideology. That follows in the next chapters. But do not expect an easy ride.

Sinha's advice says it all: "If you really, really, *really* are determined to get into advertising as a writer or an art director, then you'll find that you are entering a world where there are all sorts of conventions and rules already set. You can either play by those conventions and rules and try to win yourself fame and fortune that way, in which case you may not be stretching yourself. But if you're someone with protean creative urges inside you, someone who really wants to break the mould, and you want to do something that no one's ever seen before, then you've got to be prepared that the industry will not help you, because it's full of extremely conservative people who know the way it's been done since the year dot. Creative directors who have seen awards won on things for many years by doing it *their* way; clients who see that results are produced by doing it *their* way. And if you come in and say, I want to do it some *new* way that comes out of your spirit or some intuition of yours, there'll be a hell of a lot of resistance.

"But, by the same token, the people who do follow their own instincts, and fight for them, and *prevail*, they're the people who break new ground and end up setting the new standards and showing the new way forward. Like Graham Fink, they'll be the figureheads for the future."

It's in here. And it's no
smaller than a tumor
that's found in a real
breast. The difference is,
while searching for it in this
ad could almost be considered
fun and games, discovering the real
thing could be a matter of life and death.
Breast cancer is one of the most common
forms of cancer to strike women. And, if
detected at an early enough stage, it's also one
of the most curable. That's why the American Cancer
Society recommends that women over forty have a
mammogram at least every other year, and women under
forty have a baseline mammogram between the ages of 35 to 39.
You see, a mammogram can discover a tumor or a cyst up to three
years before you'd ever feel a lump. In fact, it can detect a tumor or a
cyst no bigger than a pinhead. Which, incidentally, is about the size of what
you are searching for on this page. At Charter Regional in Cleveland, you
can have a mammogram performed for just $101. Your mammogram will
be conducted in private, and your results will be held in complete confidence
and sent directly to your doctor. After your mammogram, a trained radiology
technician will meet with you individually and show you how to perform
a breast self-examination at home. And, we'll provide you with a free
sensor pad, a new exam tool that can amplify the feeling of anything
underneath your breast. Something even as small as a grain of
salt. If you would like to schedule a mammogram, just call
Charter's Call for Health at 593-1210 or 1-800-337-8184.
Oh, and by the way, if you haven't found the lump by
now, chances are, you're not going to. It was in
the 17th line. The period at the end of the
sentence was slightly larger than the
others. So think about it, if you
couldn't find it with your
eyes, imagine how hard
it would be to find
it with your hands.

CAN YOU

FIND

THE LUMP

IN THIS

BREAST?

CHARTER REGIONAL MEDICAL CENTER

CALL FOR HEALTH

5 9 3 · 1 2 1 0

Print creativity defies all rules. Words can be words, words can be visuals.
There are no limits, as Henderson Advertising, Greenville, South Carolina, proves.

2

HOW TO FIND YOUR VOICE

G reat advertising has never been produced by ambivalent minds.

Some very fundamental beliefs about advertising are now being questioned. At the root of it all are: how advertising works; whether or not traditional advertising research is still valid; and whether we should have more trust in our own intuitive skills as communicators.

As a cutting edge communicator, you will need a very strong, well-informed personal philosophy about advertising. You will need to take sides and take a stand. Understanding the fundamental elements of your craft does not mean simply intellectual comprehension. It means consciously accepting certain ideas, internalising them, and committing yourself to them. Otherwise your faith will not survive.

Once you have found your values, you will begin to find your true voice as a communicator.

CHANGING CONSUMER ATTITUDES WON'T CHANGE CONSUMER BEHAVIOUR

All too often, well-meaning souls write briefs for advertising which has to change consumer attitudes. It is an utterly fallacious objective.

Beware of believing that the way to change

consumer behaviour is to first change consumer attitudes. Attitudes tend to be the *result* of behaviour, not the cause of it.

Psychologist Leon Festinger showed that attitudinal change tends to follow behavioural change, rather than precede it. His *Theory of Cognitive Dissonance*, published in 1957, recognised that people desire stable opinions. When that state is upset, they experience a kind of tension, or dissonance, which needs to be relieved. His experiments explained how people justify their actions by changing their beliefs. In this context, advertising plays a vital role by reinforcing a new pattern of attitudes *after* a change in consumer behaviour. The more advertising creates dissonance, the more people are likely to *reject* it.

Dr. Herbert Krugman's research into advertising showed that identifiable attitude change occurs *after the purchase* and not before it. Attitudes, therefore, are significant only when tied to experience.

A perfect example is anti-smoking advertising. After years of exposure to dissonant health warnings, many smokers will grudgingly admit that their habit is harmful. While their attitude to smoking has in some way changed, their behaviour has not. In fact, their negative behaviour could well have been reinforced. What would more likely change their behaviour is a tragic experience: the death of a close relative or friend from cancer. If they quit smoking as a result, then anti-smoking messages would support their new attitude.

AWARENESS: A WARNING

Another fallacy worth exploring is *awareness*. Advertising briefs are written *ad nauseum* calling for campaigns to create awareness, as though awareness itself will guarantee purchase.

Andrew Ehrenberg has researched the relationship between advertising and consumer behaviour in the supermarket. His point is that awareness is not a highly emotional state. Nor does it imply an active predisposition to buy the brand. Rather, it means just what it says, and it may just stop at that: pure awareness. Ehrenberg believes that the trigger to purchase is more likely to come from the external world, such as a cut-price offer or an in-store demonstration, than from the internal world of attitudes and dispositions.

Like Festinger and Krugman, he concludes that advertising's main role is *reinforcing* feelings of satisfaction with brands already bought.

AND LET'S NOT FORGET RECALL

While we are about it, we should probably despatch that other old bogeyman: advertising recall.

The classroom model of advertising still lingers on. Sales managers still believe in selling points and like to list them in their ads. Researchers still believe ads can be assessed by measuring the amount of advertising content retained in the minds of consumers.

The theory sounds plausible enough: if the audience can remember what the advertising said, the advertising was effective. The reality, though, is completely different. The real test is how they *interpreted* the advertising, and what they did as a result.

For every study that shows a positive correlation between advertising recall and purchase behaviour, there is a study that shows a negative correlation. It is a lot wiser if you believe that consumer behaviour *cannot* be predicted by the recall of advertising, only by the recall of brand names.

HOW ADVERTISING *DOESN'T* WORK

Hugh Mackay explodes what he calls the Injection Myth. Advertising, he reminds us, does not work like a hypodermic needle.

In order to be effective communicators, the theory goes, we must first craft our messages carefully so as to maximise their impact on the audience. Then we choose a medium for injecting them into the minds of our target audience. We load our messages into the medium, inject them via the eye or ear, or both, and wait for them to work.

Mackay says: "We cling to the idea that messages are powerful and audiences are passive. We want people to absorb what we're saying without being distracted by their own opinions or by their feelings towards us. The things we want to communicate seem so interesting and important to us that it's hard for us to believe that they're not equally interesting and important to other people."

An equally dangerous delusion, Mackay explains, is the assumption that meanings are actually *in* our messages; that once our messages lodge in the minds of consumers, the meanings will, too.

"It's not what our message does to the reader, but what the reader does with our message, that determines our success. When we speak of a powerful message, we're really referring to the power of the message to evoke a response. *Communication occurs when the audience does something with the message.* The audience has the power to interpret the message. In communication terms, that's the ultimate power."

"People are not passive sponges just waiting there to receive your messages," warns Mary Stow. "There are a lot of misconceptions about shouting very loudly, and saying what you want to say, and it will work. Of course it won't. You should be thinking not what you're going to tell them, but what you want these people to feel and think after they've seen the advertising. Instead of writing propositions in briefs, you really should be writing *key responses.*"

How Advertising *Does* Work

The most lucid explanation you will ever find is in Mackay's book *The Good Listener.*

"We're engaged in a lifelong process of constructing personal *'cages'* around ourselves. The bars of our cages are all the things that life has taught us: our knowledge, our attitudes, our values, our beliefs, our convictions. As the cage becomes stronger and more complex, we feel increasingly comfortable inside it and increasingly confident in our ability to cope with the world beyond the cage."

"The cage is the most powerful element in the communication process. It acts as a *filter* in the process of interpretation. Because we look at the world through the bars of the cage, the bars impose their own pattern on what we see."

Suddenly we have a very clear picture of what advertising has to do. Our creativity has to find ways to penetrate the bars of the cage.

Armed with Mackay's Cage Metaphor, we can see why people interpret messages in ways that make them feel comfortable and secure. It lets us see why empowerment advertising has a better chance of working than confrontational advertising. If we attack people's attitudes head-on, the bars will simply filter out what we are saying. In fact, in the process, the bars could even be reinforced.

We can also understand why Mackay, like Tim Delaney, believes ads should be relevant, not gratuitous. "Relevance ensures that messages will find a ready point of entry to the cage," Mackay explains. "People pay most attention to messages which are relevant to their own circumstances and point of view."

Fortunately for communicators, cage-building never ends. New experiences add new bars, or *modify* existing bars. Travel is one experience which can produce new attitudes, new bars. Marriage, childbirth, divorce, bereavement, retirement, life-threatening illnesses also cause people to reassess their values and reconstruct their bars.

So how do we slip our advertising through the bars of the cage?

Mackay suggests we can send messages which act as **signposts**. Advertising can signpost a social change, or a change in behaviour by our peer group.

A good example of the cage at work: when Pepsi challenged Coke on taste, it challenged the beliefs of Coke drinkers head-on. But when Michael Jackson became Pepsi's icon, he signposted that times had changed, that Pepsi was now 'cool', and loyal Coke drinkers *gave themselves permission* to change brands.

Another form of signpost is **sending a piece of news**. News about a price drop can change behaviour. So, too, can offering something new; it is news which people have never heard before. Stow cites a pot noodle which actually contained fibre. "It was an extraordinary message because nobody thought a pot noodle had any nutritional value whatsoever. It was news and it fundamentally changed behaviour."

Advertising can send messages of **support and encouragement**. One scenario: people buying expensive cars might be feeling dissonant about their extravagance. They will actively seek out messages which help justify their action and bring their attitudes into line with their behaviour.

Here's another: Bill Oberlander recalls a campaign for a church. "I think people are a little tired of being yelled at, being busted by advertising slamming them against the wall. When I first got the church assignment, I thought advertising God would be very confrontational, very powerful, using fear as a tactic. The truth is, it was *cliched* and hackneyed. It was much easier to present a lighter side of God, with more whimsy. We called it God Lite. We promoted the fact you could call a phone number and give the cause you wanted people to pray for, whether it's finding your dog or helping your mother get better. The entire congregation would gather together on Sunday, and take your cause, *cause de jour*, and pray for it."

We can base our message on some **existing part of the cage**, so the audience can see how the brand is consistent with what they already believe. At the Campaign Palace, writer Lionel Hunt and art director Gordon Trembath did that for Footrest Shoes. Footrest was making sensible shoes designed, unusually, by women for women. The photograph showed a pair of extreme stiletto heels going over on their sides with the headline: *Most women's shoes are designed by men who never have to wear them.*

We can **share experiences**. The consumer inside the cage can live a moment of someone else's life, someone whose life mirrors their own. It does not have to be executed in a mundane, formulaic way.

As Nick Cohen observes: "The best advertising, in a lot of ways, is like the best comedy. If you look at stand-up comics, what they're very good at doing is getting a mirror and turning it back on people, capturing the mindset of the nation at the exact time, just getting people to look at how they live their lives, making us all smile and laugh at it. It's very human stuff. A lot of it is about intuition and observational humour."

We can **answer dreams**. This does not involve us in rattling the bars of the cage, trying to change attitudes or beliefs. Research will have told us what the dream is. The advertising will simply be fulfilling it.

As a general rule, Mackay counsels, we should focus on behaviour, not attitudes. And we should seek small changes, not large ones. "Erosion," he states, "is more effective than explosion."

If everything thus far has penetrated *your* cage, well and good. The bars of your cutting edge value system should strengthen and prosper.

The next subject, however, may well evoke a different response.

Support and encouragement for dissonant readers: a Mercedes-Benz might be a tad expensive, but at least you'll survive to enjoy the view should it ever overturn. Springer & Jacoby, Hamburg.

Not your average slice of life. Readers share the cruise experience of stockbroker Ted and his wife, Kate, "who wore sunblock 40 and not much else". There is nothing formulaic in this treatment by Goodby, Silverstein & Partners, San Francisco. Readers can relate to Ted and Kate, who returned to the envy of their neighbours and their dog who "knew them not".

Using an existing part of the cage: Mad Dogs & Englishmen show kids how Nickelodeon is consistent with what they already believe.

RESEARCH: FRIEND OR FOE?

"Focus groups are bogus. They're broken." Oberlander believes the more he knows about his target audience, the more he can craft the work to push the right buttons. But conventional focus groups are not the solution. "Anybody who's going to cut out an hour and a half of their time on a Thursday night to go to a very small, fluorescently lit, stale cookied, bad coffee'd room to talk about how they consume mosquito-bite ointment in their lives, I should think those people are losers."

The people who really make a difference to how brands succeed in the marketplace are what Oberlander calls opinion leaders. "They're very intelligent, very stylish, very together, and trust me, they're not going to focus groups."

John Salmon is equally sceptical. "If you think about the people who are prepared to go out and spend the evening talking about advertising, who *are* these people? If they are people who are fanatically keen on advertising and they're not in the advertising business, they should be eliminated from the sample. People who leave their homes and go out for fifteen quid, sit down with similar people and talk about advertising, these people have to be a subgroup like trainspotters. Otherwise, why else would they do it?"

"A lot of research in the advertising process is misguided," explains Mackay. "It asks people rational-sounding questions that create the expectation that there will be a rational explanation. If you ask people for a rational explanation, they'll give you one. *But it may have nothing to do with the truth.* How do you know that you wouldn't have got a different answer if you'd asked a different question? How do you know that the thing the person said mightn't actually exist *unless* you asked the question? It was only an answer to a question. It had no roots in their psyche at all."

Asking a question and getting an answer is the great pitfall of all social, marketing and advertising research. Asking questions, warns Mackay, almost guarantees that we have put a barrier between ourselves and the consumers.

There *are* rational aspects of behaviour which are very appropriate for formal questions and rational analysis: How many brands of chocolate can you name? When did you last visit a supermarket?

How much did you spend?

But when dealing with the process of connecting people to brands and responses to advertising, the problem is to create a research method which will allow people to reveal the nuances of their feelings about a certain category, to reveal to us the dreams they are dreaming that they would like to come true.

"When we've heard all that, we respond to it. And if we do, *they* in turn will respond to *us*."

Connections made between consumers and brands, and the passions aroused by certain propositions, are rarely a rational process, advises Mackay. "Of course there are rational elements in it, and the more money you're asking people to spend, the more you've got to provide them with rational things to support the process of falling in love."

The best way of understanding the advertising process, suggests Mackay, is to use the analogy of personal relationships. "Everything we need to know about how advertising works, we can learn from seeing how people fall in love, and how friendships evolve and prosper or break down. What you find when you look at why people connect with some people, and not with others, is rarely rational. If you said to someone, 'Why did you fall in love with her?', they'd look at you and say, 'How do you mean, *why?* I just did.' Suppose you asked me that question and I said, 'Well, she had this many dollars in her bank account, and I tested her IQ and it was this much, and I made some quantitative assessment of her physique, so I thought I might as well fall in love with her.' It never works like that, and neither does advertising."

Advertising, Mackay reminds us, should be a process where people respond to each other. "We've got to get away from this idea that we want people to respond to the ad. The overwhelming thought in any agency has got to be: *the ad must be a response to the people*."

"Research is the first thing we do," Cohen reveals. "Qualitative research to find out how people relate to a brand, what people think of it. You need three bits of information: what's good about it; what the culture of the company behind it is, in a very honest way, because you can't misrepresent the client and you can't misinform the consumer; and you need to know what people think of it, what baggage comes with it." Cohen quotes the example of Exxon. "There are some realities you've got to face. They're an oil company, they're out to make tons of money, and they're selling something we need to put in our cars, but it's pollutive, it's mishandled, etcetera, etcetera. So you have to take on board all of that before you do an ad. With Exxon, one of our problems is that there's a distrust towards them, people think that they're evil, so you can't ignore that. You have to address that. So our usual starting point is: how people relate to the brand, what people think of the brand, balanced up with what the brand truly is."

Attitudes to research vary, according to experience. Some call research a tool, others a crutch. The question is, has the crutch turned the industry into a cripple?

"You can ask some people in the target audience about how they feel about a brand," suggests Tim Delaney. "You can ask them how they feel about language in a category. If I'm writing an ad about a tampon, which I don't use, I may want to understand as a writer what women feel about the tampon category, what language they're prepared to accept, what they're not prepared to accept. That doesn't make me a cripple when I get the information. The issue then, about writing an ad, is that I can do it because I'm armed with the right kind of knowledge. From then on in, it's about my intuitive ability to use that information and make an ad out of it. What research *can't* do is take that ad away and confirm with six women down the road that I've done absolutely the right thing. All you'll get are different opinions and I'm not really interested in the lowest common denominator."

It is a sentiment echoed by John Hegarty. "We like to use research at BBH because it's another opinion. It's a way of finding out what is going on in the world, what consumers are doing, and testing out theories. But when it comes to *predictive* research, researching an ad to see if people like it, then I think it's seriously flawed."

Concept Testing

Mackay is adamant: *"The best advertising research never, at any stage, mentions advertising."*

Not surprisingly, he is opposed to concept testing. "Don't fall for it," he warns. "The best advertising research is the journey around the consumer's head. What we really want to know is what dreams the consumer is dreaming, and how we can position our brand in such a way that will help those dreams come true. It's a technique borrowed from therapeutic counselling: tell me about your life, and in that story I'll find *a point of connection*."

Besides, argues Mackay, the classic concept test is not a concept test. It is a *primitive* ad test.

"Concepts are mental constructs. They only exist in people's heads. As soon as you write some words on a piece of paper and draw a picture, it's not a concept. It's an expression. If you show someone an ad and get them to talk about it as if they are on some kind of consumer jury, almost certainly what you'll get is a spurious art director's or amateur copywriter's assessment. You're inviting them to be judgemental and you *don't* want consumers to be judgemental when they see your ad."

Pre-testing of rough executions and ads, in Mackay's view, is the refuge of the insecure. It also puts a little fence around what you can talk about with consumers. "All you can talk about is what is in the material. It might trigger some of the broader issues, but it's a big risk because you've already flagged what *you* think. The real challenge is to establish what concepts exist in the consumer's mind. If you can do that, you don't need to test. If you have taken the journey through the psyche of your target audience, and responded to that, you're going to have effective advertising. If you have really good people creating that advertising, it will also be brilliant as well as effective."

Hunt is concerned that clients will deny themselves the creative breakthroughs they need to build their brands. After all, creativity is the opposite of conformity. "The more research that goes into providing the brief the better, up to a point, but after that I really think you should leave it up to the creators of the ad. If they are genuine, and talented, and students of human nature, you are better off leaving it to them than to any focus group. Of course, the creative team needs to be really good and really intuitive, but if they aren't, no amount of research is going to save them."

Because advertising is intuitive, Delaney believes we cannot research our way to a solution. "Intuition, by definition, is something which is without a kind of absolutism. There isn't anything absolute about what we do. The problem that I have with research is that it tries to prove *objectively* that we are right, when the essence of what we do is *subjective*. Because agencies won't own up to the fact that what we do is subjective, they're happier dealing with objectivity which they know to be spurious. But because it's got a logic to it, they follow that instead of just saying that we're like footballers, or cellists, or ballerinas. We're as good as our born, innate talents and that's it. There's no point trying to prove that one footballer is better than another by using research; there are no absolutes in that sense."

"Everybody knows predictive research doesn't work, but it's convenient for them to believe in it." Hegarty paints a familiar scenario: "If you're in a corporation, you go along to your boss and show him something really provocative and different, and there's a sharp intake of breath. So you say, 'Oh, but I researched it, and the research said it was fine'. In other words, I'm not to blame if it goes wrong, it was the research."

"It's dangerous, extremely dangerous," says Ian Batey, whose agency credo publicly relegates concept testing to the same status as a Tasmanian transvestite. "We all know it's been a security blanket for advertisers and, I might add, for a lot of agencies. We've become such disciples of these practices, they've obsessed us. It's a disease that's getting worse as the years go by; that without the appropriate research, no one does anything. By and large, we're talking about brand managers and commercial managers, whose jobs rely on them achieving certain results every year, and they follow formulas, they follow a process. If you don't follow that process, they actually can't relate to you." Batey admires the businessmen who can trust their own judgement and marketing skills. "There are clients who can say, now listen, we've been around our business long enough that if *we* can't feel it, if *we* can't smell it, if *we* don't know what is going on, what the hell are we doing in this business?"

If people are insecure about their advertising, Mackay believes they should admit it. If the planner, the writer, the art director, the account director and the client are in *genuine* disagreement, or experiencing *genuine* doubt about whether they have caught the dream, testing ads would be appropriate. "But the testing should be as naturalistic as possible," he cautions, "and always done in homes. If it's a print ad, don't get a group discussion and hold it up. Give it to them in the context of a magazine or paper, ask them to look at it overnight and come back tomorrow for a chat."

A Different Drummer

There are no rules, and Britain's Howell Henry Chaldecott Lury & Partners has developed an unusual approach to research.

Stow explains: "We tend to avoid doing research early on in the process. We would not start by doing focus groups so we could understand attitudes to the product. We think by using observation and intelligence, we can get to that quite easily. Focus groups can so easily hold you back. People can only tell you what is *now*, not what might be possible." Instead, the agency concentrates on understanding the client organisation and the competition. "Usually when people do a competitive review, it means getting the graduate trainee to put together a little reel of ads. We take the competitive review really seriously. We deconstruct the ads and try to see exactly what the competition is doing."

The basic learning from one such review, coupled with an understanding of the client, provided the breakthrough for the agency's famous Orange Tango campaign. "Everyone else in the soft drink category was rushing headlong into the area of glorious American youth, bright teeth, very smiley-wonderful happy-healthy-people-having-good-clean-fun. That's the obvious place to go and a lot of people would think if those are the rules of the market, we'd better follow them. But we thought there was a great opportunity for someone to push youth on the streets, urban and gritty. That was where the tonality came from. Real life, *British* real life. There's a real resistance to Americana; in some ways we love it, in some ways we hate it. The tonality led us to the orange man, to the slap." Stow says the message, *The hit of real oranges*, came straight out of product delivery. "We could have gone the fresh orange route, but it wouldn't have been credible because Tango has a taste that hits you in the mouth."

The agency uses research for creative development and always produces more than one idea. "We tend to use research to find out what is possible, rather than just what is. It's very easy to think these are the rules of the market, we can't break them, we can't go any further than that. But by researching creative work which takes a brand in a different direction, we can discover what *is* possible."

Possibly the most controversial aspect of the agency's approach is the way it treats *likeability*. "In a lot of focus groups that are being watched from behind the mirror, everybody's looking for the 'that's nice' reaction, 'that's lovely', because the client behind the mirror will feel good. We actually have an allergic reaction to that response," explains Stow. "People can say 'that's nice', then file it away and ignore it. We're looking for the ideas that *worry* people a bit."

The agency believes that if it is going to change behaviour, any behaviour, the first step is to be noticed, to let people know that something is happening. It has an effect on people because it starts them questioning things. "After the groups, we try to eavesdrop on people as they leave. We try to find out which idea they're still talking about. It's an indication that it stayed in their mind, registered enough, did enough. That kind of reaction means the shock value is not just shock value; it's got something intrinsic to it that's both shocking and interesting to people, but not irrelevantly so."

RISK AND RESPONSIBILITY

With so many fundamental beliefs under siege, conservative voices urge caution. The pursuit of creativity, they say, has lost its perspective. We risk ignoring our basic responsibility to our clients, to produce what is called "effective" advertising. Certain rules, certain beliefs, certain methodologies have served the business well, and restraint is called for.

Most of the rules and methodologies have indeed served business. They have provided the cardiovascular systems of conventional agency structures. They have stifled evolution and innovation. They have proliferated mediocrity and made it respectable. The greatest risk in not taking risks is that advertisers will abandon the advertising industry and go in search of creativity elsewhere.

Oscar Wilde said: "An idea that does not involve risk does not deserve to be an idea."

If you agree that taking risks is a legitimate part of your responsibility, what specific risks should you be taking?

"The agency's responsibility is to go way *beyond* where the client could get to himself," asserts Simon Sherwood of Bartle Bogle Hegarty. "Clients can buy media, source production, do the analysis and strategy, but they can't take the creative step. If agencies don't take creative leaps, they're not doing the thing they can best do. We believe at BBH that we are manufacturing advertising properties which have a value to clients. We've always believed we should come to a very firm view about what the right kind of advertising is for a client. We never present clients with alternatives. If you do, it's an abdication of responsibility."

"An idea that hasn't been done before might, on the surface, look really risky," argues Bob Isherwood, worldwide creative director of Saatchi & Saatchi. "It's an area where no one has been before. There is no precedent. But usually the biggest risk lies in ideas that are predictable, because ideas that are predictable don't get noticed. You can't sell anything to anyone unless they notice you. To get a boring ad noticed, you've got to run it lots and lots of times. If you've got a really original message, you only need to run it a few times. People retain the message longer and it costs the client less."

"People think the low risk thing is not to run the high risk idea," observes Stow. "The biggest risk is to be safe, because if you're safe you're invisible and you waste your money."

"A lot of creative people think creative risk-taking means doing stuff that scares the life out of you," says Singapore creative director Garry Abbott. "The leaders of the industry, the Tim Delaneys and people like that, come up with things that are completely new which come out of nowhere; certainly not from last year's award books. They don't rely on borrowed ideas. Risk is about *freshness*. Ideas you haven't seen before. They give everyone a buzz, and they give the consumers a buzz because they're regaled with the sameness of advertising. Risk is about breaking rules." Abbott believes advertising should not have many rules. "We are supposed to be on the cutting edge of communications, yet we keep falling back on the same old things."

Risks must be taken at two levels, advises Mackay. "One is the risk of listening to the consumer, because when we hear what the consumer is thinking and feeling and dreaming, it might not coincide with our preconceptions. Going to the consumer and saying, tell me your story so I can really see what it's like to be you so I can respond to that, is a risk that creative people and clients are rarely prepared to take fully." The second risk? "I would define creativity as taking a set of familiar elements and rearranging them in an unfamiliar way so that the audience recognises both the familiarity and the *un*familiarity. In other words, present something the audience will recognise as themselves, their lives, their dreams, but with a twist, so they're actually a bit startled by it, or will get an extra insight from it. So it's not just a mirror, it's a mirror that's *cracked*. The safe thing is to say, 'Well, the consumer said I like X, Y and Z, so let's show them X, Y and Z'. But that's not creativity; that's journalism. Creativity is saying that's what the consumer feels, that's the dream, that's the aspiration, that's the *raw material* we're working with. Now we have to be creative with it, or we'll just be part of the bland advertising landscape and not be noticed."

CUTTING EDGE VOICES

As you begin to find your voice, it might help to hear some other voices: those agencies which not only do different work, but do their work differently.

Britain's **Howell Henry Chaldecott Lury** does unconventional work within an unconventional structure. Dedicated project teams are assigned to each account. Each team comprises an account director, a planner, a writer and an art director. There are no briefs as such; each close-knit team lives and breathes its account, literally writing its own brief as it burrows into its assignment.

As Steve Henry explains: "They work together more closely than would be allowed or encouraged in conventional agencies. They also have quasi-autonomy; for instance, the account director and planner will look at cuts of TV commercials *before* the creative director."

The system has produced some of the most electrifying work Britain has seen in two decades. It is not a cosmetic attachment to a conventional agency structure; it grew out of a belief that everybody should have a shared goal and a share in creating great work.

"In the early days of the agency, there were just the founding partners of the agency sitting together in one room, as it is when most agencies start from scratch," recalls Henry. "But the point about it for us was that we really enjoyed that method of working. We loved the kicks we got out of having three disciplines working so closely together, trying to solve problems as a genuine team, sharing responsibility and working towards a shared goal. As we grew and hired more people, we could have gone the conventional way and split up into different departments. But we wanted to preserve the magic, the chemistry, that happened when you mixed the different disciplines together."

Henry believes the agency has developed a more positive work environment as well as achieving work which hits its dual target of being surprising and effective. He admits that imposing a system of shared responsibility on people can take some getting used to. "But cynics who join the agency soon find that they couldn't possibly work any other way."

Meanwhile, years ago in Hamburg, **Springer & Jacoby** hived itself off into six totally independent agency units located within a 500-metre radius of each other. Each unit can call on support from media, research, planning and other agency departments.

Springer & Jacoby has consistently retained its position as Germany's most creative agency. Guido Heffels elaborates: "Our unit system was created to keep our agency flexible. After all these years, it's made us multi-cultured."

Heffels stresses that each unit is free to work on its own style of advertising. "Each one has developed its own very special way of seeing things. Each has a totally different working process, from a virtual office like Chiat/Day to an eight-person unit with no account guys."

It may sound like a recipe for anarchy, but very pragmatic controls are in place. "Each unit is continually screened; its performance is measured against our 4 K's: Kunde, Kasse, Kreation, Kultur (Client, Income, Creativity and Culture). They *all* have to be in balance. So a lot of awards and happy clients is not enough if your billings volume is low and your crew is not satisfied."

How have major clients like Mercedes-Benz reacted to working with six-agencies-in-one? "It's an important advantage for them. They only have to deal with a small bunch of people; those that really count. There's no account managing senior supervisor, no supervising creative director, no copy north/west; no nonsense like that! If they wish, a client may work with several units which always leads to new ideas and a little bit of competition, too."

Keeping the work fresh is a key objective. "After a few years, it might be advisable to change the unit on the account," explains Heffels. "Which is, of course, much better than the client changing the agency."

Santa Monica agency **Ground Zero** has removed boundaries and created autonomous cells called brand teams.

Kirk Souder describes his agency as a *community*. "Each brand team consists of strategic people, media people, creative people and the client, and is responsible for uncovering the soul of the brand. Each member's perspective is deemed integral to the development of the brand's planning and positioning. For the brand team to function fully, it must exist for the continued growth and success of the brand, not for any departmental or company agendas." Souder points to the fact that Ground Zero has dispensed with the antiquated Us-and-Them client-agency relationship. "Not surprisingly, many Ground Zero client contacts end up actually moving themselves, either sporadically or permanently, into the Ground Zero environment to be closer to their brand team. In spirit, and in reality, this is one manifestation of what we mean by a community."

While Ground Zero's work is frequently described by the industry as "fresh and edgy", Souder sees a more fundamental issue. "We set out to first uncover the souls of our brands, and then communicate that essence in a clear way to the world. Inevitably, if we do that job well, the work will be new and different because every soul is new and different. The face of the brand must emanate and express the soul of the brand. If we do that, the work will be something more powerful than 'fresh and edgy'. It will be *true*."

It is delusional, Souder believes, for a company to exist for anything other than its people. "When people come to Ground Zero, both clients and employees alike, we ask them to be selfish with their time here. We ask them to look at every task as an opportunity to fulfil their own personal growth, their own personal journey to the truth, and to try what they've never tried before. We ask that in the knowledge that if they do that, inevitably the work will feel fresh, innovative and important. And, more importantly, that *they* will feel fresh, innovative and important."

Art is the *raison d'etre* of another West Coast agency, **Goodby, Silverstein & Partners**, San Francisco.

"A lot of advertising people are afraid to even think about art, of course," says chairman Jeff Goodby. "They're proud to say they've got nothing to do with it. In our case, however, art is why we're here."

The word *art*, Goodby reminds us, has the same roots as *artifice*, something created to achieve a certain end, purpose or effect. He recalls: "We started the agency, frankly, because we believed advertising could be an interesting conjunction between art and commerce. We thought art could serve business in a powerful way."

Art, and a respect for the intelligence of the consumer, distinguish the agency's print work. "Have we proven what we wanted to prove?" Goodby ponders. "I'm not sure you ever quite *prove* art. We certainly have gotten it to serve our clients in a business sense on a number of occasions."

Art aside, Goodby talks about the agency's environment. "There's an element of fun here, which we deeply believe in. Contrary to a lot of Western thinking throughout history, we don't think good things only come about as a result of pain, introspection and torture. Study instead your freedom and exuberance each day," he suggests.

The agency's structure, he believes, is not all that different from other agencies utilising an account planning approach. "The key is to hire incredibly intelligent people and create an environment in which they treat each other, and each other's ideas, with respect. People have to feel free and secure to be as smart as they can be," he emphasises. "The rest is just procedure."

Goodby stresses that clients are a fundamental part of this equation. "We look for smart clients who want to bring their best to this process as well."

Democracy, energy and madness are at the heart of New York's **Mad Dogs & Englishmen**. Cohen calls it an inside out environment. "In most agencies, all the senior people with all the experience have fancy offices with sofas and plants. It looks like they're there forever. All the young people are in lousy offices in the peripheral part of it. What we did was turned it around and made it all much more democratic."

As a result, says Cohen, the energy flows all around the agency. "Young people, and people without experience, are full of ideas. They're naive. They're not cynical. They're very open so they're actually an amazing source of energy. As you get along in the business, you get a lot more experience and a lot more knowledge, but you also become jaded and cynical. All of a sudden, things become less possible and not more possible. By opening it up, we get a really good mixture of energy, vitality and hope, mixed with experience, knowledge and focus."

Cohen is English. He has worked in America for ten years. He admires Chiat/Day, Goodby Silverstein, BBH, Howell Henry, GGT and Abbott Mead Vickers. "I like agencies that do work that changes my mind about things, makes me think about things in a different way. I don't like agencies that stick to the same thing. I like agencies that challenge. I always thought that the British ad scene was becoming very formulaic; it was always a double page spread with some nice body copy, a well-crafted argument. What the business needed was a good kick. GGT was like what the Sex Pistols were to rock-and-roll. When BBH came along and did some of their early Levis work, I thought that they injected something deeply missing from British advertising: sex and sexuality. They were really clever; they made you really lust for things."

Mad Dogs & Englishmen started in 1991. "There was a recession. Nobody was starting ad agencies, they were downsizing them." Why the name? "We didn't want to sound like a law firm. Mad Dogs & Englishmen fitted our combination of maverick madness and British charm. It seemed like a good oxymoron."

Another New York agency synonymous with different thinking is **Kirshenbaum Bond & Partners**. Richard Kirshenbaum and Jonathan Bond believe cynical consumers have developed marketing radar as a form of self-defence. Their response is to produce advertising which gets under the radar. One of their most famous ideas actually ran underfoot, stencilled onto city sidewalks in washable paint. The message, for Bamboo Lingerie, read: *From here, it looks like you could use some new underwear*. It was under the radar before anyone realised it was an ad.

Oberlander says the agency has gone out of its way to hire a diverse range of people and personalities. "We look for *different*. Different kinds of thinking minds. Different nationalities. Different religions. Different genders. The ways that different kinds of people approach problems result in very different kinds of solutions."

Not all cutting edge agencies have conventional, big city addresses. Some prefer to do different work in some very different places. Jim Mountjoy, of **Loeffler Ketchum Mountjoy**, Charlotte, North Carolina, believes geography does not determine your fate.

"It begins with self-imposed standards and disciplines. Harry Jacobs in Richmond, Ron Andersen and Tom McElligott in Minneapolis, Stan Richards in Dallas, Dan Wieden in Portland, all believed first in themselves. All have proved it's not where your body's at, it's where your head's at."

Quality of life has become another issue, argues Mountjoy. "An environment is defined by far more than the office. Maybe that's why more young people today, still passionate about work, want a life outside the office. For some it's not The Big Apple. It's mountains, lakes and outdoor adventure just outside their office windows."

PREPARING TO LEAVE THE COMFORT ZONE

Cutting edge creativity asks a lot of you. Questioning conventional methodologies is just one aspect of it.

There has to be a personal commitment to risk-taking as well. Taking risks means you could fail.

"You've got to be willing to fail," insists Roy Grace. "It's a very important requirement. You've got to be willing to be embarrassed, humiliated, feel stupid. Believe me, I've had those moments. How do you know if an idea is a breakthrough, or if it's rubbish? Sometimes it's breakthrough rubbish! I've done things I know have never been done before, and they were awful. They should *never* have been done! At the time I was taking a big chance and they were terrible, really dreadful. Fortunately, we live in a business that forgives. It's

interesting that the stuff you do that is recognised as breakthrough somehow sticks to you, and the really bad stuff just sort of vanishes into your closet."

"*Never be afraid of having ideas.* They're the most wonderful things in the world," says Hegarty. If they fail? "Failure is fantastic. You learn so much more from it. But it's a double-edged sword; it can instil caution into you. If it does, you begin to recede and draw back from having daring ideas. You've *got* to dare to be different. That is the thing you *must* be! If you let failure control you, you'll walk away from daring ideas and that will be the end of you as a creative person."

It is odd. Most people prefer to take the line of least resistance. As Shakespeare said, "All the voyage of their life will be bound in shallows."

So those who dare to be different, those who dare to take risks and create landmarks and become the figureheads of the future, will find the field surprisingly uncrowded.

3

THE EIGHT GREATEST LIES YOU'LL EVER BE TOLD

In advertising, the world is flat. Agencies are structured on a linear basis. Campaigns are created in linear formats. There are all kinds of rails and fences and obstacles to keep creative thinking linear, too.

Agencies preach change to their clients, without pursuing it themselves. Generations of creative people have been taught to obey certain rules. Despite social change, technological change and audiences which have become highly media literate, the rules have remained the same. In some agencies, they are mandatory.

The danger with any rule is its rigidity. When it ceases to be a positive influence, when it impedes our development, it deserves to be called a lie. Such lies are counter-productive. They spawn two evils: mediocre work and gratuitous work. They make us behave unprofessionally: on one hand, we impose restrictions on ourselves; on the other, we congratulate ourselves for thinking outside the box of our own making. Clients, observing such behaviour, must question our industry's relevance.

The rules, of course, had their roots in experience. In their day, they were applicable. They were the gospel. Even now, cutting edge creatives can still detect grains of truth in each lie. So see them in perspective, not as rules carved in stone, but merely as useful considerations in the creative process.

LIE NO. 1:
YOU MUST HAVE A UNIQUE SELLING PROPOSITION

When this rule was written, products did have genuine, tangible differences. It made good sense to make those unique differences the central focus of the advertising. But, as John Hegarty tells us, those times have changed.

"We've gone from a time when products had genuine unique selling propositions, when you could genuinely manufacture a difference. Electronics firms now share research, Chrysler has joined with Mercedes, big brands come together to manufacture more economically. Products are reaching a fantastic level of quality, but their differences are fewer and fewer. We are now at such a competitive level that it's very difficult for brands to maintain a conventional u.s.p."

Now, Hegarty says, there are perceived differences, *emotional* differences. The u.s.p. has been replaced by the e.s.p., the *emotional selling proposition.* "There's nothing wrong with that. We shouldn't be ashamed of that. How one *feels* about something is incredibly important. Why do I wear a purple shirt as opposed to a white shirt? It's only a colour, but it makes me *feel* different."

As a result, Hegarty's agency sees itself as a manufacturing company. "BBH is not a service company. In a way, we are part of the manufacturing process. We make ideas that make the difference between one brand and another. We help make a brand really different. Not because we're selling something that's got an extra widget on it that no other product has, but because we make you feel differently about this product. You can feel more certain about it, more assured about it, more in love with it, more passionate about it. The emotional differences become the *real* differences."

Bill Oberlander believes in the u.e.p., the *unique emotional proposition.* "Product attributes are small fry and generic and totally vulnerable. Your competitor can duplicate whatever product attributes you have, especially in packaged goods. You have to come up with much bigger emotional propositions for the consumer to stay. The work Fallon McElligott is doing for Miller Lite does not talk about barley, hops, refreshment. It's complete entertainment. A lot of people in this business hate that campaign. They can't wrap their heads around it. I think they're cavemen. There's nothing to say about beer. It's supposed to be *fun*."

As Fallon McElligott art director Bob Barrie asks: "What is the u.s.p. for Coke or Pepsi? Their advertising has become their u.s.p."

Perhaps, then, the term u.s.p. is really a question of interpretation. Lionel Hunt elaborates: "I'm not sure the u.s.p. is dead at all. With the ever increasing number of messages competing for attention, it's more important than ever to be unique. The thing is, *it doesn't necessarily have to be a unique feature of the product itself*." Hunt provides a charming example: "My favourite brand of all is Baxters Soups of Scotland. I learned recently, in print of course, that Baxters had rejected one hundred and eighty-seven takeover offers. The Chairman of Baxters said, 'No one will ever be asked to sit on our board who does not *fish*'. Now there's a unique selling proposition and the brief for a fabulous advertising campaign."

John Salmon maintains that some kind of brand property is still needed to imply superiority. "It's not always possible today to develop a u.s.p. of the type advocated by Rosser Reeves. I like that other idea of Rosser Reeves', that everybody's got little boxes in their head, and in each little category box they have a few brand names, two or maybe three. If you want to get your brand name in, you've probably got to kick another one out, because there isn't an infinite limit to the number of names that people can contain in their boxes. So you have to provide some kind of memorable element that they can attach to the brand name, some reason for putting it in there." Salmon stresses that the manner of expressing a u.s.p. has moved on. "One doesn't have to be dogmatic. You should try to make your product unique either in style, flavour, attitude, the way you talk about it, even if you can't bring to bear matters of fact, which was what Bates did, to deliver unique benefits."

"In an effort to make account executives realise they're in advertising, because most of them wish they weren't," recounts Neil French, "we wanted to get them to write briefs. So I wrote a very short book with very short words and big print. It was called *How To Do Ads*. It said that every ad had to have a button, something you press, that changes the consumer's mind. So their job was to find the button."

According to French, the button could be a u.s.p. or something else: "The button could be contained in the tone of voice. Because it's the personality of the brand speaking, it must have a definite character. 'Warm and friendly' will not do. What is the alternative? 'Cold and unfriendly'? And anyway, used car salesmen are, on the surface, warm and friendly, and who believes anything they say?"

Finding the button presents unlimited cutting edge opportunities. Brands can be *reframed*, so people see them differently. Like Hugh Mackay's analogy of the cracked mirror, the familiar can be made *unfamiliar*, so people's interest is *renewed*. Advertising can bring to light what was hidden, overlooked or forgotten.

Mary Stow talks about reframing the AA, Britain's automobile breakdown organisation: "When you don't have the luxury of having something new to say, you have to find a new spin on it, find a new way of talking about it, a new emotional territory. The AA had been doing all this advertising about the patrolmen being very nice men. The patrolmen were deeply patronised by motorists. The mindshift we got to on that was referring to them as *The Fourth Emergency Service*."

When you cannot be unique, be the *first*: the first to express a certain thought, the first to look at something from a particular perspective. For the consumer in a cage, the first information received about any subject becomes part of the filter through which all subsequent information on the same subject must pass. Mackay quotes Hitler's propagandist Goebbels: "Whoever says the first word to the world is always right." Not always the case, says Mackay, but quite often. "A great advantage which the first brand into a market always has is that the message of its advertising is new. The fewer reference points which are available to the audience for evaluating the advertising, the more they are likely to accept what the new advertising says."

At the Campaign Palace, Sydney, creative director Ron Mather believes advertising's function has changed. "I don't believe you sell anyone anything any more; instead, you make them want to buy.

Most of the time there isn't a u.s.p., so giving brands a personality is extremely important now. If you like the personality, you're more likely to like the brand. It's a bit the same with people."

LIE NO. 2:
YOU MUST OFFER A RATIONAL BENEFIT

Saint Augustine said: "I have encountered many people who wish to deceive, but no one who wishes to be deceived."

Somehow, over the years, rationality has come to be equated with substance. If the advertising offers a rational proposition, it will be more believable and effective.

"An absolute lie," says Bruce Bildsten, group creative director at Fallon McElligott, Minneapolis. "Some of the best ads are totally *irrational*. One that leaps to my brain is the British campaign for Stella Artois, where they had fun with the fact it was overpriced. What a wonderful proposition. It's something that's as far from rational as can possibly be!"

Bildsten cites his agency's work for **Porsche**. One ad listed such irrational product benefits as *Too fast, Doesn't blend in, People will talk*. "It was a campaign that really resonated. We got so many letters from people and they said, yes, that's why I buy this car. There's nothing practical about it. I live in the United States where the law says I have to drive fifty-five miles an hour. It doesn't have room for my kids and my luggage. And that's exactly why I love it!"

Also citing Porsche is Salmon. "I think benefits can be purely emotional. There are all kinds of subrational benefits that people are quite prepared to pay large sums of money for. Take the case of somebody who buys a Porsche to drive on the Los Angeles freeways. There's no specific benefit to a Porsche other than you feel better about yourself sitting in one."

Hegarty quotes the classic VW campaign. "Volkswagen built itself on the proposition *it's ugly but it works*. The fact that a product has flaws is wonderful. Don't knock it. It's like a human being. Do you like someone who is perfect? You don't. You'd actually rather *dislike* him. Do you like somebody who comes into a room and starts knocking somebody else? Not really. Frailty is a wonderful thing in human beings. I love somebody who comes into a room and makes a joke about themselves. They seem like an interesting person, they seem *confident.*"

Mackay provides a perspective from philosopher Bertrand Russell: "For scientific purposes, I suggest the following experiment. Let two soaps, A and B, be manufactured, of which A is excellent and B abominable; let A be advertised by stating its chemical composition and by testimonials from eminent chemists; let B be advertised by the bare statement that it's the best, accompanied by the portraits of famous Hollywood beauties. If man is a rational animal, more of A will be sold than B. Does anyone, in fact, believe that this would be the result?"

French certainly does not. "Anyone who thinks you need a rational benefit is ignoring ninety percent of the human psyche which is irrational. There's no rational benefit to Pepsi and Coke." However, says French, *the irrational can sometimes be made to seem rational.* "People like to rationalise fun. For instance, it's irrational, on the face of it, to go out and get drunk. It's easy to rationalise things, it's like people who buy *Playboy* for the articles."

Stow believes that sometimes people need an excuse or a pretext to change their behaviour. "I think ads have to either be rational, or *seem* to be rational, because people are smart enough, marketing-literate enough these days not just to buy the fluffy stuff around the edges. They have to feel something substantial in there. The question is, how real is that difference? *The hit of real oranges* is the functional heart of Tango. It talked about something functional which almost gives people an excuse to say, 'I like Tango because it's got the hit of real oranges'. In fact, what they were probably buying into was the giant orange man, the sense of fun, the fact it was real, British, and not American."

While most key decisions we make are emotional, says Simon Sherwood, strong emotional propositions often need rational underpinning. "All brands are a mix of rational and emotional credentials. You have to be strong in both. Our Levis advertising talks about youthfulness, rebelliousness and sex, underpinned by rational product features like strength."

"You've got to have a balance between rational and emotional arguments," counsels Ian Batey. "There have to be core values providing rational support for the emotional proposition." He quotes his agency's campaign for Singapore Airlines. The *Singapore Girl* is the emotional icon, says Batey. "*Inflight service even other airlines talk about* becomes the rational argument."

Making love at four in the afternoon on a Tuesday, or being naked more, or putting first things last are not exactly rational. But they are intensely human. If we listen to what people are dreaming about, and respond, consumers will respond to us. Describing Hitler's powerful effect on audiences, Carl Jung said: "He is the loudspeaker which amplifies the inaudible whispers of the German soul." Advertising

Fallon McElligott's work for Porsche: irrationality that resonated.

Inaudible whispers of the human soul, amplified by
San Francisco's Goodby, Silverstein & Partners.

can do precisely the same. Goodby Silverstein's campaign for the **Norwegian Cruise Line** amplified many inaudible whispers:

"I will be naked more."

"I will memorise clouds."

"There is no law that says you shall not study a sunset."

"Beyond heavy woollens, beyond the Nightly News, beyond the reach of what hurts you, beyond politics (national, local, sexual), beyond *beyond*."

There was nothing rational in the advertising about the ships, the friendly crew, the quality of the cabins and the cuisine, the amenities on board, or getting more ports of call for your dollar. There did not have to be. The emotional aura created by the words and execution made cruising with the Norwegians seem a perfectly legitimate and rational decision.

As Gary Goldsmith sums up: "I don't think you need to offer a rational benefit. I think you need to offer a benefit that a rational person can understand."

LIE NO. 3:
HUMOUR DOESN'T SELL

"Humour was one of the phobias of the Rosser Reeves approach to advertising, which was always so absolutely stony-faced humour-less," observes Salmon. "Humour makes friends, but it's very difficult to use." Not everybody will laugh at the same things, he cautions, advocating that humour works best in a campaign format. "Within an overall campaign, you'll make them all laugh, sooner or later."

"There's always been a great debate over whether humorous ads work. There's a million case histories that they do," says Bob Barrie, who describes his own creative style as minimalist with a sense of humour. "Brands are like people. The most important questions you have to ask: what is the personality of your brand, what is the most appropriate personality to project to a consumer audience, and which personality will they most readily accept? If IBM came out with the funniest campaign in the world, I don't think it would feel right to people. If Miller Lite Beer does, then it's acceptable."

Colleague Bildsten reminds us that brands have been built out of humour. "The original Miller Lite campaign, *Tastes great, less filling*, completely changed the beer landscape in the States."

Building a brand out of humour: Miller Lite defies time and convention.
Fallon McElligott, Minneapolis.

A tactful use of humour: no one lost face, but the point was made.
Ogilvy & Mather Singapore for British Council English-language courses

WHEN UTTERING YOUR LAST WORDS,
PLEASE SPEAK SLOWLY AND CLEARLY.

When Albert Einstein died in 1955, a group of friends gathered around his bedside. The most brilliant scientific mind of this century uttered his final words and then gently slipped away. With what thought did the great man leave us? A new theory? The answer to a tricky time-space conundrum?

We will never know, as none of his friends spoke German.

So becomes apparent one of the problems with last words. Another is timing. Given the fickle nature of death, few people are lucky enough to have their final utterings recorded and inscribed into history because often no one's there to hear them.

Even when someone is close enough to hear your well-chosen words, nature can still be unpredictable, as General Sedgewick found out. The American Civil War troop commander gave us a moment of unintentional humour when he peered over a parapet towards the enemy and boasted 'They couldn't hit an elephant at this dist.... '.

Some of our finest artists have given us great works but rather lame last words.

'Now let me sleep', said English poet Lord Byron. And the best Felix Mendelssohn, the composer, could manage was 'I'm very weary'.

But others left us with gems. Novelist W. Somerset Maugham commented 'Dying is a dull and dreary affair. My advice to you is to have nothing whatsoever to do with it'. And Oscar Wilde observed 'Either this wallpaper goes, or I do'.

Prima ballerina, Anna Pavlova, was famous for her sensitive portrayal of the dying swan in Swan Lake. How apt then her parting words; 'Get my swan costume ready'.

Stan Laurel, it appears, was the consummate comedian to the very last. 'I'd rather be skiing than doing this', he said to his bedside nurse.

'Do you ski, Mr Laurel?', she asked. 'No, but I'd rather be doing that than this', Stan whispered before he left us.

Closer to home, outlaw Ned Kelly departed with the short observation, 'Such is life'.

But the most positive outlook on the final journey comes from the English poet Gerard Manley Hopkins. Rather than a clever or gloomy quote, he simply said 'I am so happy, so very happy'.

At Chippers, we're seldom privy to a person's last words; our duty is to carry out their last wishes. A task we're proud to say we follow to the very last letter.

However simple or unusual the request, their wish is our command.

Which is why, in Western Australia, we at Chippers are often referred to as the last word in funeral directors.

CHIPPERS
The Family Funeral Director

© Chippers is a Western Australian family-owned company

Will Australians die laughing? An appropriate use of gentle humour
by Vinten Browning, Perth, for Chippers Funerals.

IT IS NOT UNCOMMON TO SEE ELEPHANTS WEEP OPENLY AT FUNERALS.

Some people refuse to go to a funeral. 'I'll deal with it in my own way', they say. 'And besides, it's not natural.'

With respect, we disagree. A funeral and the healing processes of grief are two of the most natural things in the world.

And if you don't believe us, take a close look at one of nature's biggest-hearted beasts; the elephant.

Elephants show a range of emotions that are uncannily similar to ours. When they meet each other, they touch trunks and rub shoulders. When a young elephant is in danger, its mother will go to extraordinary lengths to save it, even if she has to risk her own life. And when an elephant dies, its friends give it a funeral. Yes, honestly, a funeral.

The death ritual starts when an elephant is close to dying. A wounded or sick animal is soon surrounded by members of its herd who try and help it back on its feet. Two healthy elephants stand either side of their patient and use their trunks and tusks to lift, and then their whole bodies to support the animal.

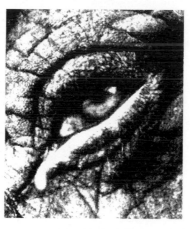

Some observers have even seen young elephants bring food and water to a dying mother to help her recover.

When the beast finally breathes its last, the extended family circles it. Very slowly and with heads hanging gloomily, they walk around the body several times before standing still.

The assembled circle then turns away one by one until the body is surrounded by elephants all facing outwards. Their trunks hang limply on the ground, and they look as if they are mourning the loss of a loved one. (We'd like to believe that they are.) Maybe they find the sight of death too painful, or perhaps this

ritual has another meaning. Only an elephant can tell you.

And then, there's a simple funeral ceremony. The bereaved beasts gather branches, leaves and clumps of grass from the surrounding area and gently lay them on the body of their dead relative to form a simple grave.

Occasionally, elephants also weep. Big, salty tears roll down their wrinkles in a river of sadness. They weep because they are lonely or hurt, just as we do.

The family stands quietly at the graveside for several hours before moving on. Elephants have clearly not forgotten how to grieve. And we should follow nature's example. Next time you are invited to a funeral, please go. You may find the experience sad, but it's a natural start to the healing process.

And next time you are in need of a funeral director, we trust you will remember us; Chippers.

CHIPPERS
The Family Funeral Director

Client Branding CHD32

© *Chippers is a Western Australian family-owned company.*

Very, very, very unconventional humour for Shelter Clothing from
Mad Dogs & Englishmen, New York.

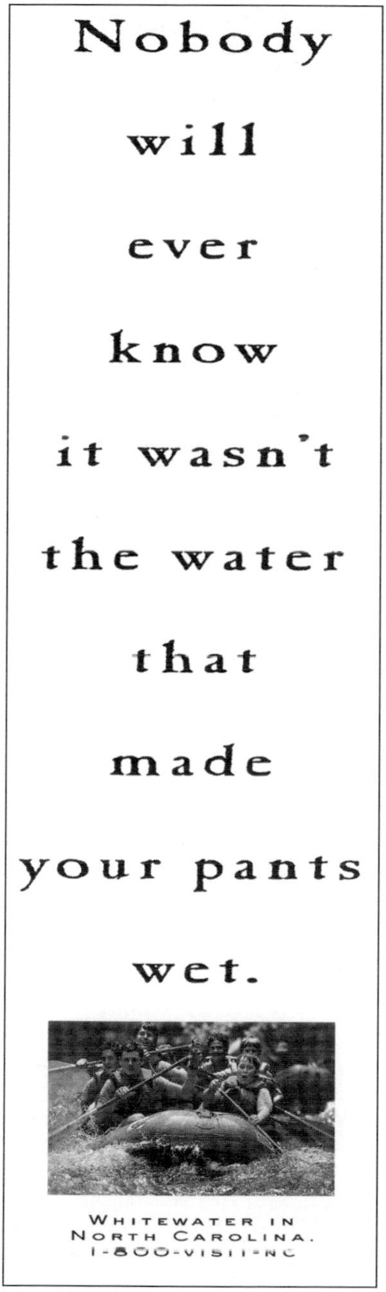

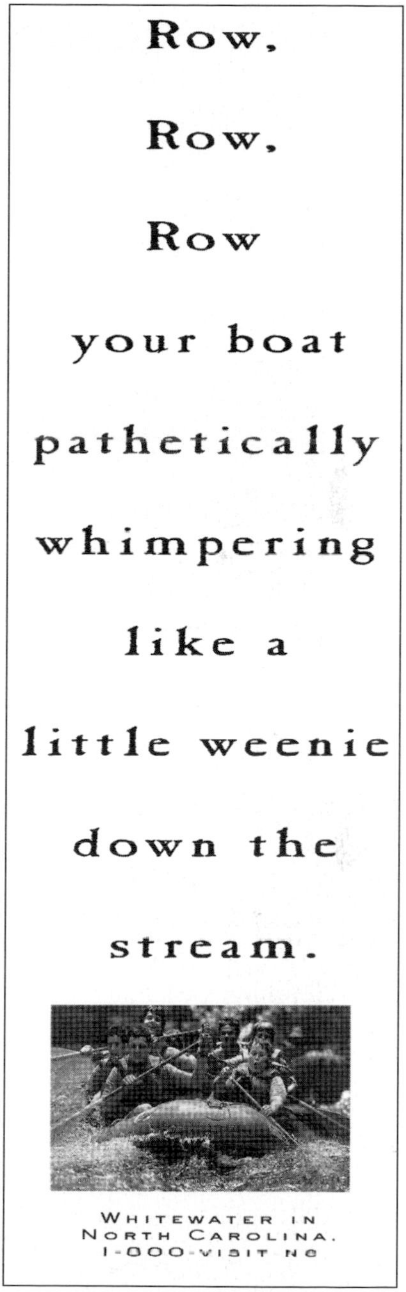

Nobody

will

ever

know

it wasn't

the water

that

made

your pants

wet.

WHITEWATER IN
NORTH CAROLINA.
1-800-VISIT-NC

Row,

Row,

Row

your boat

pathetically

whimpering

like a

little weenie

down the

stream.

WHITEWATER IN
NORTH CAROLINA.
1-800-VISIT NC

In times of war, danger and tension, somebody always cracks a joke.
It's human nature. Here, humour accentuates the adventure.
Loeffler Ketchum Mountjoy for North Carolina Travel and Tourism.

JOHN PLAYER SPECIAL.
WAHRSCHEINLICH IRGENDWIE ANDERS.

Who said the Germans don't have a sense of humour?
The headline reads: "Somehow different". Springer & Jacoby, Hamburg.

"Of course humour sells," says French. "Look at the great salesmen in real life, like the guys in the markets in London selling crockery. They juggle the crockery. They have audiences in stitches. The funniest men sell the most crockery because they get the biggest audiences. Humour crosses all boundaries, financial boundaries, national boundaries. You'd rather buy something from someone you like than someone you don't like."

In Singapore, there are many quaint abuses of the English language. Someone with a good command of English is likely to be told: "Wah, your England damn powderful." Ogilvy & Mather's campaign for **British Council** language courses did not have to look far for inspiration; malaprops and assorted howlers abounded. The use of signage was a tactful device. Nobody felt personally insulted. Humour helped people to laugh at themselves, while gently reminding them it was time to brush up their England.

"You've got to entertain people," advises Garry Abbott. "Their lives are faster, more complicated. Advertising works best on an entertainment level. It stimulates them, amuses them for a nanosecond, sufficient for them to retain the message. Collett Dickenson Pearce did that so well. They were constantly entertaining the consumer and the brands didn't suffer. Quite the reverse."

The most unlikely products can benefit from humour. Even in Stuttgart, which is hardly the world capital of comedy, the makers of Mercedes-Benz applaud wit in their headlines. The brand becomes more accessible, less imposing.

Death, however, is another matter entirely. Defying conventional wisdom, humour has proved appropriate for **Chippers Funerals** of Perth, Australia. At agency Vinten Browning, writer Steve Browning explains: "Our brief for the Chippers campaign was unusual. The client, Kim Chipper, had seen some of our work and asked us if we could do a few ads for him. He briefed us on the finer points of his profession; the importance of grief, the various customs people observe, what a funeral director actually does, and the pros and cons of cremation vs. burial. Thankfully, he spared us the factory tour." Each ad in the campaign tackles one interesting aspect of death and funerals, and then turns the subject to Chippers. According to Browning, "Writing the turnaround at the end of each ad is often the most difficult bit. That, and getting the tone of voice right. I try and remember that some people reading the ads will have lost a close friend or partner that day, so you can't be irreverent or flippant. But an injection of gentle humour into the series seems to have done no harm."

Shelter Clothing broke advertising conventions in the skateboarding market. Agency Mad Dogs & Englishmen believes humour can look at faults and vices as well as virtues. Skateboarders were no exception. Nick Cohen describes the creative leap: "If you look at how skateboarders are marketed to, and how they see themselves, it's all about being tough, being out there, on the edge. The reality is, they're just people having fun. Skateboarding magazines are full of photographs of people doing really dangerous things. Everyone's trying to top each other. We wanted skateboarders to laugh at themselves a bit, so we chose things that were very *un*dangerous." Tripping up the blind and stealing from children provided irreverent scenarios which turned the joke on the skateboarders. The cynical strapline reads: *Very, Very, Very Tough Clothing*. Simple, black-and-white on-the-street photography was a stark contrast to the complex graphics and typographically-driven ads for competitors. "The art director, John Soto, did the ads when he'd just turned thirty. It was an honest look at his sport. Blatantly honest. It came from his heart."

Cohen is convinced humour endears, providing you are honest about your negatives as well as your positives. "Advertising is about building relationships, so if you forget about advertising and just think about *socialising*. If you get two Heads of State meeting, usually it's all laughs and smiles. Breaking the ice. Finding something they can laugh at. When you see Clinton with the Chinese Premier, the magic is when something funny happens, when the two of them are laughing and smiling."

Advertising that takes the consumer seriously does not have to be serious, Mackay assures us. "It's the classic combination of heart and mind, as opposed to being simplistic, patronising and insulting. Think of the brand as friend, as potential lover, talking to the consumer in a way that will nurture their relationship. You can be funny, vulgar if you have to be. You can send yourself up. But at the heart of it, the consumer has got to recognise that I understand you, I like you the way you are, I'm not trying to change you, I'm trying to relate to you."

Lie No. 4:
You Must Have a Memorable Slogan

"It seems like there's a locker someplace in the Advertising Hall of Fame with fifteen different words," observes Oberlander, "and they keep on shifting them around. Words like *experience*, and *thrill*."

Traditionally, straplines sat beneath the logo, down in the bottom right-hand corner, just above the address and telephone number. They were intended to deliver the final convincing clincher in the ad, or to make some meaningful statement about the advertiser or the brand. Mostly, they have become either shallow wordplays or meaningless phrases like *Progress is our most important product*. Technology companies promise *Tomorrow's Technology Today*. Telephone companies are invariably *In Touch With Tomorrow*. Should we persist with such nonsense?

"There are lines that come right out of the vernacular," says Oberlander. "They feel familiar to your brain. A friend could have said them the other day. Like the line for New York Lotto: *Hey, you never know.* Lines are good for wrapping your head around what the idea is, and talking about it. They're more of a convenience than something that's necessary. At the end of the day we always ask ourselves, does it really need a tagline? Because the truth is," Oberlander warns, "consumers hate advertising, and taglines and jingles are the biggest *cliches* within the parameters of advertising."

Roy Grace believes there is no fixed rule, either way. "I think they're good and I think they're bad. Avis had one, Volkswagen didn't. My basic instinct is *not* to do them. They're usually a waste of time."

French takes a harsher view. "I think we've all been failing for the last fifty years. When clients say they want a tagline, I write down half a dozen from large companies. When I ask the clients which companies they apply to, they can never remember. Pick up any magazine on your desk and read out the taglines," suggests French, "they're a complete waste of time and energy."

Salmon raises a similar eyebrow. "There's an endline which is greatly treasured on Lexus advertising in the States, *The relentless pursuit of perfection,* tucked away under the logo. I'm sure that everybody involved feels very warm that they've got that there, it touches on their corporate aims, and I'm sure they are relentlessly pursuing perfection. But whether it has any active value as far as people reading the ad is concerned, I'm not very sure." Salmon believes endlines have a different purpose in television: "Very often the endline is the scaffold on which television commercials are constructed. They are enigmatic and inexplicable, until the moment of *denouement,* when everything becomes clear and you discover, ah, that's what they meant."

"Slogans now are becoming less and less important," considers Bildsten. "Some of the best slogans in current use are old ones that are used for their retro effect. I don't think anyone even feels compelled to write a slogan these days. It feels so tacked on, so forced. It becomes almost a crutch more than an aid to anything. It's usually reinforcing something that you weren't able to get across in the rest of the work, or for the benefit of a corporation's ego. But it's still possible to write ones that really reinforce the message," he concedes, "*Got milk?* for example."

"Great lines are great lines," says Sherwood, quoting BMW's *The ultimate driving machine*. "But they must have something interesting to say, not just corporate waffle."

Many cutting edge print ads still carry straplines, but more as the *campaign thought* than a traditional slogan. Sometimes they function as headlines. Some have become more organic, appearing as part of the visual texture. They run everywhere: top, bottom, sides.

"I think the best taglines are great headlines," Barrie argues. "If it's the right slogan, or a really great summarising thought, they still have a place. The worst tagline I've ever read in my life was for a company called TRW. It ran underneath the logo, which was a sans-serif TRW, and it said*: A company called TRW*. TRW, *A company called TRW*. I wonder what the strategy was there? Don't let 'em forget we're a company?"

"I think some of them actually do a lot of harm," cautions Goldsmith. "I hate using them, and almost never do. I can't think of too many that are very good. They're just stuck on to please the client or someone in the agency. I've always thought that if the ad does what it's supposed to do, then you don't need them. If the ad doesn't do what it's supposed to do, a strapline is not going to save it." Goldsmith shares the view that most slogans are talking to themselves. "*Just do it* is actually very good because it's about the attitude of the people reading the ad. It's not about the company, it's not *Making better shoes for the people who do it*."

There are no rules, but the consensus is clear. Unless your line is as powerful as "Just Do It", *don't do it*.

LIE NO. 5:
YOU MUST HAVE A LOGO IN THE AD

"It's a lie that you *must* have a logo in the ad," reasons French. "If you write a letter to someone and the most interesting thing in the letter is your signature, you've wasted your time. You ought to be able to write a letter, not sign it, and everybody ought to know who it comes from because it's written in your tone of voice, your handwriting, and about the things in which you're interested. Most people could write a letter without signing it and the recipient would know who it came from. If nobody knows you, then you need to sign it."

"Some logos shouldn't be anywhere, of course, they're so horrible," argues Salmon. "If the logo is there in the bottom right-hand corner, in one sweeping glance the reader can know who is talking; it colours the way an ad is perceived." For copywriters, at least, Salmon can find one benefit of a logo being in an ad: "It enables you to do headlines that don't have the product name in them."

The usual argument for removing the logo runs like this: Why advertise the fact that the ad is an ad? The less an ad looks like an ad, the more it is likely to be noticed.

It sounds logical. In most agencies, however, excluding the logo from an ad is akin to heresy. It is pure creative self-indulgence. The logo is essential for branding the campaign.

"The ad in itself, corner to corner, should look like the brand," stresses Oberlander. "The whole page is acting like a logo. If you're doing an ad for Coke, you know there's going to be a lot of red, some really beautiful script typography, and certain elements that are intrinsic to the Coke brand are going to be in the visual presentation. I would try to design a page so that the logo didn't appear in any *traditional* fashion. Because consumers hate advertising, once they see a page with a logo in the corner, it doesn't look like editorial, it doesn't look like the reason why they bought the magazine in the first place. It's a trigger that makes them turn the page faster."

If Oberlander is right, the plot has changed. It is not the logo that brands the ad, it is the *brand* that brands the ad.

"People are finding more organic ways to put a mark on an ad," Bildsten advises. "More and more, *products* are being used as logos. By making the logo more invisible, people feel they aren't seeing it. As Neil French says, the more elements you take away from an ad, the better it works, and I think logos are one of them."

Perhaps it is a question of being less literal with logos, and more lateral. Does making it the size of a pea in the lower right corner really achieve anything? In Fallon McElligott's *Time* campaign, the magazine's masthead is an integral part of every ad. In the same agency's famous Hush Puppies campaign, the actual Hush Puppies dog was the creative idea.

Making the logo more organic, less obnoxious.
Bartle Bogle Hegarty, London.

Barrie art directed both. "In Hush Puppies, the dog brought the company logo to life. It involved you and it was impossible not to remember who the ads were for."

Sherwood agrees. "If it's possible, make the logo part of the idea."

In themselves, logos can have incredible power. Some are more than just design forms or corporate devices. Some have a history. The BMW logo, for example, is actually a white propellor against a blue sky, symbolising the company's origins as an aircraft engine maker. The Levis logo harks back to indestructibility in the Old West. If logos can convey so much, why bury them?

Barrie recalls an Everlast campaign created by Goldsmith. "This obnoxiously huge Everlast logo filled the spread, with wonderfully thought-provoking lines underneath. It was great advertising, almost *anti*-advertising. It was like every rule you had ever learned about tucking the logo in the right-hand corner was just laughed at."

French returns to his analogy of writing a letter. "Sometimes the best ad is just a big logo. Everybody knows what the letter would say. Just put a tick on the page and I'll go and buy the sodding shoes. But don't try to tell a story, then put a big logo on it. That's really depressing. If the logo is so important that it's the whole point of the ad, don't try to write an important ad around it. Do one thing or the other. If you can write an ad and cover up the logo and it still makes sense, you've done a good ad. If you can throw the logo away and make people think this might not be an ad, I'd better read it, it looks interesting, *you've done your job*."

By definition, therefore, if you put a big logo on a bad ad, it will only increase the client's embarrassment, and yours.

Lie No. 6:
You Must Show the Product in the Ad

Neil Godfrey reflects on the famous surrealistic campaign for Benson & Hedges, which became the best-selling cigarette in its category. "We always had problems with the censorship authorities. I think they realised how powerful, how strong something could be that doesn't *overtly* show a piece of advertising, but is image-making based on the power the images can have." One execution showed a rainstorm of cigarettes beating down on umbrellas. It was the first

Two car makers saving the environment.
Porsche, through Leagas Delaney, London, shows the product in the ad.
Mercedes-Benz, from Batey Ads, Singapore, doesn't.

time the pack did not appear. "We had gold umbrellas. Everyone knew it was Benson & Hedges just by the style."

"We are not paid to put a product in an ad, but in the consumer's mind," says Guido Heffels. "Sometimes a colour or a special location can create an *image* of the product. It's the biggest pack shot you can put into your ad because it involves the consumer. It's like a *riddle* that the consumer will be proud to have solved. And that creates a much deeper impression than anything else."

"If you take something away," Bildsten contends, "you leave something more to the imagination. A beer with a head is a beer with a head. A can is a can. A bottle is a bottle. There are other ways you can *represent* the product."

"It's a lie you must show the product," asserts Sherwood. "Consumers can picture in their minds what things look like. Lots of Levis ads don't show jeans. People can visualise them."

"Ads should be based on what the product can *do* for the reader," Salmon reminds us. Other than that, "I think there are no rules that are unbreakable in advertising."

Grace believes showing products can impact negatively on the advertising. "Communication is far more participatory when it isn't an overt sell, when the sell is more internal. In the early days of DDB, one of the unspoken, guiding forces was that the product and the logo should never be in the ad, because it'll be an ad and nobody will read it."

The question is, what will work best for the strategy, the brand and the idea?

Generally speaking, says French, if the product has to be bought off a shelf, if pack recognition is important, you must show the product in the ad. Sometimes the name itself will be adequate. In French's own work, campaigns for Chivas Regal and XO Beer showed the pack and made it part of the idea; Kaminomoto did not, for legal reasons.

"One exception," says French, "is when you're selling something that's *so* different to anything else in its category and you really need the story to stick home. A new shampoo, say. Putting the product in the ad might stop people reading the story because they'd think it's just another boring ad for shampoo. Maybe then you shouldn't."

Showing parts of the product reveals the greater whole.
Fallon McElligott, Minneapolis, for BMW.

Showing a fashion product doesn't have to be predictable. Fallon McElligott
combines a retro look in art direction with cheeky social gambits.

Strategic reasons could also preclude putting the product in the ad. Oberlander quotes Kenneth Cole Shoes as an example. "The shoes were actually changing styles so quickly that if we showed them in the ad, it would date the brand. By the time the ad ran, six weeks later, the style was actually starting to turn out. So we kept the ads product-less and just promoted the brand itself." One of the most famous Kenneth Cole ads was a simple typeset message regretting the fact that Imelda Marcos hadn't had the courtesy to buy a pair of Kenneth Cole shoes.

Each category presents its own set of decisions. The car category is one of the most contentious.

"We've all got an idea of what a car looks like," says French. "It's got a wheel on each corner. If you've got a brilliant looking car, show it. If you're selling a Datsun, probably don't." French had the task of relaunching a famous Japanese car; one look at the current model convinced him not to show it in the ads. "It was a toilet on wheels, a terrible old nail, something your granny would drive." He made the advertising exciting instead.

"Sometimes you're selling a promise, you're not selling a product *per se*." Bildsten talks about his agency's work for BMW. "With BMW, it's so difficult not to show the product. What we've done is show bits of it, very small details of it, because those details reveal the greater whole."

Grace remembers working on the classic Volkswagen campaign with Bill Bernbach. "I was twenty-seven when I took it on. Bill was already in his fifties, already a legend. Bill said to me, 'Whenever you portray a Volkswagen in an ad, Roy, I want you to do this: either make the Volkswagen very big or very, very small'. And I said, 'Why?' Well, he just gave me a look. He just *looked* at me. So for ever and ever, I never said 'Why?' to Bill Bernbach again."

In the computer category, the products look basically the same. Therefore, Salmon questions why every ad shows a picture of a computer. "Obviously the people who manufacture them can detect the finer points of difference. But if you look at the ads, it's hard to tell one from another."

So, why do it?

The hotel category has French baffled. "I can never understand why people show hotels in their ads. Nobody ever sees the hotel! You arrive in a taxi, that's the first idea you have that you've actually got to the place. Then you see the room. I find hotel advertising hilarious because they've all got these photographs of big, concrete block-houses. It's like they're saying, please come and stay in our prison!"

LIE No. 7:
EVERY AD IN A CAMPAIGN MUST LOOK THE SAME

Nobody in their right mind wears the same clothes day after day. Yet who we are, and what we stand for, remains constant. If brands are the same as people, a similar logic should apply. If a brand wears exactly the same look every time you see it, if its advertising conforms to a rigid layout grid, won't that defeat freshness and surprise? Won't that stifle the brand's personality?

"When they measure advertising recall, rigid formats are statistically the most effective," says Salmon. "But I believe in *repetition without monotony*. I think you have to change print ads frequently. Once you've looked at an ad, you'll recognise it subliminally as you go through a publication but you won't look at it again. You could argue that a second insertion will get the people you missed the first time, and maybe it takes three exposures for everybody to see it, but after that you start to show people something they're not going to look at again with fresh attention." Salmon prefers campaigns with elastic formats. "It's important to have a campaign look, with enough characteristics in common for there to be some synergy between one ad and the next." This could be achieved by some visual device which links them.

"There should be some variables which are consistent," recommends Oberlander, "so consumers know there's that guy again, trying to talk to me; there's that brand, trying to strike up a conversation with me. We should put together what we call the *visual turf* of a brand: the kind of photography, the kind of colour panels, the kind of typography. But the format should be kept flexible, so that each ad in a campaign is like a step-brother to the ad before it, rather than a perfect twin."

"Every ad in a campaign must have the same tone of voice," says French. "Which means, in the same campaign, you could produce an ad which is entirely copy and one which is entirely a picture, and they would both work." French did precisely that in his XO Beer campaign.

"You can have a *framework* for consistency," suggests Sherwood. BBH's Boddingtons campaign was designed to work as posters on magazine back covers. Within that framework, every execution contained a new interpretation of creaminess.

Done well enough, a campaign can become a series of surprises, rather than a series of ads. A diversity of executions and formats can invite comparisons and provoke public debate. When consumers talk about the advertising, every media dollar will be doing the work of three or four.

As David Abbott argues: "There's no reason why you can't mix visual and long copy ads within one campaign or one client's advertising. I think it's quite a good idea so you can surprise people. If you look back at classic Volkswagen ads, once the campaign had been established they often surprised you with format. There were occasional long copy ads and there was a lot of talk about it. It gave the campaign a great *spontaneity*."

What makes a campaign, for Heffels, is a great *overall thought*. "Everything you create for the brand should be driven by the same thought, the same idea. A few constant design elements may be helpful for a major brand to build up a global presence, but if that's all you've got, you will end up with a series of ads, not a campaign. See what Nike did over the last few years? There was no special look, no corporate design grid. Everyone had the freedom to go for the maximum in art and copy. What kept all the hundreds of different ads together, all over the world, was having the same overall mission."

Global advertising campaigns, in fact, frequently impose the most rigid formats of all. The worst excesses are found in the hotel category. "Some genius works out a grid that every ad must follow," observes French. "Fortunately they only last for a couple of years. They become so tired that even the most rabid client cannot seriously keep running them any more."

It seems the real issue is the degree of flexibility, and knowing just how far to go. While there are no rules, there are commonsense guidelines.

"If you've a *small media budget*, if you're not as ubiquitous as Nike or Miller Lite, it would be a mistake to go off with too many different looks and voices," cautions Barrie. "You'd lose the synergy that you develop by having a unified look."

"If you're talking to a very *advertising-literate market* that's more hip, you can't be predictable," Sherwood advises. "That's why Levis talks about the same things, but doesn't look the same."

In Tim Delaney's view, the *relationship with the consumer* should always be the deciding factor. "I don't like things in advertising being non-strategic. Campaigns are things which are aimed at consumers by advertisers on the basis they're looking for a cumulative effect. Is the relationship you want, from the brand's point of view, one that requires a tidy uniformity in order to get a cumulative effect? There are markets which are so crowded that unless you get a look, you are going to be lost. In that sense, a distinctive look can give you something back. However, there are other accounts where you want to have a different kind of relationship. Someone like Adidas has all different kinds of categories. You may want to change the flavour of the relationship depending on the category, and that's acceptable."

Of course, as Lionel Hunt laments: "Most print ads are so appalling it would be criminal if the ones that followed them looked the same."

LIE NO. 8:
CREATIVE ADS DON'T SELL

"The redoubtable Donald Gunn has proved they do, beyond any doubt," French reminds us. Gunn's research was conducted when he was the international creative guru at Leo Burnett, Chicago. "Donald also proved that ads which won Gold awards worked better than ads which won Silver, and that Silver worked better than Bronze."

The problem, as French points out, is that the word *creative* has achieved its own demise. "To most people, creative has come to mean self-serving and pointless. A form of self-abuse. Which isn't, of course, what being creative really is. Creativity is merely sugar-coating the pill. That's all you're doing. At the base of it, creativity is finding an interesting thing to say about a boring thing. And the more interesting it is, the more creative it is."

"To say creative ads don't sell is definitely a lie, no question about it," asserts Sherwood. "This is something that gets talked about a lot, particularly when the industry gets attacked for awarding itself too often." Sherwood quotes a correlation drawn between advertising which won creative awards and advertising which won effectiveness awards. "In Britain, the IPA run effectiveness awards every two years. The IPA awards are taken very seriously by clients. By going back over the years, it was shown that the campaigns which were deemed to be the most effective had also picked up large numbers of creative awards."

Sherwood also believes a correlation exists between the ads which consumers like and the ads which award juries like. He quoted the fact that BBH's Levis Claymation commercial had not only been covered in creative awards, but was also voted the best ad on TV by a viewers' poll in Singapore. "There is definitely a relationship between creativity and effectiveness."

Cutting edge creativity impacts as successfully on consumers as it does on award show judges. Reaching the standard involves risk, but no rules. Having cleared away The Eight Greatest Lies, we have arrived at The One Creative Truth.

THE ONE CREATIVE TRUTH: EVERY AD MUST HAVE AN IDEA IN IT

Nothing in life, nor advertising, is easy. The value of the great single-minded idea is under siege, or so it seems. Executionally-driven work, where the idea is secondary or even non-existent, appears to have become a respectable creative form. While execution can act as a brand separator, can it ever substitute for a genuine idea?

"Of course every ad should have an idea," affirms Heffels, "otherwise it's not necessary to run it. An execution can't be an idea. It's only the vehicle to transport the idea."

"In my opinion, execution is never more important than the content," states Ron Mather.

Goldsmith recounts the joke about the art director who jumps up and says: "I've got an idea ... Herb Ritts!"

"It's a laziness," shrugs Goldsmith. "There's this illusion that if you use people who have shot good work, you will have good work, too. Execution is becoming such an equal playing field. Everyone can go out and buy all these computers. People are pretty hard to shock with execution." In Goldsmith's view, creating an idea still has the edge. "You tend to remember execution for a short while. You tend to remember ideas for a long time."

"I'm always suspicious of technique," Cohen confides. "I always feel it's a little bit self-conscious. It gets into smoke-and-mirrors land. It's shallow and gets very samey. There are agencies that do a lot of very executional, stylistic work. I like it to a degree, but I don't love it like I love a bit of work that makes me look at myself, that makes me smile." Cohen points to the great landmark ads which are still talked about in the industry. More often than not, he says, they were not that expensive to make. They didn't rely on technique or execution. They relied simply on putting a great premise in front of people. "There was nothing executional or flashy about the old Volkswagen work. It was presenting an underdog and talking honestly about it."

Ironically, it was the great Bernbach himself who said: *"Execution becomes content in a work of genius."* His words have haunted the idea-driven purists ever since. They have been quoted and misquoted in support of countless executionally-led campaigns, the last word being conveniently overlooked.

Grace was closer to Bernbach than most. The way he reads it: "There's nothing wrong with accepting it as an axiom, but like other truths, sometimes they're Big Truths and sometimes they're Little Truths. I think he was right, but I don't think it's formulaic. Sometimes, a simple photograph and no words at all can convey enormous amounts of information in a very profound way. Sometimes the presentation of a picture or graphics has some sort of emotional content that *can* be the message. But it has to be brilliant execution to work that way. It isn't something that's going to work as a formula all the time. Unfortunately, or fortunately, the majority of things that are done that way are just empty, meaningless and transparent. A lot of it is just surface decoration with no emotional content. Obviously, a lot of stuff comes out of computers. Many things are so overly designed, they interfere with the basic communication." Grace ponders whether the famous Volkswagen *Lemon* ad would look the same if it was executed today. "I would hope that whoever came up with *Lemon* now would have enough sense to understand what it is they're doing and keep it stark and lean and powerful."

French believes execution defines the tone of voice, but warns against relying on it to replace an idea. "There are occasions when the execution is so original, and so powerful, it becomes the idea. In our Bank of China work there wasn't the ghost of an idea, unless you said the Bank of China is Chinese, therefore that's the idea. But it's very difficult to be that original, because there are only so many ways of doing something. It's much easier to take the tough way and have an idea."

"I think the execution has got to build up to something, or mean something," says Stow. "It's not enough just to have pretty pictures. People are smart enough to see through that. But if it builds up a really unique and distinct tone of voice for a brand, then that makes it different."

Hegarty sees execution in terms of ambience, *adding depth to an idea*. "Our advertising is very, very simple, incredibly simple, in its thought process. Good advertising has to be that because people aren't prepared to give it a huge amount of time. People want simple things from the brand; what you can put *around* it is an ambience and an attitude that has a depth and complexity to it, a series of layers." BBH work demonstrates a textured, layered approach to simple strategies and ideas; as each layer is peeled off, another level of intelligence is revealed. But it's not about making things complex, says Hegarty. "Great pieces of communication work on a number of levels. They work on a very simple level; you get the idea straight away. But then they have a repetitive factor to them, so when you come back to them you see more things. I think that's very important when ads are repeated again and again. You can see something else in the way it was put down, a greater depth, something else is going on there." Hegarty believes the way you communicate should have a poignancy and power to it. He draws a parallel with movies. "For me, great movies are ones which are populist, but have a depth to them. On one level you can look at *One Flew Over the Cuckoo's Nest* and say it's all about Jack Nicholson, a bit of a wacky guy who can't get on in society; there are some good jokes in it, and in the end he dies, fine, that's the way life is sometimes. Or, on another level, you can look upon it as a very moving observation of society; how it excludes people who are different. It has a lot of depth and meaning to it. It approaches its audiences at all stages and at all levels, and I do like communication that does that. The more you get into it, the more it *includes*."

"Execution can be 50 percent of the ad, sometimes even more," David Droga believes, "but there is always a danger of things being overexecuted, and when you dig below the surface there's nothing. The bigger shame is when you see a great idea that's hidden below something."

David Abbott recognises the influence of a new generation. "A commonplace truism now is that we're talking to a generation bred on television and video. They have visual rather than verbal minds. They react to imagery more than the written word. I think there's some truth in that, you can't just discount that. I think that imagery is playing a bigger part in UK advertising. It's always been a strong tradition in Europe and especially on the West Coast of America. I think that's something to do with the sunshine," he quips, "and as we're getting warmer here, maybe it's got nothing to do with art directors at all."

Not surprisingly, Abbott confesses he is a purist. "I don't think I'm necessarily right, but I just do what I do as well as I can do it. I try and change, I try and embrace some of these things, but even if it's a non-verbal communication I still like to find an idea at the root of it. I think in the best execution routes there's an idea. In a lot of it there isn't, and unless the image is truly outstanding, it isn't as *memorable* somehow as a phrase, or a thought, or an insight. What happens, it seems to me, in the sports shoe market, you get your very, very quick imitators. You get everybody merging into everybody else. If that's all you've got, a panoply of images, it's easier to imitate and confuse one with the other. Whereas a statement is a statement, and it is allied to a brand and a proposition. There's more chance, long term, of being unique and individual."

The sports shoe market is at the forefront of the debate. Some argue that Nike print ads do not have ideas in them, merely an attitude. Others believe the attitude *is* the idea.

"It's okay to have attitude in an ad," concedes Barrie, "but not insincere attitude, phony attitude. Probably what I hate most is the kind of advertising that insincerely says, we know who you are. It tries to get into your head. Nike has done stuff in that vein, but done it really well and so poetically that it doesn't feel like advertising at all."

"I think Nike print ads are pretty crappy," asserts French, "and have become more crappy as time has gone on. Their line, *Just do it*, said to an extent that the end justifies the means. It was inherently baaaaaad, which was what was so good about it, which is why large black people who play netball wear Nike shoes because they're baaaaaad. 'It is easier to obtain forgiveness than permission' would have been a nicer way of saying it, but *Just do it* was snappier. Nike forgot the plot. It's supposed to be a rebellious brand that doesn't take notice of authority figures, but at one point in their lives they forgot that. Michael Jordan is one of the richest men in America, so how can he be a rebel? The seeds of their own destruction were sown at the moment they bought the very thing that made them. Almost a Greek tragedy in the making."

Delaney believes it is not a matter of saying that execution-based work is purely superficial and idea-based work is somehow deep and meaningful. "Advertising is there to capture people's imagination in the first instance, then to help them enjoy a relationship with the brand. In that sense, there isn't just idea-based or execution-based advertising; it's the kind of relationship you want. You may *want* to have a superficial relationship. Most fashion advertising doesn't have any idea in it, but it's highly successful. If you look at a brand like Prada, it's come from nowhere. It does advertising which is skilfully shot, with a beautiful model, with just a logo. That is an execution. There's no idea that I can see in it, but the brand is vastly successful. It plainly has an advertising relationship with its audience. The same can be said over the years for Calvin Klein and Tommy Hilfiger. They don't have advertising relationships that I would relate to, but they do have advertising relationships that their audience relates to, and it's *only* execution. Inside the execution, there are things that can be decoded and, on that basis, it is *more* than just a superficial execution. It's got depth to it."

Delaney says an idea should be used when the product itself does not necessarily grab people's imagination in a very crowded category. "If you're talking about a bath cleaner, or a rather ordinary, utilitarian product, that's the time when you can capture someone's imagination and delineate that product from its competitors by using an idea." As a preference, though, Delaney would try to build ideas into fashion ads as well. "You want something which is a little deeper than a photograph."

Execution, however, serves another purpose in Delaney's view. "Execution signals to people a kind of craft, which then goes on to signal that you have some conviction about the product. There's a direct correlation between the degree of craft in the execution and the fact that the advertiser really has some sense of belief and care, and even craft, within his product."

While the One Creative Truth is open to interpretation, French's logic is irresistible: "I'm trying desperately to think of anyone famous who has actually produced great advertising using only an execution. I can't, therefore it doesn't work."

4

THE CREATIVE WORK
BEFORE
THE CREATIVE WORK

Cutting edge creativity does not happen in a vacuum. As you will see, breakthroughs in creativity are often the result of breakthroughs in strategic thinking. Strategic leaps produce creative leaps.

In the same way that people are questioning the Eight Greatest Lies of print creativity, people are also questioning the conventional ways of building brands. New marketing paradigms are being adopted. Single-minded thinking is shifting to open-minded thinking. Marketing strategists are not just thinking outside the box; they are discarding the box altogether.

These changes are not superficial. They are fundamental. Not only will they disrupt the cosy rules of the marketplace, they will challenge the whole process of writing strategies and briefs in advertising agencies.

Mary Stow says, "A brief is only good if it produces good work." Yet the system used for producing briefs is based on conventional agency methodologies which have remained the same for decades.

As a cutting edge communicator, you need to know what is happening. You need to understand the changes. You need to see how they will impact on your own creative thinking process, because they will.

STRATEGIES AND BRIEFS

The joke goes something like this: a copywriter and an account director were visiting a client in Paris. The copywriter asked the account director how to get to the client's office, and the account director handed him a map of Europe.

Too often, conventional agency methodologies produce strategies and briefs which are meaningless. *Strategy* is probably the most abused word in advertising.

A strategy is not a request to produce a campaign. It should be the blueprint for the campaign, the path through the minefield.

What is a strategy? Simply put, if the objective is to get to New York, the strategic options are (a) take a plane, (b) take a bus, (c) take a train, or (d) drive there. If the client, the account director, the planner and the creative director all agree that taking a bus would be the best way to achieve the objective, that is the strategy. If the writer and art director decide to take a plane instead, they are *off*-strategy.

The analogy is crude, perhaps, but it makes the point. And a lot of creative work has to happen before the actual creative work can begin.

Simon Sherwood defines a strategy as *the single starting point for the creative process.* "Good strategies are very liberating, as opposed to very constraining. They should have a very clearly framed proposition from which the advertising can leap and a very clear direction in which the advertising can move."

Providing that single starting point is a very distinct skill. The account director and planner, often in consultation with the client, must make a series of decisions before reaching a judgement about what the advertising has to say. All too frequently, their thinking process will have been governed by logic and the rules of the category. Unless there is room for intuitive thinking, and lateral thinking, chances are their strategy will be a cookie-cutter replica of everyone else in the category.

"The trouble with logic, process and analysis," explains Sherwood, "is that everyone tends to end up in the same place. In the last ten years, our industry has been too concerned with things that can be measured. Too much value has been placed on research and getting consumer approval. People are frightened of making mistakes. With intuition goes risk." Sherwood hopes that clients and agencies can become less reliant on data, less reliant on analysis. "They must become more confident of their own ability to make judgements."

Intuitive, entrepreneurial judgements still drive the most successful marketing exercises, believes Ian Batey, from building an airline around a girl to something as bizarre as turning miners' boots into disco clogs. "We've got so much information at our fingertips, so much data, and we get driven along by it, that we forget that marketing and strategies are still esoteric things. Marketing is not a science, marketing is an *art*."

If the strategy is a mirror image of everyone else in the category, the creativity will suffer a similar fate.

If the strategy breaks new ground in the category, the creativity will, too.

As Ezra Pound said, "Make it new for me."

BRAND BUILDING

The ways brands are built, and the ways their personalities are defined and developed, are changing. In some quarters, the changes are radical; in other companies, imperceptible. Without question, though, their impact on creativity will be substantial.

According to conventional wisdom, companies used to work with a statement of the brand. It was carved in stone. This is what the brand is now. This is what it will be forever.

Some marketers would identify the single point of product difference. It, too, would be carved in stone. It would be the pillar on which all advertising was built. Now and forever, amen.

In recent years, the first cracks in the matrix appeared.

"It was amazingly constraining," argues Rod Wright of BDDP. "You cannot live on simple product differences in today's world. You cannot be so dogmatic about a brand and hope to stay relevant. As the consumer changes, how do you then shift your relationship?"

According to convention, the brand's personality is also carved in stone, and usually in an arbitrary way.

Stow has a horror of briefs which connect a list of adjectives to the brand personality. "They're meaningless," she says. The most commonly used include: Warm, Friendly, Innovative, Stylish, Caring, Contemporary, Dynamic. Pick any three or use them all.

"People are trying to establish a personality, but what they can't get their heads around is change." Stow draws an analogy with a human being. "You can't write down and fix in time that this person will always be X, Y and Z. A much more useful way of thinking about a brand is giving the sense of a living person, how they will grow and develop." She cites Tango as an example: "Tango can stay real-life, urban, young, streetwise, a bit of a lad. These quintessential characteristics can continue. The brand might dress slightly differently, and behave slightly differently, but fundamentally it will always be the young lad on the street."

Obviously a brand cannot keep changing, otherwise nothing will be built for the long term. It has to have some kind of structure. The question is, what kind?

"It should not be rigid. You have to build *elasticity* into a brand," Wright advocates. "You have to know what you can stretch with the consumer, and what is unstretchable."

As Wright points out, all successful companies and brands have core values. The task is to identify other values, other things, which the consumer would give you permission to change.

Wright likens the ideal consumer relationship to a rope. "Once, the convention was to build a rigid brand structure, with a rigid connection to the consumer. But in today's marketplace, the consumer is exposed to a constant stream of different stimuli. Their view will be moving. The brand will need to respond. So you have to allow for movement in the relationship. The consumer can move, the brand can move, but a rope keeps them connected."

Wright believes ropes are made when marketers communicate not so much what they make, but what they believe in. "Mercedes-Benz stands for brilliant product. Volvo says safety. What do other car makers stand for? There are blanks behind their brands. Brands should have points of view to which consumers are sympathetic."

Author Will Self once spoke of a *coinage of sympathy*: "I completely identify with that sentiment or that idea or that experience and I've never heard it articulated to me in exactly that way." By residing its brand in the soul of the athlete, Nike commanded such sympathies. When consumers discovered that sports shoes were allegedly made in offensive Asian sweatshops, the coinage was devalued.

Richard Kirshenbaum and Jonathan Bond describe brands as *communities of users*. Great brands, they argue, have a cultish quality, bonding consumers to the brand through a sense of belonging. A perfect example is Harley-Davidson, which has engendered a sense of community beyond its physical products, a virtual blood brotherhood where users are members.

Brand elasticity, ropes, communities of users, coinages of sympathy: dangerous talk indeed, and certainly not the way things are supposed to be. But if we reject the old brand building models, and all their conventional baggage, what lies ahead? More heresy?

What you will find is a return to the days when marketers trusted their innate intelligence. New brand building methodologies are pragmatic. Certainly, intuition and risk-taking are at their heart. But so, too, are the painful lessons derived from propping up antiquated brand structures.

Two examples demonstrate the leap from logic to ideas, promising more scope for creativity rather than less.

"Disruption"

Jean-Marie Dru, co-founder and chairman of France's BDDP agency, now part of TBWA Worldwide, uses the term *Disruption* for his revolutionary approach to marketing.

"If you don't create change," explains Wright, "change will create you. The Disruption Theory starts from the premise that every company exists in a world where things are constantly changing in the context of the company, the brand, the marketplace and the consumer. Every company builds up a set of conventions about the way it operates, about the way its culture works. If a company is to move forward, it has to be able to break through its own way of looking at things; it has to disrupt its own conventions."

There are four spheres of conventions. "Corporate conventions are about how a company sees itself and how it works. Marketing conventions are the way companies in a category go to market, like banks offering friendly, personal service. Communication conventions are the way companies in a category advertise their products; shampoos always show silky hair, pizza ads always show melty cheese. Consumer conventions are the way consumers see products in a category. Using Disruption methodology, you can plan for different scenarios," suggests Wright. "If a company wanted to disrupt its marketing conventions, if it wanted to go to market in a different way, it may need to change its corporate conventions, too. A disruption in one sphere may well be the *vision* which drives changes in the other spheres."

The real challenge is for companies to make sure that the external brand and the internal brand meet. "You can't offer a brand relationship unless you have connected all the spheres. The corporate culture has to want to deliver the marketing. The marketing culture has to want to deliver the communications. And the consumer has to see the consistency."

According to Wright, Sony has achieved this consistency. As a result, it continues to offer credible brand relationships. But for many other companies, the dream has soured.

"They start off brilliantly," says BDDP planner Fiona Clancy, "but lose their edge, their motivation, their specialness. They get themselves into a stagnant or even vicious circle. Often they try to rectify it through communication, in the hope that a better, brighter advertising campaign will revitalise the relationship with the consumer. And sometimes it works; communication can have an extraordinary effect on all aspects of a business. But it's rarely the communication alone. Behind such breakthrough communication, there's usually a new evangelist, a visionary, changing the energy in the company."

But "just saying something", Clancy believes, will not transcend the turbulence of the marketplace. Companies must identify where key brand relationships lie, what makes them solid, and who and what can sustain them. Advertising must help build *sustainable* brand equities.

To help bring advertising disruptions into focus, Clancy uses a tool called the *Ladder*, offering six different areas called registers in which campaigns can be developed: Top of Mind, Attribute, Benefit, Territory, Value and Role. Shifting the advertising message from one register to another can be highly disruptive, as when Pepsi abandoned Benefit (taste) in favour of Territory (*The Choice of a New Generation*). The ladder provides a clear picture of advertising activity in any category. If the brand's competitors have situated their advertising in the Attribute and Benefit registers, the strategist can disrupt the category by claiming a Role or upholding a Value.

Once the fear of change is removed, companies gain a new sense of control. "Disruption is all about brands in permanent transition, all about control in permanent turbulence," says Wright.

"In this context," he adds, "we don't talk about share of market, but share of the future."

"The Unthought Known"

At Howell Henry Chaldecott Lury, over twenty dedicated multi-disciplined project teams search for the *Unthought Known*, a key principle in the agency's brand building methodology.

"A lot of people produce communications which play so obviously to the rules of the market," observes Stow. "If they were talking about cars, for instance, they'd have lots of shots of the car, and sex would be a subtext. We'd say, hang on a minute, that might be the perceived wisdom, the rules of the market, but let's see if we can break one or two of those rules and see if that makes us stand out, which it usually does."

According to Stow, the agency has done away with the typical agency relay race. The account director, planner, writer and art director work as a team the whole way through. They do the research together, they set the strategy together, they develop the creative work together. "Because the teams work so closely, you don't have that awful ownership issue," says Stow.

The agency's methodology defies both conventional and *uncon*ventional wisdom. Brand building begins with research, but not with consumers.

"We tend to do a lot of research into the client organisation which is either behind the brand or is itself the brand," Stow elaborates. "That's

Howell Henry Chaldecott Lury, London, discovered the Unthought Known for the AA.

where the point of difference will be. It will be in the cultural values of the organisation, or in the beliefs of the people working there."

Stow describes the process which led to the creative leap in the agency's campaign for the AA. "We did a lot of research into the way the Automobile Association worked. We interviewed the patrolmen, talked to them about their jobs, their lives. What we were looking for was the Unthought Known. We found it in some of the things the patrolmen said. They told us things like, 'Often we get to the scene of an accident before the other emergency services'. Just off-the-cuff comments like that. The team was throwing around what the patrolmen had said. It was the art director who was the first person to articulate the idea of *The Fourth Emergency Service*. It was a great strategic thought!"

It was not just a reframing of the AA in advertising terms; it required the organisation to change fundamentally.

As Stow points out: "If your car does break down, it's a genuine emergency for you. But the AA had to ask itself if it was prepared to stand up and compare itself to the police."

What had been a traditional breakdown service with nice, friendly patrolmen completely restructured and rebranded itself. "They changed all the old vans; they now look like police cars. They answer the phones and say, 'AA Emergency Service'. They give priority to lone women motorists in certain cases. In every sense, they became *The Fourth Emergency Service*."

From a declining membership of 7.5 million, the AA now has 9.5 million members and growing. Membership retention is running at an all-time high of 89 percent.

STRATEGIC INSIGHTS

Reading about brand building is only a start. Strategic thinking must become the subtext to your creative thinking. It must become instinctive. It helps to be what Lionel Hunt calls a student of human nature. The best creatives have this quality, as you are about to see. Their work is unconventional, so is their thinking. Yet, in the final analysis, their creative processes are disciplined. And they all share one thing in common: the ability to produce what in retrospect seems so clearly obvious, but somehow was not in the first place.

Outward Bound. Jim Mountjoy of Loeffler Ketchum Mountjoy, North Carolina, puts his creative leaps down to disciplined chaos. "Discipline means being an advocate for the consumer versus a mouth for the client. It means listening to and understanding the consumer's nuances, emotions and desires not readily apparent on the surface. It means steeping yourself in the product and the consumer to find the common ground. Once you've disciplined yourself, then you're free to create with intelligence and purpose. You let the chaos happen. A bare wall gets papered with ideas. You attempt to do more than meet the strategy. You try to top it. Make it smarter. Go a little crazy. Fire at will."

The North Carolina chapter of Outward Bound faced a classic perception-reality problem. Their previous advertising had convinced teenagers, the core audience, that Outward Bound was a cosy summer camp which their parents would like. The kids craved adventure and challenge, precisely what Outward Bound really offered. When Mountjoy's agency researched the under-20s, it unearthed diaries and journals written by young people who had endured the programme.

The agency had found "the common ground". As the creative team riffed through the accounts of the wilderness-from-hell, they started making connections for stark, simple visuals. Kids told how they had answered the call of nature whilst being surrounded by it. How they had become incredibly resourceful. How scared they had felt on rock climbs.

The images of the hand, leaves and knots symbolise the soul of an Outward Bound adventure. The art direction preserves the rugged honesty of the woods and the handwritten experiences in those diaries. The brown sepia tone conveys a taste of roughing it.

Visa Gold. When Antony Redman was creative director at Batey Ads, Singapore, a pan-Asian campaign for the Visa Gold credit card presented both strategic and creative opportunities. "In Asia, there was burgeoning wealth," recalls Redman. "There was an almost wanton look on people's faces which you don't see in the West. Their idea of success was to amass all material possessions possible, to have it bigger, faster, stronger, shinier than anyone else. When it came to the credit card product category, those kinds of people wanted American Express Gold. It was the epitome of everything,

A strategic, unconventional solution to a perception-reality problem.
Loeffler Ketchum Mountjoy's campaign for Outward Bound
was inspired by first-hand consumer experiences.

the equivalent of a Rolex or a Mercedes-Benz. Yet within that environment of the *nouveau riche*, there was a younger group aged from twenty to thirty-five, maybe forty; in amongst all the uniformity and respect for authority that you have in Asia, they were trying to assert their individuality. They still wanted the same things, but they wanted to be seen as more individualistic, more international. They'd been educated in America or Europe or Australia, they had a more worldly outlook. The brief was to reach them, to get them to switch from Amex Gold to Visa Gold."

Redman knew that Visa Gold would have to break the convention in its category. "All those gold credit card *cliches* of people in restaurants, or driving a Porsche, wouldn't talk to our target audience."

His first decision was to make the campaign visually-led. "It had to work regionally. Also, the audience we wanted didn't have time to read. And because everyone knows what a credit card is for, what it does, there was nothing truly interesting to say. Instead, we asked ourselves, what is truly interesting about the people we're going to advertise to?"

Two creative teams explored four different directions. Ultimately, one campaign led through its originality, tonality and strategic appropriateness.

"It took the conventions of wealth and *subverted* them. When you're in the luxury market and you want to say something different, you need to subvert, to flip it on its head a bit. Some ideas were funny, but didn't show the wealth. The people we were talking to still wanted to be told they were wealthy and successful. What this campaign also tells them is that they have a sense of individuality, as well as a sense of humour."

Over sixty different concepts were tabled; five ultimately ran. The first ad which set the tone for the series was an impeccably shot bottle of rare vintage wine. It was, in itself, a parody of classic wine advertisements. On second glance, however, the reader discovered a cheeky straw poking out of the bottle. "It totally subverted the imagery associated with gold credit cards," says Redman.

The *cliche* of the facial was another target. "Someone who is wealthy goes to a spa. They lie down, and they've got all their fluffy towels, and they get a facial. So we subverted that. We said if someone is wealthy enough, and individual enough, they could treat their dog to a facial as well. Then we went the other way. We took a cheesy bit of popular culture, the hot dog. We said someone who is wealthy enough, and individual enough, could decide to put the finest caviar on it, rather than mustard."

Another ad showed pigeons wearing diapers sitting on a branch above a collection of luxury cars. In another, the owner has put his pet dog on the treadmill. Ideas which did not see the light of day included a mansion with Beavis and Butthead statues outside and a wealthy estate where all the bushes had been trimmed fastidiously into the shapes of famous cartoon characters.

"Originally, the line we had was *Whatever*, meaning whatever you want to buy, whatever you're into, whatever. But in Asia, whatever is also used in another way. If someone is lecturing you, ticking you off, and you want to annoy them, you say 'Whatever'. So we had a campaign, but no line."

Eventually the strapline came from the agency chairman, Rick Scott-Blackhall. "Rick had a passion for the product and the campaign, and it's integral to have that in an agency, from the top down. One morning he came in with a list of anonymous quotes. When I saw the line, the play on gold, I knew it said everything we wanted to say. *He who has the gold makes the rules* said you've got the money, you've got the power, you can do whatever you like, you can break the rules and make new ones, and damn anyone else who says otherwise."

Redman believes great ideas just do not come from the creative department. "I think it's important to have your ears out, to listen. You should open up to opinions. Some are damaging and boring, but some are worth listening to. Take it in, suck it all up, then edit out what you don't need."

The campaign was shot by Mike Skelton in Australia and art directed by Redman. "The visuals had to tell the story, deliver the humour. I kept the rest simple. The line was set in plain, boring Bembo. You need a simple, classic face for the luxury category."

As the full colour pages rolled out across Asia, eyebrows were raised from Taiwan to Thailand. Ultimately, though, the healthy dose of subversion left an indelible, highly successful footprint in Asia's conservative financial services category.

VISA GOLD. He who has the gold makes the rules.

Visa Gold subverted the conventions of wealth when it targeted wealthy young Asians keen to assert their individuality. Batey Ads, Singapore.

Sol Mexican Beer. The award-winning Sol ad is virtually a photograph of the strategy. According to creative director Jay Pond-Jones:

"There were two Mexican beer brands in the British market. Corona, the other one, was almost generic for Mexican beer. People would always ask for a Corona. Actually, the thing that was really generic about Mexican beer was the slice of lime in the top. Our thinking was if we could find a way of owning limes, then hopefully that generic would transfer to Sol."

Pond-Jones set out to brand the generic. The original idea was to brand every lime with a Sol sticker as it came into the country. "There were twenty times as many limes being sold as there had been previously, but unfortunately the fruit importers refused to believe this had anything to do with the phenomenon of Mexican beer. They couldn't be fussed with it." Unable to brand the actual fruit, the idea was pursued in a print ad.

The concept broke conventions, yet it took less than an hour to sell. "The client didn't even see a rough. I just described it to him. I think it helped that I knew more about Sol than he knew himself. I'd read the history of Sol. It was initially brewed by a German, a kind of black sheep of his family, who'd left the Black Forest and gone off to live in sunny Mexico. He happened to be living in a part of Mexico which had particularly good water so he figured he could start brewing beer again. I think it was having a real passion and understanding of what the brand was all about that talked him around."

At no stage were captions or copy considered. "The picture said it all. We mulled over other ideas for the background, but yellow seemed appropriate because it said sun. The beer got its name when the German held it up to the sunlight; it was sparkly and sunny and clear, so he called it Sol."

The photographic style was also unconventional. "I didn't want it to look like a piece of fruit, I didn't want a food shot. My brief to the photographer, Charles Liddall, was to photograph it like a piece of jewellery, so it had a fashiony feel."

The ad first ran in magazines, then later on illuminated adshells. "We managed to buy lots of outside back covers. Because our offices were in Soho," Pond-Jones confesses, "we used to send runners out to the local newsagents to turn the magazines back to front. You'd go into the newsagencies and there'd be piles and piles of this Sol image all over them."

*Branding the generic:
if Sol could own limes,
it could own Mexican beer.
Photographer Charles Liddall
is now based in
Kuala Lumpur, Malaysia.*

The Village Voice. What, on the surface, might appear an extremely outrageous campaign was created to address two strategic issues. Both were critical to the newspaper's survival.

"*The Village Voice* was about to change its business structure," explains Nick Cohen of Mad Dogs & Englishmen. "After being sold by subscription for years, the *Voice* was about to be given away free. From a business standpoint, they wanted to increase circulation. If they got more copies out there, they'd get a new audience. But there was a concern on the part of the client that it would be a real negative. Like, suddenly the paper wasn't worth anything any more, it was free because it wasn't worth paying for any more."

The agency had to grapple with a second strategic issue. The *Voice* wanted to attract a younger audience. "The problem the *Voice* faced was that they'd been around since the late 1950s. The kind of people who had co-opted the *Voice* when it first came out were the hippie generation. Young people thought, well, that's *their* paper, it isn't *our* paper. So we wanted young people in New York to realise how important the *Voice* was to them. The *Voice* was a pioneer. It was a newspaper that made it very possible for young people to live a kind of lifestyle that wouldn't be acceptable in other parts of America. If you're gay, for example, it's very hard to practise, to be open about the fact in most parts of America. But you can in New York, you can in the Village, that's what it was all about. It was about

Turning the mirror on the enemy, Mad Dogs & Englishmen solved two strategic problems for the Village Voice.

people being allowed to be themselves. Young people had forgotten that. They were all too ready to slag off the *Voice* rather than give it credit for what it had made possible."

In order to win that credit from younger people, as well as retain the paper's credibility among existing readers, the campaign focused on prejudice and hostility. Rather than turn the mirror on the target audience, the agency turned it the other way: on those most opposed to the paper and all it stood for. In so doing, the interests of both younger and older readers were unified.

"We reminded them that it's *Not America's favourite paper*," says Cohen. "The kind of people who live in Idaho, or wherever, are not going to accept the *Voice* at all. They're going to reject it, and reject anyone who reads it. So what the campaign was saying was, Thank God for *The Village Voice. The Village Voice* has made it possible for you to live the kind of lifestyle that you want to live. Give them credit. Support them. Don't forget that this paper is for you, and if it went away, it would be a worse world for you to live in than if it's around."

The campaign worked, paving the way for the *Voice* to go free without losing any credibility. The message also resonated for younger readers. As Cohen muses: "Everyone who's young, eventually they're all going to become fifty, but is our spirit going to be alive? The *Voice* is for people who are free spirits."

XO Beer. When Singapore Press Holdings briefed Neil French to promote its newspapers to the local advertising industry, they little realised the train of events they were setting in motion. XO Beer is essentially a study in lateral thinking. An unconventional strategy evolved, leap by leap, eventually reaching a highly unconventional creative solution. In the process, the need to be creator-and-critic emerges clearly. A schizophrenic function, it separates cutting edge communicators from the rest.

The XO story began routinely enough.

"The first thing I did was produce a campaign based on all the facts that said newspapers are as powerful, maybe more powerful, than television," recalls French. "I wrote it and sold it and they thought it was jolly good. But the next day I called up and said, look, we can't do that because I've just realised that those facts are totally available to everybody, and the fact they're ignoring the facts means there's no point in telling them again. That'd be silly. So I apologised very much and said I'd do some new ads.

"They said they wanted to get the FMCG business, detergents, shampoos, beer, that kind of stuff. So I said, let's pick one for a start. Beer seemed like the more relevant to me than shampoo, because I don't have any hair. What we'll do, I said, is go out and find a small, unadvertised brand of beer, do some great ads for it, put them in a newspaper, sell lots of beer, thereby proving print to the big beer advertisers. The clients said, right, okay, and off they went."

"The next day I rang them up and said, sorry about this, I've changed my mind again. We can't do that because if we do it success-

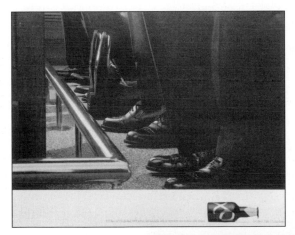

The campaign which Singapore breweries could not take lying down. Neil French, for Singapore Press Holdings.

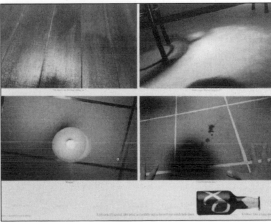

fully, the big brands will say we've been taking the rice out of their ricebowls and they'll never advertise with us. So we were forced into the position that if we can't tell them the facts, and we can't advertise a real beer, we'll advertise a fake beer. It was that easy. There didn't seem to be another way to do it."

French believed it was crucial to make things as difficult as possible for the new beer to succeed. "If we gave ourselves an easy trot, everyone would say, yeah, well, of course, anybody could have done that. We looked at the research which said that all beer must be light in colour these days, so we decided we'd make ours *black*. It must be light in alcohol, so we decided we'd make ours, toss a coin, *12% alcohol*. The ads must have photographs of girls, so we decided

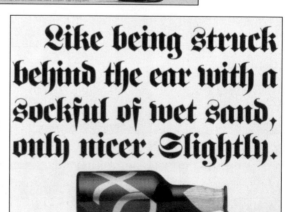

In research, consumers could recite the copy-led ads word-for-word.

not to have any photographs of girls. They must have status symbols, so we said *no* status symbols. They must have crowds of blokes having a jolly time in a pub, slapping each other on the back and pouring beer down their necks, as though people don't know what beer is for, do they rub it in their hair or something? Really, it's pathetic. Anyhow, we said we'd have *none* of that, either. Every rule we could find about beer advertising, we decided to *break*."

However, before he could do the ads, French had to name the product and design the packaging. "In naming it, in saying this beer was going to be powerful and expensive, I just ripped off the idea of the cognac which is XO," French explains. "I found out that XO wasn't ownable because it was a degree of cognac, so we could use it and no cognac company could sue us. I also found out I couldn't register it for beer as such, but that I could register the trademark. Which I did, in my own name."

French designed the XO logo so that it could be read on its side or the right way up. "There was a purpose in that. Most beer clients I've worked for are the most reactionary people one could ever come into contact with. They tend to forget that beer drinking is a rather jolly thing to be doing and they all get very serious about it and follow the rulebooks. It struck me that if you're selling a very strong beer that makes you fall over, then the bottle should have fallen over already."

The fallen bottle became a powerful campaign mnemonic. "If you look at the ads, there's no cap on it and it's dripping rather sadly. It's a drunken bottle, as well as a beer that makes you drunk. It seemed to me to be an important part of the message. It says this gets you very, very drunk."

The campaign was a celebration of inebriation. Singaporeans opened their morning papers and stared in disbelief at the ravages of alcohol. Collapsed drinkers, blood-flecked floors, a man about to drink XO with a pillow tied to the back of his head. In one execution, a barroom floor was sketched with coroner's chalk, showing where the bodies had fallen. In another, a naked man stared morosely down at his diminished manhood, thoughtfully framed out of shot. Beneath the visual, the little neck of the XO bottle was also drooping, "as things tend to do in my experience", observes French.

Another flight of ads were simple cryptic captions, set in Munich Beerhall Bold. They became so popular that readers could recite them word-for-word.

As one half page colour ad followed another, barmen and waiters found themselves harangued and abused. "It was getting a tad violent out there. People were saying, 'Give me some of that XO Beer', and the barman'd say, 'We haven't got any', and he'd be called a bloody idiot, 'Of course you've got it, *I saw it advertised!*' It was really very funny."

It was not so funny for the major breweries as they tried to trace their newest competitor. The newspapers, naturally enough, refused to disclose who was placing the ads. "We really covered our tracks," French confides. "We'd started a company called Xerxes & Osborn, which purported to be the importers. We knew some smart guy would get onto it, hey, there's a new importer, Xerxes & Osborn, *XO*, I reckon it's *them!* So we got a phone number and put a girl on to answer it. If anyone asked for Mr. Xerxes or Mr. Osborn in the morning, she was instructed to say that they had very bad hangovers and would not be coming in. If anyone rang after lunch, she would say, sorry, but they've had a very large lunch, they've gone home to sleep it off. So the company was apparently run by two alcoholics who were never in the office and that really annoyed the breweries."

The campaign climaxed on the night of 31 March when a big party was held, ostensibly to launch the beer. Brewery executives and the advertising fraternity were invited. However, when they arrived, there was not a drop of XO to be had. They were told it had been held up at the docks. There were plenty of other beers to drink while they waited.

"At midnight, the boss of the newspaper got up and said, 'April Fool!' The breweries were very, very grumpy, but we'd proven our case. You *could* create demand for a beer in newspapers."

There was a postscript to the story. "When the beer people got stroppy, the newspaper people got stroppy back. The beer people said it was a product that didn't exist so it was easy, which is of course nonsense, so the newspaper people said in that case, we'll make the damn stuff. We got a microbrewery to start making XO, ran two more ads, and they were sold out in three days. They could see they were going to have to make a lot more, but they were having to pay me a dollar a glass, which was very nice, thank you very much, because I owned the brand. But they didn't want to pay me any more, so they took down all the XO posters and when people turned up they said, sorry, we haven't got any XO, but we've got this other stuff which is exactly the same. They were quite right, of course, it was the same, same recipe, same barrels, but people didn't want it and the place went broke. *Which is the power of the brand.*"

YES, VIRGINIA, THERE ARE *RETAIL* STRATEGIES, TOO

Hurry – Last Days is not an idea. Neither are *Giant Birthday Sale* nor *Special Offer – Save up to 25%*. Retail print is one of the world's biggest advertising categories, and creatively one of the most disastrous.

Most retailers perceive themselves as outlets, a good plumbing term which says a lot about the advertising they pump into our daily papers. If you think of yourself as an outlet, you will simply run defensive price-led ads with stamp album layouts crammed with merchandise. You will never strike up relationships with customers and build something for the future.

In reality, retail stores are *brands*. Like any other brands, they can either follow convention or develop a real point of difference. A retailer who has nurtured strong brand relationships can override transient price differentials and survive a crisis. No brand, no image, means no loyalty, no visibility.

The same strategy applies to dealerships and service providers. As technology makes everything the same, the *dealer* becomes the difference. Smart dealers who build brand relationships cut the cost of generating leads. They come to own their categories.

Building brands in the retail sector does *not* mean abandoning sale ads or never showing merchandise and prices. It just means making a more conscious effort to communicate the flavour of the relationship, to surround the retail offer with some long-term substance. Retailers are actually in a luckier position than other brand builders: they can measure response instantly, and fine-tune their art direction and tonality accordingly.

Retailers will find many case histories to support their shift from

Gorilla tactics. Australian retail advertising guru David Mattingly recommends one compelling visual with an unexpected twist.

Cashing in on Christmas wine sales, while remaining consistent with the Harrods image. Leagas Delaney, London.

Read the Parker Knoll brochure in the discomfort of your own armchair.

Are you sitting uncomfortably?

Then we'll begin. The Parker Knoll brochure has 40 full-colour pages of contemporary and traditional suites, chairs and sofa-beds. And it's free.

To reserve your copy (together with price list and stockist list) send the coupon now.

Please send me your colour brochure, stockist list and price list. To Sue Black, Parker Knoll Ltd., P.O. Box 22, Frogmoor, High Wycombe, Bucks HP13 5DJ.

Name _____

Address _____

_____

Postcode _____

Parker Knoll
A CORNWELL PARKER COMPANY

*Striking up a relationship
with consumers,
with a smile, and making it easy
for them to respond.
Abbott Mead Vickers, London.*

*Most people would have said "Save 50%", but not Leagas Delaney.
Shoppers respond to propositions they haven't seen before.*

A big bang for small bucks. DDB Needham, Sydney.

As technology makes everything the same, the dealer is the difference. Here, dx.com promises sanity and value-added service in human terms. Internet-style art direction makes sense of the copy, service listing and address. Mad Dogs & Englishmen, New York.

The horrors of a foreign summer holiday versus the joys of staying home and shopping at IKEA. A human insight which everyone can recognise transforms pre-sale ads into brand builders. Abbott Mead Vickers, London.

price-led to brand-led advertising. Many guidelines exist to help them, as well as much good advice from people like David Mattingly, founder and chairman of Y & R Mattingly, Melbourne. Mattingly is Australia's retail advertising guru, the first Australian, in fact, to win an International Lifetime Achievement Award from the Retail Advertising and Marketing Association of the United States.

Mattingly believes a good retail ad should have four elements: a simple headline, an attractive visual, good copy and an effective layout. He argues that one great visual will hold a reader's attention, compelling him to read the headline and copy, whereas nobody will read a page crammed full of merchandise. Ads set the image, he says. The future direction of retail advertising, he predicts, would reflect that of retailing itself, where stores which are quick to pick up on trends will dominate.

Of course, it does not help improve retail advertising when so many people in creative circles look down with scorn on the category, or when agencies assign retail work to the juniors. The truth is that some of the world's best-known cutting edge creatives have happily turned their talents to retail print with exceptional results.

Sweeney's. Who said you cannot do something creative with a retail product shot and a small budget? Not Gary Goldsmith.

"It was a case of working backwards from where the restrictions were," says Goldsmith. "We knew we had to show the jewellery, we knew what the message basically had to be. So instead of trying to resist those things which we all so often try to do, instead of fighting what needs to be in the ads, we said how can we do it in a way that's different from anybody else?"

The jewellery sits on the page, as it has done in thousands of retail ads. "But instead of telling you why you should buy it, we tried to tap into emotion, to find a *device* that hadn't been done."

The breakthrough came by presenting the positive side of buying the jewellery, using the negative side as a foil. "It was a Jekyll and Hyde effect, reaching into the reader's generosity and meanness."

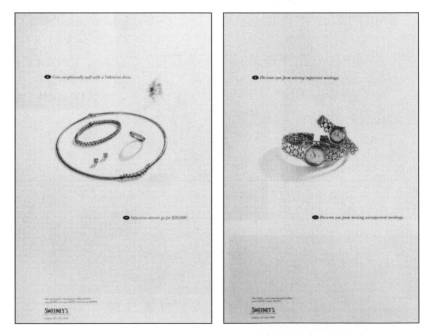

A breakthrough campaign for a jeweller. A simple idea, executed with wit and restraint, proves there are no such things as good or bad assignments.
Goldsmith/Jeffrey, New York.

The pros and cons are superbly argued. On one hand, the jewellery *Goes exceptionally well with a Valentino dress.* On the other hand, *Valentino dresses go for $20,000.* In an inspired touch of art direction, the positive and negative points of view are preceded by little battery symbols. The product copy, kept to a minimum, is tucked discreetly above the logo, located in the lower left corner. The ads are refined and restrained so the idea can breathe.

Goldsmith believes the campaign proves an important point to young creatives. Very often, he believes, the so-called bad assignments end up being the ones you do great work on. Even a routine brief for a jeweller, with no glamorous photography budget, can still be turned into a high profile piece of work. "Too many times, young people come into the business and they're waiting for an assignment that appears to be a great assignment," he says. "I really don't distinguish between good and bad assignments. I think you can do something great with just about anything."

By definition, it is not the assignments which are good or bad, merely the creative people.

IKEA Singapore. These days, it is unusual to find a campaign which has been running for ten years. It is even more unusual when the campaign is retail and has collected well over fifty international and local awards including Best of Show in its home market.

And, in a further paradox, the campaign's wit and intelligence is pitched deliberately *above* the heads of its target audience. Patrick Low, creative director of Dentsu Young & Rubicam, Singapore, explains why: "We want to talk to everybody, but if we did, the tonality of our ads would be just like everyone else's. Therefore we write the ads to appear as though we are talking upscale to the yuppies. Because everyone aspires to be better, they find the ads appealing." Low points out that the majority of Singaporeans are English-literate. "Some of them won't understand all the nuances of English. So if they don't get it right away, they will still try to get it, which is good. If they don't get it, they will feel they aren't in the right social bracket so they really make an effort."

The logic may seem inscrutable, but it works. "Everyone wants to own IKEA, to understand what the ads are talking about, to understand IKEA humour. If we lower our tone, we will lose our edge."

A consistently witty, irreverent tonality for ten years. IKEA pitches its humour
above the heads of the target audience to support its positioning.
Dentsu Young & Rubicam, Singapore.

The ads have always looked retail in style, but clever art direction and craftsmanship have elevated the stamp album approach to a minor art form. Invariably the ads are single-mindedly focused on one range of merchandise and related accessories, for example, beds, bedding and bedroom accessories, or plants and garden accessories. "We start with the main picture," says Low, "and build everything around that. We vary the sizes of other products. Laying out each ad can take a few hours. Before we had computers, we used to use photocopy machines. It took forever."

Low has been involved with the campaign virtually since its inception. "We do two new ads a month. We always use full pages and always in colour. Black-and-white ads don't stand out; they blend in with all the other retail ads. Response to black-and-white wasn't as good as colour."

Occasionally, IKEA's humour ruffles a few feathers. References to sleeping partners, for example, are not exactly commonplace in a typically staid Asian culture. When the Singapore government reshuffled its cabinet, IKEA jumped on the bandwagon, or, to be more precise, the back of buses which plied the Prime Minister's electorate, and promoted its storage systems.

Thom McAn. The scenario is familiar in retailing: a major retailer falls behind the times, and the public votes with its feet. As time marches on, winning back market share becomes harder. Cohen at Mad Dogs & Englishmen describes one such case.

"Thom McAn used to be America's shoe store. Everybody bought their shoes there. What happened was that they stopped being innovative, they stopped selling really cool shoes. Young people wouldn't go into their stores any more. They wouldn't be caught dead walking around with a Thom McAn bag."

The agency's brief was to win back the younger customers. "The company had revitalised the product. They had some good buyers. They got some better stuff in. So we had to do a campaign that said they'd changed, it was safe to come back."

Agency research discovered some surprising attitudes. "Young people said, oh yeah, that was the store where my parents took me, they dragged me in by my ears when we went to buy school shoes. So we showed them the new shoes and they said, these are quite

108

nice. We asked the kids, well, if you hate Thom McAn, if they went out of business would you really care? People held it quite dear to their hearts. They didn't go there, but they had a fondness for it, like an old uncle or something. They didn't want it to go away, but they didn't want to support it."

The agency also researched the client organisation. "They're very salt-of-the-earth, honest, really nice people."

It was that honesty which set the tone for the campaign, says Cohen. "Basically we *apologised* for the last two decades, for all the terrible shoes."

The apology was conveyed in a series of disarmingly frank yet funny statements. *Please excuse some of our shoe styles in the past*, begins one, before going on to blame a fluke computer error which resulted in the company being sent twenty-year-old calendars. The engaging message is overlaid on a section of integrated circuitry.

"Young people looked at the work, liked the fact that the company was being honest, and said, we'll give them a chance," recalls Cohen.

"Sorry, we screwed up, give us another chance": the strategy behind Thom McAn's campaign to woo back younger shoe buyers. Mad Dogs & Englishmen, New York.

Please excuse some of our shoe styles in the past.

Through a fluke computer error, the office supply store repeatedly sent us the wrong desk calendars and we still thought it was 1976.

THE NEW

T H O M M c A N

Your feet won't believe your eyes.

Thom McAn's dilemma had been a textbook one; but to solve it, the rulebook was ignored. The solution emerged through studying the corporate culture, and identifying honesty as the means to tap into consumer perceptions. In hindsight, it all sounds very logical and sensible, very easy and straightforward. At the time, however, it was not.

"We did something radical," Cohen reminds us. "We just said – sorry, we screwed up, give us another chance."

DEFYING CONVENTION

Strategic disciplines are arduous. We cannot rely on logic, because real life is not logical. Nor can we be disruptive just for the sake of being different. Stepping beyond the accepted conventions could well mean suffering a little time in the wilderness. But then, most of our advertising heroes were heretics once.

If you believe that most advertising today is still formulaic, superficial and transparent, take heart from Neil Godfrey.

"What I hated about advertising when I first started was that advertising was *advertising*. What we helped it become was something that slipped into your life, *an elbow touching you*. I tend to have chosen writers, or maybe they chose me, who really weren't advertising people as such. David Abbott, Tony Brignull, Indra Sinha. They were writers outside of advertising, who wanted to move away from the kind of *brashness* that advertising has. Somehow, if you're in advertising, you're a commercial person. It was the last thing I ever wanted to be. My mother used to introduce me to friends as a commercial artist, and it was the biggest insult I ever had."

By learning how to think strategically, by understanding more about human nature than brash formulae, by being your own creative self, you can respond to the new cutting edge disciplines. The industry will need your contribution if it is to stay relevant to its clients.

As Hugh Mackay says: "The rate of public sophistication and technological change is speeding up. Anyone under thirty knows what the advertising tricks are. Many have done media studies so they know all about propaganda, the impact of quick editing. They're very comfortable with it. From the point of view of the advertising industry, this is a very good thing. One of the myths about advertising is that it has some kind of mysterious power, that it can influence people without them knowing. The more people are educated, the more they understand the advertising process, they won't be scared of advertising. They won't think it's manipulating them in a secret way. They will be more *confident* as consumers. That should mean, if we do our job properly, they will enter the relationship with us more confidently. We should not fear the media-literate young. Quite the reverse. We can be more daring with the young. We can actually take *more* risks."

5

How to Get an Idea

We have some notions how advertising does and does not work. We have accepted that a lot of advertising truths, for the most part, are lies. We have seen how new brand building methodologies are replacing the old. We have a deeper appreciation of strategic thinking. Having consciously prepared ourselves to understand the advertising process, we can now enter the creative process.

Creativity, according to Dorothy Parker, is a disciplined eye and a wild mind. The question is, *how* disciplined and *how* wild?

Creativity is supposed to rely on inspiration. But as any author, artist, actor or composer will tell you, inspiration is unreliable. We cannot wait for inspiration. We have deadlines. We have to deliver. We have to reach our creative peaks *without* it.

We have to develop our own personal creative methodology. Rather like slipping on a comfortable old jacket every morning, our methodology will become second nature. It will be a reassuring series of steps, a mental checklist. Nothing formulaic, just a few things we can do to get ideas happening, to generate concepts. While we are focused and working, the inspired ideas will invariably surface.

The alternative is to stare into space.

Is There an Idea in the Product Name or Logo?

Some of the world's greatest campaigns have kicked off from this point. When the product name or logo becomes the idea, there is less risk of creating a generic campaign. The brand will brand the advertising from the centre out. And if the campaign thought contains an alliterative device, so much the better.

Ariston. You want to communicate that Ariston appliances are more durable. In fact, you want to own the word durability in the appliance category. The idea: *Ariston and on and on.*

DHL. You want to position DHL as the world's most reliable courier. You want to communicate the risks of packages ending up in the wrong hands. The idea: *DHL or else.*

Silk Cut. If you cannot talk about smoking, at least you can get people to talk about your advertising. The idea: *cut silk.*

Cow & Gate. Baby food advertising is riddled with generics. How can you make your ads unique when you cannot avoid showing a happy, gurgling baby? The idea: behind every happy, gurgling baby *show a cow and gate.*

Castlemaine XXXX Beer. How do you convince the British that XXXX is the beer Aussies would die for? XXXX, easy, mate! Everyone knows Australians swear a lot. And XXXX is often used to replace the four-letter word. The idea: *Australians wouldn't give a XXXX for anything else.*

The Independent. You want to differentiate the newspaper's beliefs. You want readers to identify with them. The idea: *The Independent. It is, are you?*

Time. Fallon McElligott's campaign for *Time* has been running four years. Art director Bob Barrie has chalked up over fifty executions.

"The truth is, it was the third campaign that we'd shown *Time.* We'd liked the first two quite a bit. In retrospect, they killed them for very appropriate reasons; they were tonally wrong, and they couldn't have been owned as well by *Time* as the one we eventually ended up with."

After the first two ideas were killed, Barrie recalls how he went back to his drawing board quite depressed. "I don't know exactly what happened, but I think that the *Time* red border was just emblazoned into my brain. I'd actually grown up with the magazine; my parents subscribed to it when I was a child in Green Bay, Wisconsin, and I'd subscribed to it all the way through college. I just started playing around with it on some photographs from the magazine, using it to isolate different parts of the image. It became the look of the ads. Then with some fine copywriting by Dean Buckhorn, the campaign kind of sprang to life."

Barrie believes the writing in *Time* magazine is as big a part of the product as the photography. "We tried to come up with a way to fuse the two in the advertising. When you're dealing with a product like *Time*, where you have access to what are basically some of the world's greatest photographs on a weekly basis, it would be idiotic not to use them. You can use a killer photograph of a man like Bill Clinton that ran in *Time*, without getting permission from Bill Clinton, because it's the product."

Having established the campaign based on the magazine's border and masthead, Barrie then looked into the craft details. "Rather than have big, bold headlines in the traditional Minneapolis look, I actually borrowed the typography from the editorial itself. If you look at it, it's spaced and set in the same point size as actual copy written in *Time* magazine."

Over the years, Barrie says, the campaign continued to evolve strategically. "While there's been no change in the look of the ads, the tagline has changed. It was originally *Understanding comes with Time* and the ads tended to be competitive against other media like television and newspapers. Then they wanted to take more of a high road and they positioned it as *The world's most interesting magazine*."

Creatively, Barrie sees the campaign has become more playful. "We've isolated ears, and a hand that took kickbacks, and we used double borders when cloning was a big debate. The Bill Clinton ad came out at the height of Zippergate. It was the first *Time* ad we did that has no headline. We approached them with a couple of ideas, but they said they didn't want to do an ad about Zippergate, they didn't want to pass judgement. Then we saw this photo which had run in *Time* where he's perspiring profusely. So we simply framed the perspiration on his forehead and said, here's an ad you can run because you're putting the onus on the reader."

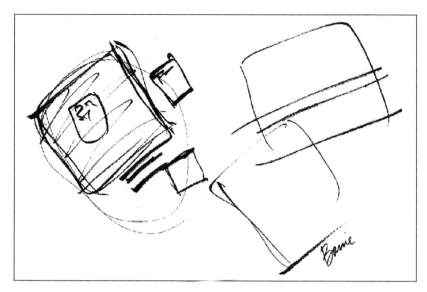

Back to the drawing board for Bob Barrie.

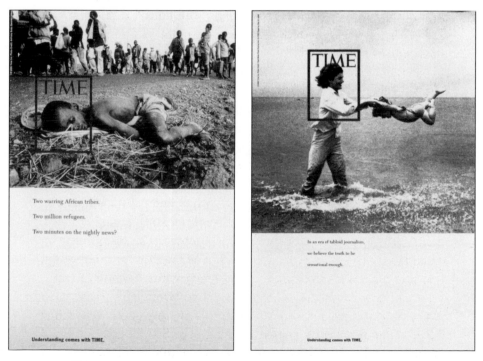

*"I love it when the design of the advertising comes out of the product,"
says Fallon McElligott art director Bob Barrie.*

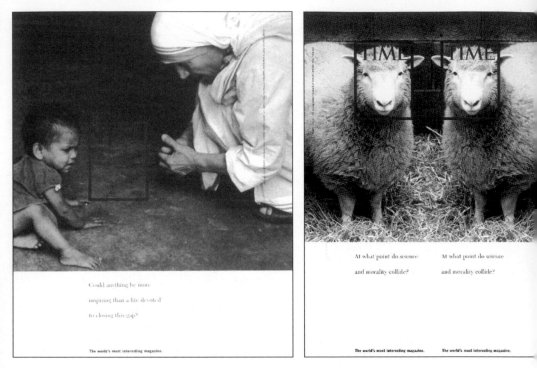

How a campaign can keep evolving and keep fresh.

The Economist. One of the great British campaigns, with its hallmark white on red, had its genesis when David Abbott, lost for an idea, sat staring at the magazine's masthead.

"I had a notion that you couldn't really spell out what we needed to say in long copy. It would be banal, and even rather offensive, to actually seriously try and say, read this and you'll be successful. Whereas you could probably get away with it with the kind of lateral, funny, witty lines that in themselves didn't take the notion too seriously, but would leave a kind of trace element of the idea in people's minds so, over a period of time, this would become a club that you wanted to belong to."

"I was sitting, wondering what to do, with the magazine in front of me," Abbott reflects, "with no real media direction, against a background where we'd done quite nice ads for *The Economist* over the years but nothing that really hung together as a campaign, and against a background where it was almost impossible to get body

Branding the beer that Aussies swear by. Saatchi & Saatchi, London.

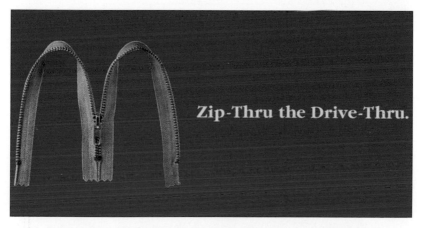

DDB Needham, Sydney, builds an idea around an unmistakable logo.

Staring at the magazine's logo led David Abbott from one kind of
Economist ad to another.

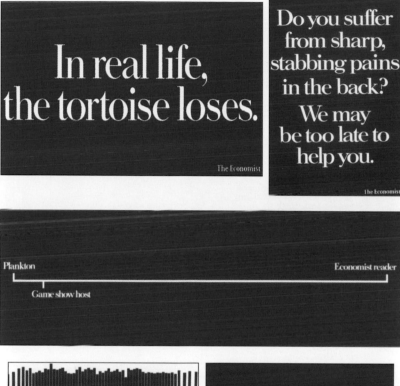

One of Britain's great, enduring campaigns continues to evolve.
Abbott Mead Vickers, London.

LOW TAR As defined by H.M. Government
Warning: SMOKING CAN CAUSE HEART DISEASE
Health Departments' Chief Medical Officers

Cutting silk and owning the colour purple.
Saatchi & Saatchi, London.

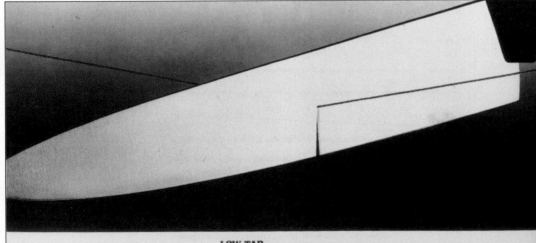

LOW TAR As defined by H.M. Government
Warning: SMOKING CAN CAUSE LUNG CANCER, BRONCHITIS AND OTHER CHEST DISEASES
Health Departments' Chief Medical Officers

Abbott Mead Vickers, London, can always find a cow and gate.

Some shipping companies hand off your package to someone else for international delivery. That's no good. Especially when there's DHL. We use our own delivery people in almost three times as many countries overseas as FedEx and UPS. So make sure your package ends up in the right hands. Phone 1-800-CALL-DHL.

DHL OR ELSE

Branding the world's most reliable courier.
Goodby, Silverstein & Partners, San Francisco, gives you a choice.

*Seeing things which others couldn't. Fallon McElligott's tour around the
Knob Creek label (a product of the agency's design affiliate) makes the
whiskey more visible and familiar on the shelf.*

copy through *The Economist.* They had a great list of people who had to see all written words of advertising, and they were all journalists, and they all felt they were better writers than the copywriters at the agency. So getting ads through with philosophy statements or even comments on the contents was always a laborious, heart-breaking business; so there was part of me trying not to write body copy."

It suddenly dawned on Abbott that the white-on-red masthead of the magazine happened to be the same shape as an outdoor poster.

"I was just looking, and I thought, well, why not outdoor? And I was prompted absolutely by staring at the logo, and thinking, yeah, maybe. And I wrote the first one, *Management trainee, aged 42*, very, very quickly. They all came very quickly after that and we presented a raft of them to David Gordon, who was the client, and he bought it. That typeface, and that white on red, have become great branding. It was just using the livery of the magazine in a way they'd never really done wholeheartedly before. I think it *is* often about going at something with gusto, and being single-minded."

Posters and print ads proliferated. Occasionally, the words vanish; once they were replaced by a white keyhole on the familiar red ground.

"They've got harder to do as the years have gone by," confesses Abbott, "simply because we've been in most areas. Now in the agency, everyone has a go at them. I collect a big pile of maybe sixty or seventy, and I choose the ones that either haven't been done before or that tickle my fancy. We end up with five or six a season. The terrain is so tightly defined, whether it's irony or whatever, and some people can do it, then they use up their supply of ads and they need a rest from it before they come back. Maybe people have only got so many *Economist* ads in them."

Is There an Idea in the Packaging?

It could be the shape. It could be the colour. It could be the material it is made from; how it feels when you hold it or use it. It could be the way it opens or reseals. It could be something on the label: a phrase, a list of awards or gold medals, somebody's signature, maybe something as bizarre as the factory address or telephone number.

For that matter, it could be the label itself. In which case, your idea will belong to the product exclusively.

Is There an Idea in How the Product Is Made?

Is it handmade by robots? After they paint the car, does somebody paint the paint? Is there a tough man behind all those tender chickens? As Britain's Robin Wight says, "Interrogate the product until it confesses its strengths."

Bob Isherwood agrees. "Every time we had to do a Parker Pen ad, we would go down to the factory and walk around and we would see things there that would just write the ads for us," he recalls. "For instance, one day when we were there, we saw a big pile of walnut shells. We asked what they were for, and the guy taking us around said, well, we use them to polish the gold. We asked why walnut shells and the guy said, dunno really, we just put them in a barrel, the shells with the gold, and we roll them round and they polish it better than anything else, must be something to do with the walnut oil. There was a fantastic ad in that and you could never make it up sitting in your office. Offices are the worst places to write ads." For his trouble, Isherwood received a Gold Pencil at Britain's Design and Art Direction Awards.

Nine times out of ten, manufacturers will take their own manufacturing processes for granted. It takes the disciplined eye and wild mind of a writer or art director to find the stories. And if you find them, and they excite *you*, your excitement will convey itself to the reader.

The Volvo 460 is cocooned in a multi-layered shell of anti-corrosive material. No wonder Abbott Mead Vickers could shower it with 6-inch nails.

IS THERE AN IDEA IN WHERE THE PRODUCT IS MADE?

Very often there is. It could be something unique in the air, a special property in the water, found nowhere else. Do the grapes grow better there? Do the tomatoes grow fatter there? Is it the only place on earth where they craft that kind of steel or blow that kind of glass?

In the north of England, for example, the bitters are very creamy. Boddingtons is no exception. It is the kind of beer you drink through the cream. John Hegarty recalls the brief.

"It was the idea of making a beer from Manchester famous, staying true to its roots, in a way that would talk to a younger audience. We believe you've got to find something in the brand which elevates it. It doesn't necessarily have to be a unique thing within the brand. It might also elevate other products as well. You find that one thing, and you build your advertising around it."

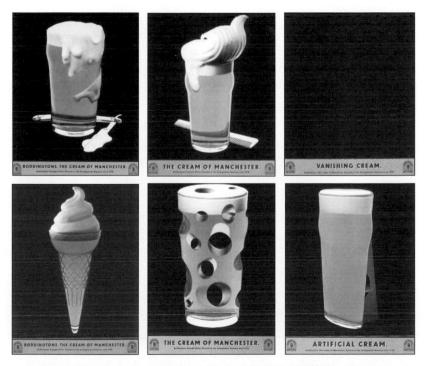

Bartle Bogle Hegarty, London, making a beer from Manchester famous.
Creaminess is not unique, but the advertising is.

That one thing for Boddingtons was its *creaminess*. "People described Boddingtons as a creamy pint," says Hegarty. "They liked it. But the creaminess is much the same as Guinness and the other Northern bitters, so it wasn't unique."

The solution was to present the creaminess in a very unique way. "We put beer into an ice cream cone, photographed it against black, made it very graphic. It demands attention, but the message in it, the thought in it, is very simple. Creaminess."

By presenting the familiar in an unfamiliar way, Boddingtons owns creaminess in its category. In terms of perceptions, cream now equals creme. The strapline, *The cream of Manchester*, became so well entrenched that it no longer appears in every execution.

Is There an Idea in the Product's History?

Stuck for an idea in the present? Go back to the past for a solution. (Or, thinking laterally, if the product has no past, you can always invent one.)

The Royal Peacock Hotel. Advertising for this charming boutique hotel celebrates its days, or, more precisely, nights of infamy. Singapore's historic red light district is now an exotic memory, which Saatchi & Saatchi deploys to differentiate the Royal Peacock from its competitors. Wisely, Rowan Chanen's copy exercises restraint; style and elegance are communicated. Each execution, art directed by Ted Royer, pays tribute to Chinese posters of a bygone era, preserving mellow illustrations and quaint borders. The choice of typeface avoids the Chinese Checkers look; it is complementary, without being *cliched*.

Lee Dungarees. Seaminess of another kind is celebrated by Fallon McElligott. There is no rule that says product heritage must always be presented in long copy, nor that it should always be treated with reverence. Miners minus their Lee Carpenter Pants make history more accessible, more engaging.

North Carolina Travel and Tourism. When history itself is the product, there are some tough acts to follow. According to the copy in this campaign, the folks in North Carolina are partial to storytelling. They "turn the spigot and let it burble". Which is exactly what agency Loeffler Ketchum Mountjoy does in its affectionate tour of

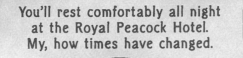

You'll rest comfortably all night at the Royal Peacock Hotel. My, how times have changed.

THOUGH A GENTLEMAN never tells, it was not long ago that a night spent at the Royal Peacock meant forgoing only one thing. Sleep.

Enticed by the red lanterns that hung from the innocuous shophouses, many a lonely sailor and weary traveller would often find themselves wandering along Keong Saik Road.

Far from home, they would take comfort in the arms of an "Ah Ku"; politely known as a lady of the evening. No doubt leaving a good deal happier than when they arrived.

SO IT MAY RAISE MORE than an eyebrow to learn that ten of those very shophouses have now been artfully restored to create one of Singapore's most elegant boutique hotels.

Though the Ah Ku no longer grace the sidewalks, resplendent in their delicate silk Cheong Sam, the Royal Peacock offers much to keep the modern traveller entirely satisfied.

A EUROPEAN SLEIGH BED adorns every room, certainly a fitting inducement for a restful night's sleep. Voice-mail allows one to deal with the telephone when it suits; a choice of newspapers is delivered directly to your door every day.

You may prefer to while away a few hours with a movie (perhaps "THE WORLD OF SUZIE WONG"). Then again, a book from our modest library may do. Suffice to say, these are the comforts one expects to find in a small, luxury hotel.

AND WHEN MORNING COMES and you fling open the cherry-red shutters to greet the day, it may cross your mind to explore the curious lanes below.

For the fragrant medicine shops, exotic spice emporiums and colourful provision stores will surely beckon. But not before a splendid complimentary breakfast, European or Asian, served in the restaurant downstairs.

AS YOU BID the front desk staff a hearty good morning (by now they will already know you by name) you will set off from the Royal Peacock as happy as those many travellers who called there long before you.

Of course, you will be rather considerably better rested.

For that is the charm of the Royal Peacock. A BROTHEL BEFORE, A HOTEL NOW. GOOD SERVICE ALWAYS.

THE ROYAL PEACOCK

55 KEONG SAIK ROAD SINGAPORE 089158 TELEPHONE: (65) 2233522

Exotic memories building the brand for a boutique hotel.
Saatchi & Saatchi, Singapore.

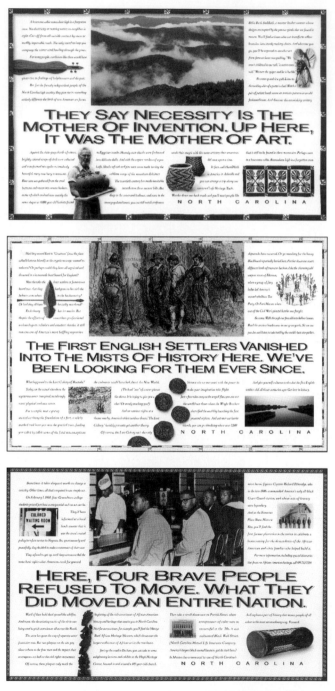

History crafted by Loeffler Ketchum Mountjoy, Charlotte, North Carolina.

North Carolina's historic attractions. The copy weaves tales of lonesome cabins, homely corn shucks, lost colonies and noble causes. The art direction is a classic in the genre.

History revealed by Fallon McElligott, Minneapolis.

IS THERE AN IDEA IN THE PRODUCT'S OLD ADVERTISING?

Robin Wight is a strong advocate of resurrecting old advertising icons and slogans. He calls it *advertising archaeology*. In a world of rapid change, the deeply familiar can be deeply reassuring. There are, of course, no rules. Retro campaigns can preserve the original, or parody it.

Simmons Beds. When McCann-Erickson, Singapore, explored Simmons advertising archaeology, they struck gold, literally, at America's One Show awards. Writer Malcolm Pryce describes how he resisted doing the campaign at first.

"We'd been briefed to do very practical demonstration ads. The traditional sort of ads, show me a wine glass balancing on the mattress with somebody lying next to it. We dutifully started work on that because the bed was based on this unique pocket-coil spring and we did a lot of ads with elephants, and trampolinists, and all that sort of stuff. Then the client changed his mind and said he wanted to do some ads on heritage. I'm ashamed to admit it," says Pryce, "but me and my art director just burst out laughing. How can you do heritage ads for a bed? We just ridiculed the idea with the arrogance which creatives quite often have."

Malcolm Pryce's favourite ad from the Simmons campaign. "It was like finding Rembrandts in the attic," he says. McCann-Erickson, Singapore.

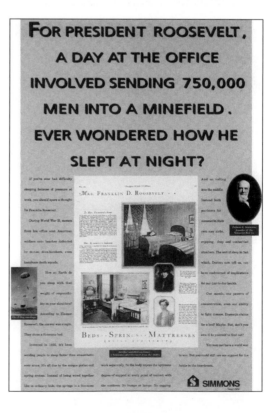

FOR PRESIDENT ROOSEVELT, A DAY AT THE OFFICE INVOLVED SENDING 750,000 MEN INTO A MINEFIELD. EVER WONDERED HOW HE SLEPT AT NIGHT?

Fortunately the client stuck to his guns. "To underline his passion, he sent over what was basically a corporate brochure," recalls Pryce. "I read it, and I was so blinkered by my derision for the fact that you could do heritage ads for a bed, that I failed to notice all the nuggets of gold in it. Ironically, it was my art director, Marc Schattner, who was also the creative director, who came back and said, look at *this!*"

In the 1930s, the Simmons Bed Company had run ads which were testimonials to the product from some of the greatest people in the twentieth century: President Roosevelt, Marconi, Henry Ford. As Pryce would later write in one of his headlines, *They all slept in the same bed*. The corporate brochure which the client had sent reproduced one of these ads, a testimonial by Eleanor Roosevelt.

"It was like finding Rembrandts in the attic," declares Pryce. "It was unbelievable, because when you're creating ads, you're always looking for a great hook to hang your hat on. When I saw that ad with Eleanor Roosevelt, the bell just went off in my head. In the 1930s, having President Roosevelt's wife talking about what bed they used was quite normal behaviour, but these days the idea of getting the President of the United States to advertise your bed would be just unheard of."

Because the testimonials were matters of historical record, Pryce and Schattner knew they could resurrect them freely. Once they had reached that point, says Pryce, the headlines came quite easily. "They seem so obvious when you think about it. I think the best ads you see are always like that."

IS THERE AN IDEA IN SOMETHING THAT'S HAPPENING AROUND YOU?

"Ideas are all around you," believes Hegarty. "They're *everywhere*. If you spend your time looking at award annuals, all you'll ever do is repeat what other people have done. But if you open your eyes and observe what's going on around you all the time, the humour and the charm and the fun of things, then you will get ideas that really do surprise, and charm, and are fresh. You can't invent some of the things that happen."

Hegarty talks about the way you can put two seemingly random thoughts together. "One of my best TV commercials came out of a personal experience, an incident I observed. I saw two people walking along in the rain. They only had one umbrella. So one got immediately behind the other, and walked along completely in unison, as though they were glued together, so they wouldn't get wet. I thought at the time, what a wonderful image that is. It just stuck in my mind. Then, much later, I used it for Audi, the commercial about the designers who follow each other around." Hegarty does not recommend keeping such thoughts in a notebook. "Your brain is the most fantastic place to keep things. You put all these things into your brain, because what your brain is brilliant at doing is suddenly putting them together. Something you saw six months ago can be put with something you saw yesterday, and together they make something incredible. In a notebook you can't do that. One thought is on page 17, the other is on page 217."

Neil Godfrey also believes that observation is a great source of ideas. His famous Pyramids ad, in the Benson & Hedges surrealistic campaign, happened as a result of something he saw on a plane. As Godfrey explains, his agency, Collett Dickenson Pearce, had originated the surrealistic images to overcome the banality of cigarette advertising.

"It was a case of what do you do when you're faced with a product where there was nothing you could say, except that it might kill you in so many years. They had done the mousehole at ground level, and Stonehenge, and the one with the pack transposed into a bird cage, but the shadow was still in the shape of the bird. Then one day, I was flying to Italy with Frank Lowe. I was reading a magazine and there was a picture of the Pyramids in it. Just at that moment, I looked up and I saw someone smoking a pack of Benson & Hedges, and I just *happened* to notice the angle that the pack was at, and I thought when you turn the pack on its side like that, it makes the shape of a pyramid. It was as *simple* as that."

Godfrey had been to the pyramids and knew how dramatic they were. "For the ad, though, I had to put together an amalgam of several pictures, because the pyramids don't actually look as pretty as that at sunset. On the day the ad ran, I had a call from the Egyptian Tourist Board. This official congratulated me on my beautiful photograph of the pyramids. He said he'd never seen anything like it before and he asked if they could use it on their tourism brochures. I asked him what he was going to do with the Benson & Hedges pack, and he said, 'What pack, *effendi?*' He hadn't even noticed it."

Is There an Idea in Showing What Happens With the Product?

This route is a bit like showing the "After" without first having shown the "Before".

It is a far cry from those old-style product demonstration ads. It means asking yourself, what will happen when somebody uses the product? What effect will it have on them? How will it change things? As you explore this territory, your ideas could well become more and more outrageous. But at least you will be having ideas, and as creator-and-critic, you can revisit them later and cull out the least relevant.

Mitsubishi Spacewagon. The brief Antony Redman received asked him to communicate that the Spacewagon was a people-mover. It could comfortably seat seven people. The conventional approach would have been to show a big family of seven, with lots of luggage, all piling inside. Or seven fat people. Or, for a quick executional thrill, seven nuns or other supposedly quirky people. Redman's mind worked a different way.

Showing what happens when seven claustrophobics go for a ride in a Mitsubishi Spacewagon. Euro RSCG Partnership (The Ball Partnership), Singapore.

"I started from the point that Mitsubishi had gone into the public bus realm. It was a Spacewagon. It was about space. A lot of space in the interior. Enough for seven people. So my process was, not who is comfortable in a big space, but who is uncomfortable in a *small* space? That got me to claustrophobics. A claustrophobic fears being caught in an elevator. You could say, therefore, that a claustrophobic would fear sitting in a car with six other people. So that was it. Claustrophobics are fearful of small spaces, so what do we do? We throw seven claustrophobics into a Spacewagon with big smiles on their faces. It was very straightforward, really."

The next problem was to identify them. How would the reader know they were claustrophobics? Would the headline tell him?

"I wanted to keep the ad visual. I wanted to make people think a bit about the ad. So we stuck this big sign on the outside of the Spacewagon. *The Society of Claustrophobics.* It was like they were all members of this society, all happy and gleeful, driving around. So the sign became the headline. I didn't need copy, either."

Redman hastens to add that the society is entirely fictitious. "I happen to know because the account executive was worried about it, so I asked him to check it out."

Actal Anti-Flatulent Antacid. "So often you get very fuzzy propositions," laments Steve Elrick. "This brief came in two parts. There was the main antacid product, then there was the anti-flatulent antacid. Antacid is just another me-too product, but anti-flatulent was a very distinct proposition and, to be honest, we latched onto it straight away."

The first issue Elrick tackled was the term anti-flatulence. "It isn't a colloquial term for the problem, so what do we refer to it as? Do we call it wind, or gas, or the devil's bad breath? The answer was actually on the packet. There was a very small line that said, 'No wind'. So 'wind' was the colloquial, homey way to say flatulence, if in fact 'wind' could ever be described as homey."

Elrick talks about the process that led to the creative leap: "The first stage was knocking out all the cheap schoolboy gags about wind, and embarrassed faces in lifts, and so on. They wouldn't have done the product justice and they wouldn't have got past the client. After we'd been round the houses a few times, we went back to a

Showing what happens when you take
Actal Anti-Flatulent Antacid.
Ogilvy & Mather, Singapore.

couple of sketches we had on the pad earlier on, which were just very simple visual expressions of no wind, meaning wind as in weather. That was the leap, from saying no wind as in gas, to no wind as in no wind blowing. Once we got to that, it worked for itself."

The thought, an absence of wind, led to a complicated variety of executions. "One idea was windmills," says Elrick. "We had Don Quixote sitting down because there's no wind, so he doesn't have to attack the windmills, how weird is that? Then there were kites just lying on the ground. Then we had stock images where wind was a part of the picture; the flag going up on Iwo Jima, and all the guys were looking up but the flag wasn't blowing. So we stepped back from it and got some images that everyone would instantly recognise, the more simplistic ones like the wind-sock and the weather-vane, and then the famous image of Marilyn Monroe standing on the grate with her skirt blowing up. It was a very recognisable icon that said wind and it was the one that made everyone laugh. I think it's because everyone has seen this image of Marilyn Monroe a few

Showing what happens to girls when they drink Jim Beam whiskey.
Fallon McElligott, Minneapolis.

thousand times in their life. It was the twist of seeing something which you've always seen one way, to suddenly seeing it slightly different."

The famous Monroe picture had to be completely reshot to get around the copyright problems. "Our shot is actually *three* transparencies comp'd together. We just couldn't get quite the perfect pose on the day. Sometimes the legs would be fine, sometimes the arms would be fine, sometimes the tilt of the neck was just right, but we couldn't get the perfect pose in one shot. If you look at ours and the original, you will see differences. In the original, the pavement is stretching back to some brownstones in the background. But even in the genuine one, your attention is so much focused on what she's doing."

Other layouts were considered. "At one stage we thought it looked too simple. So we tried some with copy, and some where the visual was in a circle like a tablet. We tried some with the pack offset. We even had the pack on the ground inside the shot. But we thought it

Showing what happens when you drive a Mercedes-Benz with ESP.
Springer & Jacoby, Hamburg.

was too tricky. So we came back to basics and decided that the visual was strong enough by itself."

Elrick experimented with other typefaces, too. He always imagines how a headline or tagline might sound if read aloud. He believes the typeface should reflect the way you would want the line spoken. For the Actal campaign, the statement was very simple, very matter-of-fact. "So it had to be set in a very simple, very plain typeface."

At one point they debated whether the line *No Wind* was even necessary. "I think it would have been asking too much of the audience to read anti-flatulence on the pack and then get the joke. We were trying to involve and reward them, not give them a test."

IS THERE AN IDEA IN SHOWING WHAT HAPPENS *WITHOUT* THE PRODUCT?

This route is a bit like showing the "Before" without ever showing the "After".

Some people call it the negative sell, yet ironically enough it has produced some of the funniest and best-loved ads in the world. Many ads from *The Economist* campaign belong in this territory. Abbott's *Management trainee, aged 42* conveys what happens without *The Economist*; in itself, it is not a happy thought, but it brings a positive smile.

Why is this genre so popular? Is it because the most penetrating human insights have been always inspired by adversity? Or simply that it leaves the reader to close the circle?

Nature's Course Dog Food. At Fallon McElligott, Dean Hanson remembers thinking that an all-natural dog food was a kind of silly idea. "The incongruity of it, going to that length to make sure your dog has pure, natural food, seemed ridiculous."

Hanson's thinking process began with a very simple proposition. "It was a natural dog food. So it meant putting down all the fundamental truths I knew about additives and artificial ingredients and how they apply to *human* food, then taking them in the context of a *dog*." Connections were made between pesticides and a dog wearing a mask; between artificial colours and a Dalmatian with multi-coloured spots. "It wasn't a complex proposition to put forward. We wanted to make the statement clearly, hopefully in a humorous way. When you're talking about dogs, people want to smile."

Hanson's art direction was minimalist. The visual occupied well over 80 percent of the ad. The product neatly integrated with the copy. The layout was clean and spare.

"There wasn't a lot of information to put across and I wanted to use the dog to full advantage. Dogs are entertainment in themselves. There's an old *cliche*, dogs and babies. Norman Rockwell, the American illustrator, once said if a thing is not going well, put a dog in it; if it's *really* not going well, put a dog with a bandage on its foot in it. If you're lucky enough to have dogs as a subject matter, you sure as hell should take advantage of it. If you can't do a great ad with a dog, you should be horsewhipped."

*Showing what happens without
Nature's Course Dog Food.
Fallon McElligott, Minneapolis.*

Tip #26:
Try a zoom lens when photographing nature.

The Nikon School

Tip #34:
Remember to compensate for backlighting.

The Nikon School

Tip #44:
To get animals to hold still, give them something to focus on.

The Nikon School

Tip #39:
Remove foreground distractions before shooting your subject.

The Nikon School

Showing what happens without taking a class at the Nikon School.
Fallon McElligott, Minneapolis.

Preparation H. "It was all about being close to the product," contends Elrick, discussing the campaign for a haemorrhoidal ointment which he and art director Phil Marchington created at Bates, Hong Kong. "It was a case of one of us asking the other about the affliction."

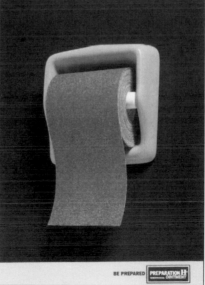

Showing what happens without Preparation H haemorrhoidal ointment. Bates, Hong Kong.

The product eases discomfort in the early stages of haemorrhoids. Previous ads had used lengthy, medical copy, but Elrick and Marchington wanted to reach sufferers in a more direct way. It was a question of finding a visual means to express the problem and the pain. The creative leap came when they talked about how the most innocuous, innate objects hold special terrors for haemorrhoid victims.

The bicycle seat was the first execution. "We wanted to get inside the heads of the sufferers, *to see what they saw.* A bike seat doesn't

Showing what happens without Epilady depilatory, using the Chinese characters for woman, arm and leg. Bates, Hong Kong.

look threatening at all," says Elrick, "but to someone suffering from piles, the idea of sitting on a bike seat is horrific. It's one of the most extreme situations a piles sufferer would try and avoid. So we asked ourselves, how would the sufferer see a bike seat? It would be something very sharp, excruciatingly painful."

The connection was made by transposing a razor sharp saw in place of the seat. "It was like doing a crossfade on television, only doing it in print."

Is There an Idea in Showing What Happens With and Without the Product in the *Same* Ad?

In this route, "Before" and "After" are shown side by side, for easy comparison.

It is the modern manifestation of that great old advertising formula called the "Problem-Solution" ad. The convention is to show the "Before" (or the "Problem") on the left, and the "After" (or the "Solution") on the right.

The tackier version, of course, emerged in the bad old days of hard sell advertising. The "Villain Product", better known as Brand X, failed on the left, while the "Hero Product" triumphed on the right.

Nothing much has changed. It is still a valid concept ground. Sometimes two separate pictures are used, left and right, or even above and below. Sometimes both scenarios are contained within the *same* picture, with the headline statement positioned under the solution. And who needs pictures? Typographical devices can represent both sides of the story.

There is only one rule which appears unbreakable: the problem must always *precede* the solution.

The genre continues to evolve. There are endless new variants, many of them narrative by nature. What happens when someone has the product and someone else does not? What happens when the product works so well that other things go wrong? At its heart, though, one truth remains: it is still one of the most effective ways to signpost a change to the consumer in a cage.

Kaminomoto Hair Restorer. As Neil French explains, the creative process behind his classic campaign was fraught with complications.

"Kaminomoto was close to my own heart, or possibly close to my own head, because I'm also as bald as a badger. I know, from honest experience, that when you open a paper and there's a big headline screaming 'BALD?' at you, you might read it if you're at home. You say to yourself, yes, here we go, come on, what have you got to sell me, and you *never* believe it. But if you're out and about, the last thing you're going to be seen doing is reading an ad that says 'BALD?' because it's embarrassing! You may be bald, but you don't want everybody else to know that it bothers you, and it *does* bother you, no matter what anybody says. I was lucky; I went bald when I was twenty-one, so I've had plenty of time to get used to it. Those poor blokes who go bald at about thirty-five are constantly worrying about it, and it's really tragic. So the one thing we couldn't do in our ads was shout 'BALD?' ...

(Be careful with the Kaminomoto)

Neil French's classic Kaminomoto campaign demonstrates the potency of visual suggestions. Nudge, nudge, note the use of brackets. Euro RSCG Partnership (The Ball Partnership), Singapore.

(Be careful with the Kaminomoto)

(Be careful with the Kaminomoto)

"The other thing we couldn't do is show the bottle, because the laws in Singapore don't let you say hair restorer, and that's what it says on the top of the bottle. So that was the pack shot gone, and that was the basic product description gone!"

The further French investigated, the more restrictions he found. "We weren't allowed to show bald men, because that was against the law, because it might indicate that this was a baldness cure, which you can't advertise. And we weren't allowed to show blokes *with* hair, because that was also against the law, because it might indicate that you'd actually grown hair on them. So if we weren't allowed to mention what the product did, and we weren't allowed to show it, we were up against it somewhat, really."

French's creative solution was visual. "We had to indicate what had happened by *suggestion*. The first thought that came into our head was bald as a billiard ball. So that was easy. We just put two billiard balls down on a table, stuck hair on one of them, and said *Be careful with the Kaminomoto* underneath. Which indicates to a bald person that if you spill this stuff on a billiard ball, it might grow hair. To anybody else, of course, it doesn't mean anything at all; but we're not talking to anybody else, so it doesn't matter. It's not a threatening ad, it's a funny ad. If you're seen reading it on the train you're not seen as some poor, desperate bloke trying to find some way to grow some fluff on his head; you're seen as a normal person trying to decipher a completely indecipherable ad. But of course to a bald person it speaks loudly, and you can tuck away that little piece of information about Kaminomoto and trot into a pharmacy and buy it along with all those other things you buy in the hope that no one will ever notice you bought."

The billiard balls execution was followed by two eggs, one of which had also sprouted hair. "The photographer's wife plucked out his assistant's eyebrows, one by one," recalls French, "dipped them into superglue, and stuck them onto the billiard ball and the egg with tweezers. By the end of it, the poor bloke had only got one eyebrow."

The most significant detail of crafting was in French's treatment of the headline. He located it outside the picture, in small type, between brackets.

"You can make a person read an ad in the way that you art direct it," says French. "So if you want something to be shouted, it's big. 'BALD', in really big letters. But if you want something to be a kind of nudge, I like brackets. I think brackets indicate a nudge, an afterthought. Small type is quiet, but smaller than small between brackets, is a nudge. It's like saying, nudge, nudge, *be careful with the Kaminomoto*, out of the corner of your mouth. It makes it more of a whisper, more of a joke. It makes it become less important. The fact that the whole point of the ad is apparently the *least* important thing on the page makes me laugh."

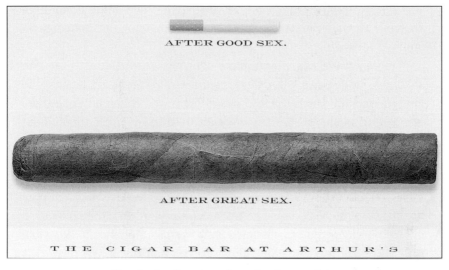

The simpler the comparison, the stronger it is.
Loeffler Ketchum Mountjoy, North Carolina.

There are no rules. Comparisons can be made in one picture or two. Photography and illustration can coexist in the same campaign. Euro RSCG Partnership (The Ball Partnership), Singapore.

While French was amused, an advertising watchdog committee was not. They descended on the agency, demanding the campaign be stopped forthwith.

"They said the ads would make people buy a baldness cure. We said, yes, well, that's what we're paid for. They said, it's against the law. So we said, here's the law, where have we broken it? Then there was a long silence while they went away to have a little think about it. When they came back they said, well, you haven't broken any laws, but the fact of the matter is, you can't run the ads any more. And in future, they said, in addition to no bald men and no hairy men, you can't show *anything* that didn't used to have hair that now has hair, therefore no eggs, no billiard balls, and they thought they'd got us. So the next ad that came out showed a chihuahua looking at a little Skye Terrier. The chihuahua's got no hair at all; the terrier's a very hairy little dog. Well, of course, the committee went completely ape and we said, no, they're both in their original state, neither has been changed. But they said, people will remember the *other* campaign! So we said, what to do?"

Crisan Shampoo. Hair was obviously a growing concern at The Ball Partnership, Singapore. The agency's next challenge was an anti-dandruff shampoo, and once more, the side-by-side comparison formula resurfaced.

The category convention is to show silky clean hair of the feminine variety; men, according to convention, do not have dandruff. If Crisan was to have any hope of standing out in the category, the last thing the ad could show was hair. The solution had to be lateral.

According to writer Danny Higgins, the worst-case scenario for any dandruff sufferer, male or female, would be having to wear white clothes to conceal the evidence. The Crisan concept emerged with two pictures: a wardrobe full of white clothes on the left, and a huge shot of the pack on the right. The headline read, *Two ways of solving a dandruff problem.*

The problem-and-solution were clearly demonstrated for dandruff sufferers of either sex.

The moral of the story is, never be afraid to show the product, as big as possible, if it is part of the idea. By doing so, all the text on the label could be read, so there was no need for additional body copy.

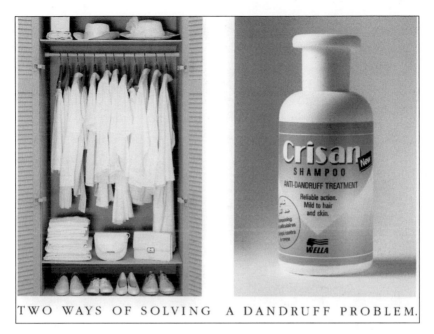

TWO WAYS OF SOLVING A DANDRUFF PROBLEM.

Breaking the category convention within a classic advertising format.
Euro RSCG Partnership (The Ball Partnership), Singapore.

And because the manufacturer's logo was also prominent, there was
no need to repeat it somewhere else. So that the brand could brand
the ad, the blue from the Crisan pack was replicated in a blue
headline and the toning of the wardrobe shot.

Mitsubishi Spacewagon. Everybody knew what the Spacewagon
looked like; besides which, the newspapers were full of car ads,
crammed with colour and black-and-white photographs. Could the
medium be used in some other way to communicate the feeling of
private space and comfort which Spacewagon offered?

Chinese readers opened their morning paper to find full page ads
shouting abuse, curses and insults, courtesy of copywriter Peter Soh.
The dense, angry typography occupied half the page, recreating what
happens when too many people are squeezed into an ordinary car.
The other half of the page remained white and empty, except for a
strip of copy communicating the space and calm of the Spacewagon.

For diversity, one ad presented the contrast left and right; another,
top and bottom.

Who needs pictures? Anger and abuse in a crowded car,
compared with space and calm in a Spacewagon.
Euro RSCG Partnership (The Ball Partnership), Singapore.

Can you spot the Range Rover in this picture?

Goodbye road. Goodbye traffic. Goodbye 5 m.p.h.

A Range Rover does something far more impressive than get you through a traffic jam in air-conditioned, arm-chaired, stereo-surrounded comfort.

A Range Rover takes you where there are no jams. Because there is no traffic.

Through the woods. Along the beach. Across the desert. Range Rovers, after all, are so extraordinary, they drive for years in places ordinary cars couldn't drive a quarter of a mile.

So it's not surprising that to many a Range Rover's most luxurious feature isn't its elegant interior, optional sunroof, or the

RANGE ROVER

security of 24 hour roadside assistance.

Its most luxurious feature is its ability to provide an experience a bit more exhilarating than a highway to the suburbs at six p.m.

Why not call 1-800-FINE 4WD for the Range Rover dealer nearest you?

We won't deny that at somewhat above $34,000 a Range Rover is hardly inexpensive. But after all the time you've spent in trafficlikethis, what could be nicer than going off on your   own?

The problem on the left, the solution on the right, with two
brilliantly subtle typographical tricks in the last two lines of the body copy.
Grace & Rothschild, New York.

Because every language has its own treasury of insults, the concept would work just as well in English, French or Swahili.

IS THERE EVEN AN IDEA IN *WHERE* THE AD WILL RUN?

Let the medium become the message.

The newspaper page has a smooth vertical edge, with jagged trims top and bottom. What better place to demonstrate the superior cutting power of a lawnmower, let alone a hairdresser?

Clemenger Advertising, Melbourne, showed how a full page could be cut into twelve pieces and used as toilet paper. *Life's harsh when you run out of Sorbent*, said the message in the corner.

Butterfield Day Devito Hockney turned the bulk of a newspaper into a demonstration of how deeply the sun's UV rays can damage skin. The headline, for Uvistat sun cream, jolted complacent readers: *If your skin was this newspaper, the sun's rays would have reached the sports page.*

The way a magazine is opened and closed might suggest how other things can be joined or separated. Euro RSCG Partnership, Singapore, used a centre spread in *Reader's Digest* to demonstrate how Crisan repaired split ends.

As always, there are no limits.

Everlast. Gary Goldsmith's famous Everlast ad came out of very pragmatic concerns.

"The brief was probably worse than many of the briefs young people get," he recalls. Everlast was in a bleak position. "They were being outspent by all their competitors by a ton, so we knew we had to be kamikazes and go after those other people," Goldsmith strategises. "We knew we had to do with *one* ad what Ralph Lauren or Perry Ellis could afford to do with twenty ads. In a media sense, we had to be able to place one ad amidst twenty of their ads and have people talk about our ad. We had to place them as an enemy, and trade off of them. That gave us a start."

Goldsmith studied the media environment. Kamikaze thinking led to the idea of trading off a scratch-and-sniff concept.

"Knowing that everybody was saying the same thing in there, everybody was showing beautiful clothing, perfectly photographed,

When you are being outspent 20-to-1, you can disrupt your category by disrupting the media environment. Goldsmith/Jeffrey, New York.

Turning the newspaper page into an X-ray. Saatchi & Saatchi, Sydney.

we said let's show some sweaty old T-shirt and make a comment that's against all the fashion correctness." The line that disrupted the category: *This is not one of those scented ads. Good thing.*

How to Get Better Ideas

The concept grounds will always be there. What will determine success or failure, greatness or mediocrity, are individual creative processes.

Are great advertising people born great, or can individual creative processes be trained, honed and perfected? If great advertising people are like great athletes, there is a good chance they can be.

"We all pay less attention to the process than we should," observes Goldsmith. "If doctors and scientists operated in the same manner that we do, it'd be a scary world. What they do is creative, too, in its own way. They've devoted a lot of thought to the way in which they arrive at a diagnosis, and the way in which they treat it. But with us, it's almost like we have this thing in our head, we don't need to do that, we should just sit down and come up with ideas."

Goldsmith believes the best creative people do have their own processes, whether they call them such or not, that they work by. He thinks there are certain learnings which can help every writer and art director improve their individual process. "After an assignment is over, stop and think about it. What happened when you did good ads? What did you do *differently* than the times when you did bad ads? Then think about how you've got to do those things more often than not, like an athlete. If great athletes could only perform that way occasionally, it'd be terrible."

Goldsmith is right; the best creative people do have their own personal methodologies. For many, they are a defence mechanism against the panic factor.

"I think you discover, over the years, ways to get yourself going. For me, the discipline is to pick up a pencil," says Abbott. "Before I really start scribbling, I've absorbed all the information I can get hold of, though that's not always true. I find I have to start scribbling or drawing. I always think on the pad. I always draw the outline of the ad, usually quite small, whether it's a double page spread or a 24-sheet poster, so I know the boundaries that I'm working within.

Generally speaking, I get a kind of mixture of tone of voice, a feel of the ad, I often see the ad in my mind before I actually know the details, a feel for the way the ad should be. I very often think of the picture before the words, if there are going to be words. But there isn't a set rule really. If I'm stuck, I change the tactics. I might work backwards on something. I might start from a new endline, though I don't always accept that you need an endline, but I might just start there. If that's not working, I might start with a picture, or go back to the strategy and rewrite the strategy. One of the ways of getting going is to walk away from it, to go and think about something else. Over the years, you learn not to panic."

Abbott likens his creative process to playing tennis. "I was always very relaxed, but as soon as the points began to matter, I seized up. I was less interested in winning a tennis game than hitting a great shot that I could remember, which is part of my personality I suppose. I now don't panic really, and I don't seize up with ads, because I sort of think that I may not get it out on time, but I will get it out."

Bruce Bildsten also starts by scribbling ideas. "I do these little drawings which only make sense to myself. Even though I'm a writer, I like to think very visually. I know I can always write a line later. Sometimes, I'll often think of ads in terms of a layout as much as what the visual is. It helps me to do a little layout of something so it's a complete idea. Sometimes, I'll just write lines." Bildsten never shows his layouts to the art director. "I'm a terrible artist. I end up explaining them. It might be talking about something as simple as the style in which something is photographed, or the size of the headline, because the size of the line is as important as the line itself."

Ron Mather works with a small notepad and pen. "Layout pads are a bit difficult to fit on restaurant tables. Very rarely does the big idea pop up first." Mather goes through a few ideas that are developed or rejected totally before something comes out that he is really happy with. "A great visual might prompt the idea, or it might be a great line that inspires a great visual. There aren't really any rules." Mather believes you are more likely to come up with a great idea in a great agency than in a mediocre agency. "I think it's the atmosphere. Being around very good people in an environment that promotes great creative thinking. I think experience plays a big part, too. *Good* experience, not just lots of years in the business."

Before Tim Delaney starts thinking, he has to believe in the strategy. "The strategy comes first. I can't think of anything until I know the area in which I'm writing. The premise has got to be right. If the issue seems muddled or plain wrong, then I can't start. So the first thing I do is sort out what I'm going to say, and check on it, and *believe* in it, and make sure that it's what everybody wants me to say." Inevitably, Delaney says, if you are worried about it, somebody else back along the line will be worried about it, too. By the time the strategy is sorted, his first thoughts are forming. "They could be visual or verbal thoughts, it doesn't really matter. If it's television, I'll be thinking of storylines, narratives, a way a thing can unfold."

Goldsmith also begins analytically. "I was an architecture student before I got into this crazy business. So I tend to break the problem down in terms of who we are talking to, what we want to say, what's the tone of the company. I'm very conscious of *tone*, because I work on a lot of big corporate stuff. The company might tell you, well, we're customer-focused, our company is about integrity, honesty, trust for the consumer. And you realise there's nothing you can say that's very different, it's all going to be tone. What's a great ad for IBM may be a terrible ad for Everlast. The tone is like a piece of clothing; it has got to fit the client. If it doesn't, they're not going to feel comfortable in it." Goldsmith's first thoughts are generally *rational*. "I don't work like some people do; they tend to start purely intuitively. I can't do that. I try to build *outwards* from the rational. Once I have a rational thought, then I ask how can I add some spice, how can I make it more intuitive." Goldsmith advocates finding out where the ads will run. "Maybe there's an idea there, like the Everlast scratch-and-sniff ad. But one thing has never gone away," he adds. *"The panic."*

"I think it's good to feel scared," says art director John Messum, "otherwise I think you're going to fall into the trap of doing something that's too easy." Messum describes how working at Howell Henry Chaldecott Lury has impacted on his creative process. "We've been involved in the strategy in the first place, in writing the brief with the client, and the planner, and the account team, which I think is really exciting. So we've actually got a head start rather than just having the brief forced upon you, and wondering first about whether it's right or not, and then wondering what you're going to do if you think it's right. When you've been involved in the strategy, you've already started forming ideas as to what your advertising is going to be. But," he admits, "I still feel a bit scared sometimes."

At Saatchi & Saatchi, London, art director Bill Gallacher says the panic begins at the execution stage. "I don't panic when I first get the brief. I think, this is going to be great, like another journey to go on. There are just so many things you can do. You find out about yourself, what you're capable of. I always start with *words*. Sometimes I'll write the sense of the headline first. If I get really frustrated, I'll sit down and draw loads of visuals. The hard part starts when you see the words, when you see how they're going to make sense to a lot of people. You see a kind of hazy vision of what you're after. You start to panic, because you think this is a really good idea, how am I going to do it, if I screw this up I'm never going to forgive myself. Once you're over the panic bit, which doesn't last long, you start working your way into the idea and try about twenty different ways of doing it. But without the panic, I don't think you'd be working as well. If you just sat back and said, well, that's easy, I know what to do ... I couldn't work that way."

"A lot of times, briefs are just laundry lists of things they'd like to do," says Dean Hanson. "Isolating the key ideas is critical for me. It's the very first step." Hanson starts by collecting his thoughts. "I put down all the basic truths that I know. Then I try and put down in a sentence what it is we're trying to communicate. I'll put it up on the wall in its flattest, most mundane way; a sentence on the wall that says exactly what I'm going to say. And then I'll break it down. I'll think about the personality I want to project, the chemistry of the ad that I want, if it has to have dignity, if it has to be broad and humorous."

Hanson believes it is easier to get ideas for products on which you haven't worked before. "There's always baggage that comes with something you're familiar with. If it's something you've worked on for a long time, you know all the tricks, you stop yourself making connections. But if it's new you're learning, you're just like the people you're talking to. If you have a bit of ignorance, just partial knowledge, you're like young people, new people, you have the advantage."

Hanson describes the creative process in terms of jumping over a wall. "You run up to the wall, try to jump over it. If you don't get there, you try another tack. If you get stumped, you go to a bookstore. Bookstores are fabulous places to get ideas. You look up the subject, just immerse yourself in it a little bit, to get off that roadblock you've hit. Or get a *Shots* reel, or *Archive*, sit down and see how other people have attacked problems. I never just sit there and look at the wall. You either talk to somebody, or you try to get stimulus from something to break through."

French often finds inspiration from the product itself. "I always try to put the product on the table in front of me and look at the thing. You don't actually get that much information off products these days, but somehow you have to understand what it's all about. You have to suck in the essence of it so your ads can't contradict it. If you try to turn something nice and reliable into something frightfully hip and trendy, of course it doesn't work. When people turn up with their money at the moment of truth and it has all been a lie, they will never come back to you. You should look at the product from every angle. If it's going to be sold on a shelf, look at it on a shelf. See how it reacts to light and different angles, until you really *know* the thing. Then put it to one side, and never look at it again. Write your ads, and remember you're writing to a person who's going to pass hundreds of other products on a shelf."

Barrie agrees. "Hold the product. Stare at it. Imagine situations where you'd use it. Enjoy the product yourself. If you're working on Miller Lite, it doesn't hurt to have a Miller Lite in your hand."

Barrie's colleague Mike Lescarbeau believes writers and art directors should often start work in isolation. "The first thing I really like to do is sit down and say, if I was working on this thing by myself, what would I do? I ask the art director to do the same. Then when we come together, our ideas have come from completely *different* places. We haven't influenced each other. We haven't thought about it only one way." At Fallon McElligott, writers and art directors work in separate offices, rather than shared ones. Teams do not work as married couples. Everybody moves around, works with everybody else. "We think that's healthy. It keeps you fresh, keeps you from getting into ruts." Getting stuck for an idea, though, is an occupational hazard, and Lescarbeau suggests talking it over with colleagues. "We'll show each other what we have in terms of ads. *Why* is this not going anywhere? *What* is it we're missing about this brief? Honestly, a lot of times it's just twenty more minutes until you get something you really like. It's not like you have to work another two days."

John Bevins, of Sydney's John Bevins Advertising, describes himself as a loner. Bevins, the doyen of Australian copywriters, is wary of writing naive advertising. "A lot of the briefs now aren't for things you automatically know about. They're in whole new categories like technology or financial services. You suddenly have to become an instant expert in order to write about the subject. You have to quickly scramble up the learning curve and you can only do that yourself, I think. I don't believe you can sit back and expect other people to distil it for you." Bevins relies on the Internet to become knowledgeable. "You can't just sit around and brainstorm with an art director. You have to have the confidence that you know what you're writing about. But I don't worry it to death, though, because I've learned that if you don't enjoy writing it, nobody will enjoy reading it. Otherwise it will come across as grudge copy."

For Godfrey, it was often a process of elimination. "Sometimes, there isn't an obvious direction to go in. You can sit there for a couple of nights and feel completely panic-stricken. There doesn't seem to be anything. You dig a little borehole into every aspect of the problem. You look at little tiny details. If you can't think of anything to do for your product, turn to the competition. Look at a product that's not as good a product as yours. Find out *why* it's not as good. Ours is a stage better *because* ... and that might give you a clue." Godfrey is a firm believer in the investigative process. "Talking to the client in detail, going to factories, even talking to other companies who make similiar products. I always found I related their view of the product to my view of it, and immediately you would start thinking of things. You try to hone what you think is the personality of the client into something you can use as a statement. This would be a kind of starting point."

Godfrey was art director to two of Britain's most accomplished writers, Tony Brignull and Indra Sinha. Invariably, the ads would come out of conversations. "It was not just me putting a picture to a line. We used to talk, not do ads, and we'd realise that one of the lines in our conversation was actually a headline. We didn't desperately think an ad has to have a headline. We would sit in a room and talk. Once we had something really interesting, then I would see if I could tip the balance and make it look great just by doing one or two things."

Godfrey believes that what distinguished Brignull and Sinha was their understanding of people's motivations. "As writers, Tony and Indra were very human people, not advertising people overtly. Tony would write a line of copy, and it would seem like nothing, unless you'd been sitting with him for days talking about the problem. Then you'd realise he'd captured something that was very *essential*. Someone walking into the room wouldn't understand it, so people were never allowed in our office while we did ads. Tony wrote lines that weren't spectacular, but were *right*. We worked on a campaign for Dunne & Company. They were gentlemen's outfitters that were a bit behind the times. The sales people were very restrained. Some of Tony's headlines didn't seem like headlines at all: *We train our salesmen not to sell you anything; Are you old enough to buy a suit at Dunne & Company?* Indra and I would sit in a room and just talk, too. Indra liked being sparked. He always scribbled on a pad, he'd listen to everyone's conversations."

Listening and observing are a critical part of Isherwood's creative process. "Ads actually write themselves. It might be something a client says without realising it." He remembers working on a campaign for a finance company that was lending money to small businesses. "We got a group of small businessmen together and we asked them what the issues were. They came out with lines like, the trouble with banks is I can only get a bank loan when I don't need it. That's a great ad. *How come I can only get a bank loan when I don't need one?* Then another guy said, yeah, my employees make more money than I do, and that's another great ad. If you just listen, and you take the trouble to actually get yourself into that environment, into that understanding of the product and the market, the ads actually do themselves for you."

Like Delaney, Isherwood insists on having a clearly defined

strategy, a defined problem. "I have to know what the problem is that I have to solve. And, this is a personal thing, I find I have actually done my best work when I've had a lot more mandatories put on me; you know, you can't do this and you can't do that, and we have to keep this, and you've got to keep that. I take all those elements and actually work through them, each one is a problem that has to be solved." Sometimes your first idea is best, Isherwood says, but you often have to go through a long process to realise it. Not getting bogged down, keeping yourself a bit free in your mind, is essential. As Isherwood admits: "Sometimes it's easier to solve a problem as a creative director. You don't take the problem so personally, the pressure isn't on you as much. You can walk in, take a short look at the issues, and you often get a very quick flash of the whole thing."

Flashes are how Hegarty gets his ideas. "I get a vision of the finished ad. That's how ideas have always come to me. And I know this will sound very plonky and pretentious, but I see an idea as a *person*." Hegarty thinks having ideas is the closest a man will ever come to giving birth. "When you've had an idea, and it's a really good idea and you know it, it has a *life*. You can see what's right for it, you can see what's wrong for it, you can see what it should be, what school it should go to, what kind of street it should live in, what clothes it should wear."

The first things that enter Bill Oberlander's mind are positions, angles and propositions. "I don't think about what I'm thinking in. I'm just thinking. I'm just trying to come up with some conceptual way to have the brand be more hip, cool and urgent in the consumer's mind."

Nick Cohen's ideas usually arrive as funny juxtapositions. "Sometimes it's words, sometimes it's pictures."

The tonality comes first for French, the detail later. "I tend to see the look of the ad, before I see a picture or any copy. I know more or less what the thing should look like. Then, I tend to think in pictures first. Afterwards I might think that's a rather wimpy picture, what it needs is a much better line, and then I'll let the line take over. If I can do it with a picture, I prefer to. Although I have this reputation of being a long copy freak, I'm really not. Only if I'm forced into a corner."

How to Know When Your Ideas Are Great

Developing a personal creative methodology is one matter; being your own critic is another. Is there an infallible way to tell when you have come up with a good idea, maybe even a great idea?

Some creatives become jubilant; others, uncomfortable and uncertain. Godfrey thinks you can *never* be sure. "We all have that problem. You see some ads and you think that they're never going to be anything else but great. But when the people were doing them, they were completely unsure. If there's somebody alive who thinks that once they do an ad it's going to be fabulous, I think they're probably not very long in the business."

Lescarbeau believes it is easier to tell if you have done a good ad. If you have to wonder about it too much, it is probably *not* good.

Goldsmith takes an equally pragmatic view. "If you still like it two or three days later, once the tiredness has gone away and you're feeling more detached. A lot of times, when you first come up with an idea, you're just so happy to be out of that state of worry and overimmersion."

Bildsten relies on experience to tell him. "But I always have this fear that there's somebody else, somewhere in the world, doing exactly the same idea. The more I judge shows, the more I realise that people do come up with similar ideas. That's why the presentation of an idea can make such a difference. Because people are thinking in similar ways, it's more and more incumbent on you to execute everything to the finest detail."

Some creatives talk about physical symptoms. For Guido Heffels, sweaty hands and insomnia. For Redman, butterflies in the stomach.

"It's the one thing you can still truly enjoy in advertising," Redman elaborates. "When you've come up with an idea, and you look at it, and through its simplicity, or its uniqueness, or its vitality, you know you've come up with something special. It's not something you can teach. Sometimes, you know it's great. Sometimes, though, you're not sure if it's too far ahead of its time, if it's too weird, and it's good to push those boundaries. It's good to be unsure. If you surround yourself with people you respect and admire, you can use them as a sounding board. And sometimes, *they* won't know either."

Barrie values the opinions of peers. "Like most creatives, I'm one of the most insecure fellows you'll ever meet. I only *perhaps* begin to think I've done a great ad when a number of people tell me so, or when it wins an award. Even then, I'm still filled with self-doubt, that's the honest-to-God truth. I always look back and imagine how I would have done things differently." As Barrie confesses, he rather likes the feeling of uncertainty. "The times I thought campaigns were the best things I'd ever done, people would be very polite and say, that's interesting. If somebody says something is interesting, then you know it's lousy."

Cohen sticks ads on the wall and waits for reactions. "That's the only way I can tell. That's one of the reasons we opened up our environment. So many agencies operate in a closed door environment where everyone's competing with each other. People are too scared to show their ideas to other people, in case they don't like them. Actually that's pretty important information: if people don't like them, it's just as important if people do like them. It's all about seeing how people respond. And you don't have to be an expert to respond, just a human being. It could be the receptionist or the cleaner, it doesn't matter. If they walk straight past it, don't look at it, don't respond to it, it's probably not a very good ad."

For Oberlander, there is a sense of irony; for Abbott, a little smile in his head.

"It's what mathematicians talk about, the elegance of a solution. You know when you've got the bits working together. And you've used an insight." Abbott recalls working on a pitch for a holiday company. "I wrote an ad based on the fact that the sign of a great holiday for a woman is that her nail polish lasts for a fortnight. After I'd written it down I realised it was an observation my wife had made; that when she's at home, her nail polish lasts three or four days, but when she's on holiday, and not washing up and cleaning, it lasts a long time. And so I felt this was a nice way of talking about what women get out of holidays, the absence of routine. I was conscious that I hadn't read that thought anywhere else and I got a little kind of buzz that I was saying something that maybe hadn't been said before, and something that was also likely to be persuasive and work."

French describes what he calls a moment of epiphany: "There's a moment at which you suddenly realise you've done something as near-original as you ever will. Of course, nothing is ever original, but there's an indefinable moment when you sit back and look at something and think that's it, *that's* the one. I can't write any better than that. The art direction is about as good as it gets. The moment you realise it's not only a great ad, but it's going to work. And it doesn't happen very often in your life. I *knew* XO was going to work. I *knew* Kaminomoto was going to work. I *knew* Chivas Regal was going to work. There's a moment when you say, that *can't* fail. You just know it in your heart. I don't know if I knew it when I was younger, perhaps I didn't; but with experience, you just *know*. Other stuff you do which you know is going to work, but isn't great, is funnily enough less obvious than the creative highpoints. You can look at some stuff you've done which worked, and which a lot of people liked, but it's not one of the ads that's going to be shown in history books in fifty years' time, whereas XO and Kaminomoto might be." As French observes ironically: "It's kind of tragic that you can spend an entire lifetime turning out four great pieces of work, and they're all ads. Nurses and ambulance drivers do something a thousand times as important, five times a day."

6

THE FIVE CRITICAL CHOICES

A concept ground is selected. A campaign idea is taking shape. The next question is: what kind of print ad should be done?

There are really only five choices. Creatives will make them intuitively, with little conscious debate. In many cases, the ideas themselves dictate the choices. There are some executional rules, though, if the cutting edge is to be achieved.

WILL YOU SEND A POSTCARD OR A LETTER?

It is all a question of words, and whether you want to be more visual than verbal.

Mostly, a postcard is a *visually-led* ad. Not always, but mostly. Certainly, by definition, postcards always have very few words; *very, very* few.

On the other hand, a letter is always a *copy-led* ad. Letters have hundreds, even thousands of words.

Oddly enough, some of the world's best-known postcards and letters have been sent in the footwear category: Fallon McElligott's Hush Puppies campaign (*postcards*) and Leagas Delaney's Timberland campaign (*letters*).

As Neil French defines the choice: "A postcard is something you send from a holiday; a letter is something you might send when you are on your deathbed. Somewhere between those two extremes of human experience are the answers to your ad. Something that's jolly and light and not terribly important can be a postcard. The more serious it gets, the more like a letter it has to be. It's that simple."

David Abbott has sent both postcards and letters. "It's mostly guided by what would work. But it's also tied up with trying to do it differently. A kind of competitive thing comes into it as well. If I were pitching for *The Economist* now, and some other agency had done the poster campaign, part of me might be saying, well, they've done it short, now we'll try and do it long."

But hasn't advertising become more visual and less verbal? Surely sending a postcard would be a wiser decision?

"For as long as I've been in the business, this discussion has been going on," says John Salmon. "Art directors have always said copy is finished; it's all going to be visual from here on. I think the fact of the matter is that certain propositions demand words, certain propositions demand pictures, and you have to make the decision based on the product, the market, *and* the proposition."

There is also no reason why postcards and letters cannot coexist in the same campaign. Attitude, tone of voice, typeface and campaign branding can all contribute a sense of continuity.

Fortunately, there is only one rule: postcard or letter, *be single-minded*. It must be one or the other. Either the visual must dominate or the words must. There is no room for compromise; for example, if a lot of copy is sandwiched into the base of a visually-led ad, the effect will be totally lost.

As we are about to see, the best postcards are simple and focused.

Hush Puppies. This classic Fallon McElligott postcard campaign started life as a stopgap measure. As art director Bob Barrie tells us: "We had gotten the Hush Puppies account with a campaign called Match the Faces to the Hush Puppies. It had celebrities on top, with their legs and shoes on the bottom, and it was all mixed up. It was meant to show a range of shoes, and the fact that cool people wore them, and get readers involved in the ad. But before this campaign could be executed, there was a small problem of some media space which their previous agency had bought. Because the celebrities campaign couldn't be turned around in time, Jarl Olsen the copy-writer and I were called in to execute some quick ads."

The idea seems really obvious in retrospect, says Barrie. "We took the Hush Puppies dog as an icon, and used it as a vehicle to show the variety of shoes by doing little visual puns with the dog. It was a very easy to produce campaign."

Easy to produce, but not easy to sell. "It was *not* something they wanted to do. The company wasn't doing very well at the time

Famous postcards from
Fallon McElligott.
Dominant visuals,
minimal copy.
The logo came to life
and branded the ads.

and they associated their mascot with their perceived dowdy image. The *last* thing they wanted to do was ads with a basset hound in them. Primarily because deadlines were looming, and because we could produce the dog campaign fast, they said they'd try it. The ads ran nationally in *USA Today*, big colour pages. When floods of requests for reprints came in they thought, maybe we have something on our hands here. Then one of the celebrity ads ran, and one of the stars, as is often the case, got into a bit of trouble with the law. So it had to be pulled and the dog campaign just took over."

Barrie continued executing dog ads for two years. Then came television. "They weren't used to spending a lot of money, so I went to the stills photographer here in town, Rick Dublin, and we ended up shooting six 15-second spots for about US$125,000 I think, which is nothing. They were the print ads, coming to life, which I don't always recommend, but this was one case where it was very charming, very filmic. The very first commercial we shot, and the very first commercial Rick *ever* shot, *Ventilated Hush Puppies*, won a Gold Lion at the Cannes Advertising Festival."

American adman George Lois had advocated the idea of moving print ads; the Hush Puppies commercials are often upheld as the perfect example of his technique. Barrie cautions: "When people try to turn or extend print ideas into television, often they make the mistake of just literally doing that; putting a print visual on TV and making something move. They forget that it has to be filmic and interesting."

Burger King. A French fry that looks like a match was the creation of Andrew Clarke at Saatchi & Saatchi, Singapore, for Burger King's spicy Mexican promotion. Now that it has been done, it looks so easy.

"The connection came when I was just doodling a French fry," says Clarke. "I had it dipped into a bit of ketchup and I thought, that looks vaguely like a match, and I knew instantly it *would* look like a match if I did it properly, and that was that!"

It was a first thought, an obvious first thought, and one which many creatives would have dismissed as too simple, too *un*complicated. And therein lies a big lesson: Clarke's minimalist ad has won a

Gold Lion at Cannes, a Silver at the One Show, and acceptance into D&AD. As Clarke explains, it was a case of Love and Protection.

"I could have put a black background behind it, I could have put an orange background behind it, I could have put it in a matchbox, I could have had a hand holding it. I could have done a million things, but at the end of the day, I have this thing I call Love and Protection. Obviously, if you love an ad, you want to art direct it to the nines; you want to play with borders, different typefaces, and that's called the Love. Then, there's the Protection. And that's where you protect the idea from all the stuff you *shouldn't* be throwing at it, and that's what I based my decisions on. When I had it up on the Mac at the agency, there was a lot of *umm*ing and *ahh*ing. Shouldn't there be something else? Somebody wanted to change the typeface, it was far too simple for them. Somebody said, put a red border around it, and I said, why? *Why?* I knew instinctively it was right, but I could also see that it was tough, really tough, for some people to actually do it this way."

Clarke talks about the typeface, Cooper Black, and why the caption and logo are tucked together into the lower right corner. "It was a face I've always wanted to use, because it's really ugly, and it's a bit trendy. By putting *Fiery Fries* near the logo, it reduces the ad to two elements. I did try *Fiery Fries* just below the picture, and I also tried it centralised under the picture at the bottom, and both times

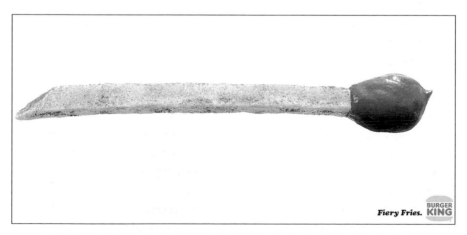

Resisting the temptation to complicate a great, simple idea. A postcard from Saatchi & Saatchi, Singapore.

the logo was in the corner. So there were three elements, picture and caption and logo, and what it did was break up the pureness of the white, so I just tucked it all into the corner. That's the thing about the white background, you have to be very careful with it. If you start putting little bits all over it, it suddenly doesn't become a white background; it becomes a background with a lot of bits on it. So you have to let the white do its job, and put everything else neatly where it belongs. Don't try and complicate it."

Adelar Pet Training and Grooming. As Simon Mainwaring explains, animals acting like humans is the thought behind the Adelar campaign which he created with Dean Mortenson.

Obedience training was the first execution. "We started out by wondering that if you could teach a dog to, say, catch a ball, what else could you get it to do? That eventually led us to the thought of humanising their skills. Animals acting like humans have always made people laugh and it seemed like a good way to dramatise the benefit. And that's where the toilet training ad came from." Once they had the dog at the urinal, they had the basis for a campaign. "It was just a matter of pushing each subsequent idea until we had the funniest and most relevant execution for the subject."

Humanised pets in a layout which carefully balances the logic of the ad.
Postcards from DDB Needham, Sydney.

Placement of captions and logos will always tip the balance in cutting edge work. One element was removed by not having a headline as such. Once you read *Obedience training* or *Pet grooming*, you get the idea. The issue was, how big should it be, and where should it be?

"We gave it prominence by reversing it out of black," explains Mainwaring. "We tried putting it top left, then top right. We even tried putting it in a dog tag at the bottom. But as soon as we strayed from the basic bottom-right-hand-corner solution, the logo started to overwhelm the picture and ruin the logic of the ad."

An unusual circular edge around the logo panel helps distinguish Adelar ads. "Dean and I felt that a black corner jutting out into the image lessened the impact of the picture. So we softened it by rounding the edge." As Mainwaring admits: "We did try several things, but in the end, staying simple proved to be the best."

UTA French Airlines. This ad, from Euro RSCG Partnership (The Ball Partnership), Singapore, breaks conventions in the airline category. There are no planes, no smiling stewardesses, no happy passengers; there is nothing, at first glance, which suggests it might be an airline ad.

The brief was to communicate that UTA offered more non-stop flights to Paris from Singapore than any other airline. The creative thinking was to find a French visual which demonstrated either something uninterrupted, or something which had been deliberately interrupted. The idea was a first thought. A French baguette, sliced four times, would symbolise a flight with four stops.

Many art directors would have added "some nice atmosphere": a checked tablecloth, perhaps, or a nice wine glass, or a French newspaper, or all three. Art director Norman Alcuri shot the sliced baguette without adornment: "Nothing could get in the way of the reader's mind latching onto the *cuts*; we were demonstrating cuts; we had to focus the reader on the cuts; then they had to follow that little headline running down the right-hand side of the baguette. We allowed ourselves a few crumbs, that was all. It was such a weird idea, just cutting a baguette, that anything you put into the picture would have got in the way of the idea. We had to pare it down, which was its strength."

A TYPICAL

FLIGHT TO PARIS

WITH OTHER

AIRLINES.

UTA HAS MORE NON-STOP FLIGHTS TO PARIS THAN ANYONE ELSE. EVERY MONDAY, TUESDAY, FRIDAY AND SATURDAY. SO WHY SPEND ALL THAT TIME IN TRANSIT, WHEN YOU CAN SPEND IT IN PARIS!

FOR YOUR TRAVEL ARRANGEMENTS TO PARIS CALL UTA ON 737 6355 OR YOUR TRAVEL AGENT

UTA

Minimalist art direction lets the mind latch on to a weird idea.
The baguette was life-sized on the page. A postcard from
Euro RSCG Partnership (The Ball Partnership), Singapore.

Alcuri's art direction was minimalist. The ad ran in full colour, on a broadsheet full page. The picture occupied 95 percent of the page; the minimal body copy and logos were tucked away at the base. Why? "Having the baguette life-sized on the page added another dimension," says Alcuri. "You opened your paper and saw this full-sized bread. Yes, it could have been done in a half-page vertical, but it would have lost its boldness, the slight cheekiness of it all. I struggled with the headline typeface; it had to be pared down, too. The logic was to focus on the cuts; then the headline, also cut into four pieces; then the copy."

How did Alcuri determine the way the baguette should be sliced? "Normally, you cut a baguette into smaller pieces. But that would have pushed credibility. Cutting it four times was more acceptable; like Singapore to Bangkok, Bangkok to Delhi, and so on. If you go too over the top, people won't believe you. The credibility factor evaporates."

Institute of Mental Health, Singapore. When writer Ben Hunt was looking at a picture of a brain one day, he suddenly saw that it could make the shape of a crouching man. "I just looked at it, and I saw the visual of the man," recalls Hunt. "I got an art director to draw it up, and I stuck it on my wall and left it there for two months. I often think the best things are accidents. You're thinking of an idea for something, and your subconscious is working. As soon as I got the image of the man and the brain, I knew I could use it one day, even if it was just for the cover of a book of lousy poetry."

As luck would have it, Hunt was commissioned privately to write a brochure on clinical depression. "I was going to do something quite straight. Then I saw the picture on the wall and I thought, hang on, this would be a great ad for depression." Sadly, Hunt's client could not afford the production costs. The picture was about to go back up on the wall when his client put him in contact with the IMH Clinic for Anxiety and Mood Disorders.

"I later found out that IMH stood for the Institute of Mental Health, but they don't call it that because of the stigma involved. The Institute loved it."

Photographer John Clang took two shots. "We had to experiment with lots of different models of brains before we got exactly the right image," explains Hunt. The man huddled over in a position of torment proved easier. "He was an account guy from another agency."

Cutting edge digital imaging, so often squandered to layer technique over weak ideas, added a new dimension to Hunt's concept. "Art director Francis Tan put the two shots together. He made them come alive. He had the vision that it should be very dark, so the first time you look at it you only see the brain. Then the second time you look, you see the man."

Hunt quotes a famous novelist who once wrote that the pain of depression could be so intense it was beyond description. "People who see this image have told me that it's exactly how they're feeling. What you can't express in words, you can express visually."

And, having expressed it visually, and with such power, Hunt and his team had the good sense to minimalise copy and position it sensitively.

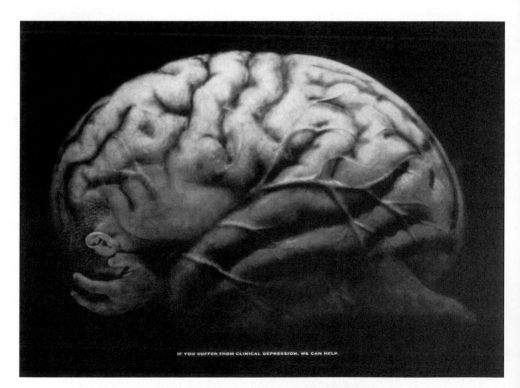

IF YOU SUFFER FROM CLINICAL DEPRESSION, WE CAN HELP.

A postcard from DMB&B, Singapore. A powerful message about clinical depression which happened by accident.

After Doyle Dane Bernbach's Volkswagen and Avis work, this is arguably America's most famous campaign. Created by Fallon McElligott in Minneapolis, it is a classic postcard concept. Minimalist art direction locates the copy and logo beneath the Reality picture.

A postcard from Abbott Mead Vickers, London, an agency traditionally known for its love of copy. On this occasion, only three words and a logo relate the cage-like construction of a Volvo to protection from danger.

177

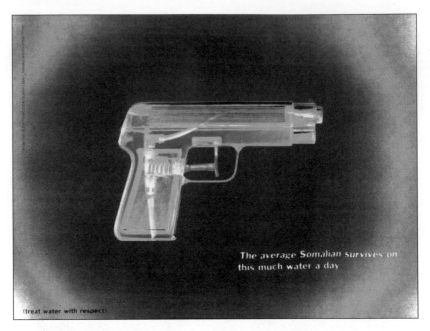

The average Somalian survives on this much water a day

(treat water with respect)

Charles Liddall's eerie photograph of a water pistol focuses attention on a distressing message: the pistol holds enough water to keep a Somalian alive for one day. A postcard from Batey Ads, Singapore.

Before sending a letter, two questions have to be answered with brutal honesty.

Is the product story interesting enough to warrant long copy?

And if it is, can it be written well enough?

Two masters of the genre elaborate.

"The quick hit of the picture has always been the first line of attack," reflects French. "If you can find a great picture, it may not say a thousand words, but it will say the important ones quickly. Long copy came in as a reaction against just a rather naff picture. There was a slew of heavy copy ads in the 1960s and 1970s, and to a lesser extent in the 1980s, caused by the fact that there were suddenly a lot of great copywriters around. Unfortunately, an awful lot of people who shouldn't be allowed near a pen also started writing long copy, which actually brought the genre into disrepute. But long copy will always work if the occasion calls for it. Long copy isn't dead any more than the book is dead, and the book is actually growing; you're reading one now."

Stay in school.

Friends of Public Education · 1-800-353-4374

A public service postcard from Fallon McElligott. Further proof that strong visual ideas work best when supporting elements like captions and logos are treated simply. Nothing should distract from the idea.

"I don't think there's a hard and fast rule that nobody reads it or everybody reads it," considers Mike Lescarbeau, "although I think it's closer to nobody. But even as a visual, long copy, whether it's read or not, gives a strong implication that the product has a lot to be said for it. We're writing less long copy at Fallon's these days, but if we felt we had a relevant story, and that the specific market for the product would read it, we'd write it."

Timberland. One of the world's most admired long copy campaigns was penned at Leagas Delaney, London. The Red Indian ad has been singled out universally as one of the half dozen classics of

WE DON'T LINE OUR BOOTS WITH FUR. WE LINE OUR BOOTS WITH BOOT.

IN ONE AMERICAN STATE, THE PENALTY FOR EXPOSING YOURSELF IS DEATH.

WE STOLE THEIR LAND, THEIR BUFFALO AND THEIR WOMEN. THEN WE WENT BACK FOR THEIR SHOES.

Breaking convention,
pushing conviction.
Letters from
Leagas Delaney,
London.

the genre. As Lionel Hunt says, "It's one of the best print ads I wish I had done. It's rightly famous. Outrageously, wonderfully, politically incorrect."

Ironically, the headline started life as a throwaway line in some body copy. Tim Delaney recalls: "I wrote that headline in the first bit of copy for another ad, and it was in parenthesis. I'd got to the Indians and I'd written this short thing that literally just went, *We stole their land, their buffalo and their women, then we went back for their shoes.* Then I went along to my art director, Steve Dunn, and I said, look, I've written this thing, I think it's a headline. He put it out and we had it there in two minutes and we just liked it. It was a headline that just popped out."

The whole campaign, in fact, originated with an ad for the Timberland department in Harrods. At the time, Delaney and Dunn would sit down and work on ads together.

"What was important about that first ad, we wrote it in a certain way, with lots of little silly puns in it, it talked a certain language. The big leap for us was when I started to create a little world in New Hampshire which is completely obsessed by boots, and cold, and extreme conditions, and Red Indians, and moccasins, and all that sort of stuff. This world sort of evolved and I could keep writing about it till the cows came home. It wasn't easy, but I could do it, and then I had America on top of that. I found out there were more miles of water on the inland coasts than there were on the outside of America. I also found out there are seventy-five thousand nerve ends in the foot. I'm a mine of useless information on all things to do with boots, feet, America, Red Indians, all kinds of stuff. That's where you find yourself. You've got to have an inquisitive mind. It's one of those things about a creative guy, you've got to be a bit of a Nosy Parker. You've got to be curious about how everything works around you, how people work. Out of that comes a sense of being able to connect and pull things together."

Delaney's little world of New Hampshire also set the tone for the art direction. "Out of that world came the look, black and white, it was more honest. The essential honesty of the product was definitely reflected in the honesty of the medium and the treatment, which I didn't get from the colour magazine ads in the States, like the guy lighting a fire. He looked immaculate, yet he was supposed to be in the wilderness."

What draws people to the Timberland campaign? Why has it become an international icon for copywriters? For its clever headline structures, the copy and art skills working so deftly in unison, most certainly; but there is something more, a lesson for anyone attempting a similar standard.

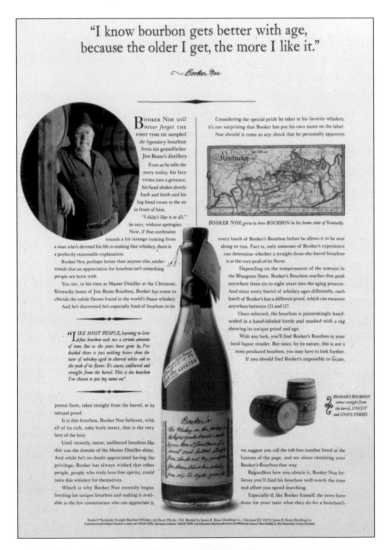

At $50 a bottle, Fallon McElligott thought letters were appropriate.

"How much can you write about a boot?" Delaney muses. "I wrote two thousand words an ad, or whatever it was. We wrote about things that people *never* used to write about boots. *We pushed the conviction we had about the product.*"

Booker's Bourbon. Before joining Fallon McElligott, Lescarbeau worked at Leagas Delaney. With Tim Delaney, he co-authored the award-winning long copy campaign for Ordnance Survey maps. He shares French's view that the genre is a victim of abuse.

"It's on a decline because products that didn't necessarily need long copy were getting it. But it still works when you have products like Booker's Bourbon, because people need to know why it costs $50 a bottle."

Lescarbeau describes how the long copy strategy was formulated. "We imagined, and it turned out we were correct, that men would want to pour this for a guest in their home and impress them with it." Booker's Bourbon comes in a hand-labelled bottle with a tag certifying its proof and age, signed by master distiller Booker Noe, grandson of Jim Beam. "They needed the lore that went with it, in order to have something to converse over, because unless you're an absolute maniac, you're going to take a little time to drink it."

According to Lescarbeau, it was a given that the ads would have a big bottle in them. "We fought it for a while. Then we said, what if the bottle was the hero, and we put in some secondary visuals of Booker Noe?"

The anecdotal ads scored Gold and Silver at the One Show. They disavow pretension and favour Kentucky folksiness: *I know bourbon gets better with age, because the older I get, the more I like it* begins one.

Lexus. In Singapore, one car in every ten is a Mercedes-Benz. Elbowing Lexus into that market required Dentsu Young & Rubicam to break several conventions.

"Mercedes-Benz had years to build its reputation," explains writer Mark Fong. "We had literally a few months. We had to show that Lexus stood for something."

Mercedes-Benz and arch-rival BMW owned engineering. "We had to sell engineering, too, but we wanted to show all the small things, all the small details, that make a car great," elaborates creative

Before we subjected the Lexus to the mercy of the critics, we first exposed it to the mercy of the elements.

Life in the desert, as any Bedouin will tell you, can really be tough.

In the day, the temperature here can easily swell past boiling point.

While in the night, the mercury level can plummet all the way to freezing point.

Naturally, this seemed like the perfect place to find out exactly how well the LS 400 would fare against a car's most unforgiving critic: Mother Nature.

So we left a pristine Lexus LS 400 out in the desert with nary a roof over its roof.

Not just for a couple of weeks or a few months. But for a period lasting more than two years. Sounds a tad fanatical, it is.

Too extreme? Has to be. Overkill? Perhaps.

So what did this admittedly unorthodox test reveal?

"If there is a paint job deeper or clearer or more lustrous, let me know where I can find it." The Freeze Bar

Quite simply, nothing the people at Lexus hadn't already before predicted.

It proved (without a shadow of a doubt) that even prolonged exposure under the scorching sun had little effect on the five-coat and four-bake paint process.

The stint in the desert also showed that the whipping gales of sand storms had left hardly a scratch on the car's chip-resistant lower body.

While the specially-formulated sealers under all the door hinges had over the years, kept minute grains of dust and sand out of its elegant interior.

Even the stainless steel exhaust remained ever so stainless.

In fact, up to 100 individual items on the LS 400 were identified to see how well the meticulous anti-ageing methods and materials had stood up to the test of time as well as the pain of performance.

Not just in the desert. But also in the sub-zero Arctic.

On speed-limitless highways, country roads, mountain trails and terrains which were better suited for creations with four legs rather than four wheels.

And all this, because Lexus believes the secret to eternal youth lies in a disciplined programme of cross-training.

It's a programme that puts to the test not only the endurance of the car but also reaffirms the ingenuity of its making.

For instance, in accelerated corrosion tests, the galvanised steel body of the LS 400 was confirmed to be four times less likely to rust than other luxury cars on the road.

Even the luxurious leather sheets which were used to upholster the seats testify to the maxim that beauty is more than skin deep.

Hand-selected leather samples are first stretched under a ray lamp for over 200 hours just to see how durable it is.

A show-to-wrinkle and hard-to-fade plush leather interior rewards you with years of comfortable travel.

After which, the chosen sheets are carefully tanned and then coated with a protective UV finish to help it resist fading under the merciless tropical sun.

And when it comes to prolonging the longevity of full-grain hide, the buck doesn't just stop here.

You see, even the leather that surrounds the steering wheel has been specially treated to protect it from the oil left behind by the driver's palm.

So the leather on the steering wheel will age not only gracefully but also in unison with the rest of leather inside the cabin.

Time, like the LS 400 doesn't stand still. That's why the Lexus V8 quad-cam 32-valve 240 bhp 4.0 litre engine has been torture-tested

to perform in any condition you can imagine.

In one particular experiment, our engineers chilled one of the engines down to minus 30°C, which is cold enough to make oil flow with the fluidity of sticky toffee. Yet with the very first start of the electronic ignition, the sweet hum of the V8 melted away any doubt of cynicism.

While this would have sufficed for others, the perfectionists at Lexus decided to take it a few steps further. *(The brutes.)*

So they ran this engine until it reached over 250km/h. And then continuously so for 24 hours a day for a week. (That's the equivalent of driving it at race track speed for a distance long enough to circle the entire world once over.)

To further ensure even more kilometres of trouble-free motoring, we cast the engine from a metal that proves to defy the onslaught of corrosion.

Service intervals will be infrequent, upkeep costs will be low and overall quality will be unsurpassed. Automotive Industries

Likewise, a number of the Lexus' most critical connectors have been plated with gold for uncompromised conductivity and durability.

While the spark plug tips on the V8 are made from platinum, a material even more expensive than gold.

After considering everything that went into it, it's no wonder why Car and Driver predicted after

A multi-process, multi-layer, hand-buffed paint finish is key to the pristine beauty of the Lexus.

"I can't think of a car in the entire history of the automobile which has set such high standards. Not even the first Rolls Royce." Whale Magazine

a 100,000km test. 'When it comes to providing quiet, elegant and powerful transportation, the Lexus shows every indication of doing so for another 100,000km.

So will the allure of the Lexus remain long after the appeal of these words have faded?

Only time will tell.

Mind you though, not on the Lexus.

For more details on the other wonders of the Lexus LS 400, please call your Lexus Consultant at 740 3288 for a test drive.

LEXUS

For Perfectionists. By Perfectionists.

Lexus Division, Borneo Motors (S) Pte Ltd (An Inchcape Company), 17 Ubi Road 4, Singapore 1440. Tel: 740 3288. Fax: 743 4079. Open on Sunday 10am-5pm.

Selling a US$200,000 Japanese car to a country in love with Mercedes-Benz.
Letters from Dentsu Young & Rubicam, Singapore.

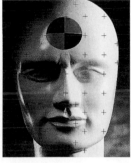

director Patrick Low. "So we decided to marry the high standards of the owners with the high stardards of the car, to show how the driver's values are reflected in the car. We took the positioning, *For perfectionists, by perfectionists.*"

The decision to use long copy print ads defied the conventional wisdom that Singaporeans do not read them. "We ran the ads in English and Chinese on Sundays, when businessmen had more time," says Fong. "The mass of information presumes high quality. The Chinese-educated reader assumes that because there is so much to write about, it must be a good product."

The campaign's tonality was more Western than Asian. As Fong recalls: "Toyota had many of the same features in other models, so we had to sound different. We had to couch the features in a different tone and manner, one which would appeal to the kind of people with money, who were at a stage in life to drive a Lexus." There was no shortage of subject matter. "The product manager was very passionate, he kept feeding us nuggets of information, all kinds of trivia, and we soaked it up like a sponge. Every headline was a point of entry to the key subjects like power, silence, safety, ageing well. My copy ran one third over length on average," he laments. "Every cut was painful."

Low crafted the visuals so all seven ads shared a campaign look, without being exactly the same. "Some pictures were bigger, some were smaller. I wanted to create little pockets of interest with sidebars. People always read captions and quotations."

The new marque captured both market share and consumer imagination. The salesmen were surprised when customers could quote facts and figures from the ads. For the agency, there was a bonus: a Silver at the One Show.

Hamburg Police. Not all letters are letters; some are more like telegrams. This little transit ad, with its appropriately distressed execution, demonstrates the principle.

It was designed to instil civil courage and prick the consciences of apathetic bystanders. The translation reads: *Yesterday, seven people stabbed a foreigner here. Six of them were reading the timetable. Doing nothing is taking part.*

> # GESTERN WURDE HIER EIN AUSLÄNDER VON SIEBEN LEUTEN NIEDERGESTOCHEN.
>
> ## SECHS DAVON LASEN DABEI DEN FAHRPLAN.
>
> ### WER NICHTS TUT, MACHT MIT.

A Cannes gold-winning telegram from Springer & Jacoby, Hamburg.

WILL YOU HAVE A BENT HEADLINE WITH A STRAIGHT PICTURE?
OR A STRAIGHT HEADLINE WITH A BENT PICTURE?

Again, there are only two choices. But this time, the choice is made consciously.

If the idea in the ad is being carried by the headline, it means the headline will contain a twist, a trick, a turn, a shock factor; it will be *bent*. Therefore, the accompanying visual must play a subservient or *straight* role.

And vice versa.

If the idea in the ad is being carried by some creative twist in the picture, the picture will be *bent*. Therefore, the headline must be absolutely *straight*. No puns, no wordplays, no embellishments. The words could even be taken from the product statement in the brief.

It is a truth in which Lionel Hunt absolutely believes. In fact, he coined the terminology. "It was to do with the importance of thinking about print ads as words and pictures that work in unison. If a copywriter only thinks about the copy, he will never write a straight line because, in isolation, it won't appear clever enough. However, in conjunction with the right picture, it might just be a brilliant ad. It's the same with the art direction."

John Hegarty agrees. "You're using words and pictures. What you don't want to do is make the picture do what the words are doing, and the words do what the picture is doing. So you've got to decide which is *leading*, which is taking you forward, and if it's the picture then almost certainly what you want is a very simple headline. Or it's the other way round: a very simple picture and you've got an intriguing headline. So there is a kind of juxtaposition. But you *can't* have both. Then it's bland, and they work against each other, one's fighting the other rather than complementing it."

The classic example is having a straight photograph of a car. If you write a straight headline, the ad will be boring and forgettable. If you write a bent headline like *Lemon,* everybody will sit up and take notice.

Every ad in this book conforms to this truth.

If you are sending a letter, by definition you must have a bent headline. The headline carries the idea which extends into the long copy. Delaney's Timberland is a campaign of bent headlines with straight pictures of boots, Red Indians and New Hampshire trivia.

If you are sending a postcard, however, you will have to make a conscious decision whether to bend the headline or the picture.

The cream of Manchester is a very straight headline; a beer in an ice cream cone is a very bent picture.

Two old ladies talking on the steps is a very straight picture; *It's so nice that homosexuals, Jews and terrorists have a newspaper to read* is a very bent headline.

Cutting silk is a bent picture; the brand name *Silk Cut* is the invisible straight headline.

Management trainee, aged 42 is a bent headline; the colour red is a straight picture.

For his Kaminomoto postcards, French bent the pictures and wrote a straight headline. For XO beer, sometimes he bent the pictures, other times he bent the headlines. But he never bent both in the same ad.

If both the headline and the picture are bent, the ad will lose its focus. Neither will work.

If both the headline and the picture are straight, the ad will be bland and lifeless.

All letters have bent headlines. Because the words are carrying the idea, the supporting pictures must be straight.

Leagas Delaney, London.

Leagas Delaney, London.

Not all postcards have bent pictures.

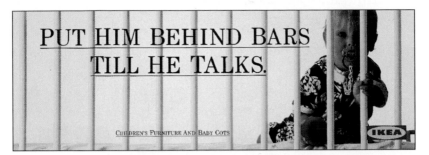

Dentsu Young & Rubicam, Singapore.

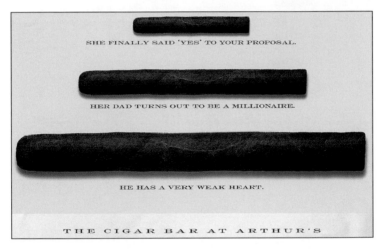

Loeffler Ketchum Mountjoy, Charlotte, North Carolina.

*Leagas Delaney,
London.*

191

A straight picture can always be saved by a bent headline. If all you can afford is the product shot, you can still achieve the cutting edge.

Saatchi & Saatchi, London.

Abbott Mead Vickers, London.

Fallon McElligott, Minneapolis.

The more you bend the picture, the straighter the headline should be. If both are bent, one will fight the other. Sometimes it is as simple as hanging a bent picture on the product statement in the brief.

Saatchi & Saatchi, Sydney.

Lowe & Partners, New York.

Abbott Mead Vickers,
London.

HOW TO IMPROVE A GOLF'S TURNING CIRCLE.

Mad Dogs & Englishmen,
New York.

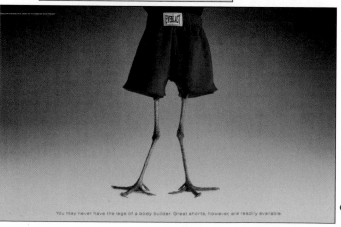

Goldsmith/Jeffrey,
New York.

*Springer & Jacoby,
Hamburg.*

*Fallon McElligott,
Minneapolis.*

*Euro RSCG Partnership
(The Ball Partnership),
Singapore.*

Having a beautiful picture is *not* an idea. Thousands of ads have beautiful pictures and become beautiful wallpaper. You will still need a bent headline for a cutting edge juxtaposition.

Leagas Delaney, London.

Fallon McElligott, Minneapolis.

Being weird, provocative and in-your-face is *not* an idea. If that tonality is relevant, you cannot assume that bizarre visuals of pierced nipples and pregnant women work automatically as bent pictures. Shock factor alone does not put the copywriter out of a job. Some cutting edge bent headlines demonstrate this principle.

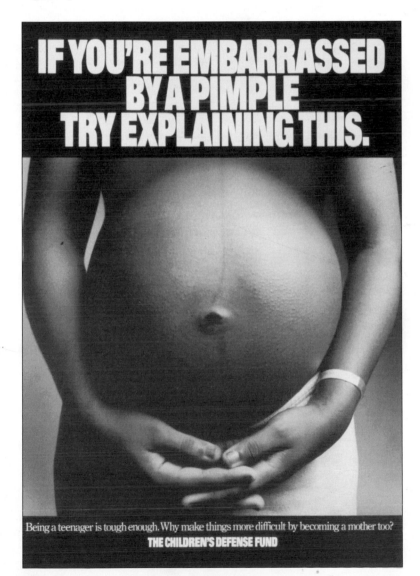

Fallon McElligott, Minneapolis.

Leagas Delaney, London.

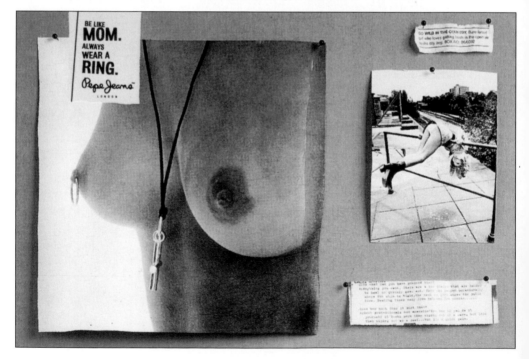

There is no law that says you cannot mix ads with bent headlines and ads with bent pictures in the same campaign. It is like mixing postcards and letters in the same campaign; it adds spontaneity. For WFLD-TV Chicago, Fallon McElligott bent their headlines whenever they used straight library pictures. When they could create their own pictures, they bent them and wrote straight headlines. They are doing the same for BMW.

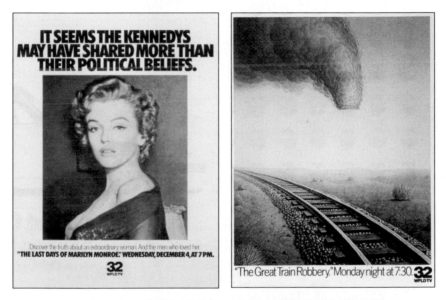

Fallon McElligott, Minneapolis.

WILL YOU USE TYPOGRAPHY INSTEAD?

You can still send a postcard with a bent picture, even when there is no picture.

A typographical ad communicates the idea solely by typography. There are no other visuals whatsoever.

The two rules of the genre are simple. The headline or copy should be straight; the typography provides the bent picture. If the words are bent as well, it does not work. And, if a shape or an object has been formed typographically, there should always be enough space in the ad to frame it. If the shape runs edge to edge, there is a risk it will not be recognisable.

Typographical ads can communicate ideas which cannot be expressed in traditional ways. Agency Houston Herstek Favat of Boston formed a typographical message into the actual shape and size of a two-month-old baby's lungs. The copy described the effects of second-hand cigarette smoke on babies for the Massachusetts Department of Public Health.

When competitors all use visuals, a typographical campaign can disrupt the category. For example, the Mates Condoms campaign formed straight product statements into the shapes of copulating couples. For property consultants Jones Lang Wootton, Australian agency OMON constructed a headline in the shape of a skyscraper. It posed the question: *What happens to your new building if experts aren't handling the finance?* The answer appeared alongside; the headline had collapsed into a pathetic jumble of tangled letters.

Typographical ideas can turn low-budget print ads into highly visible cutting edge print ads.

Everything is possible.

Not all typographical ideas are based on making shapes out of words. Some communicate what might happen without the product by removing key letters or words. Others represent the product typographically as an intellectual challenge to sophisticated audiences.

At a time when people are debating whether print ads should be visual or verbal, the typographical genre comes into its own. As Guido Heffels says: "You can't make a distinction between words and pictures any more. Words have become pictures, pictures have become words. This is the rich language an art director or copywriter should use to express his ideas. The choice between words and pictures is only the search for the best expression, and the 'words' which express the idea best are the ones you should use."

If Heffels is right, the typographical option could well be where visual and verbal meet best.

Charter Regional Medical Center. Scott Sheinberg, writer and executive creative director at Henderson Advertising, Greenville, South Carolina, discusses the strategy behind the breast cancer ad seen in Chapter 1 of this book.

"In concepting the ad, our goal was to force the involvement of the audience. Women typically don't read mammography ads or literature because it's something they would rather not think about. So we sought a solution that had a sufficiently provocative headline to lead the reader to the body copy."

The headline, *Can you find the lump in this breast?*, led readers into copy typographically shaped as a breast. The breast, however, served more than a visual function.

"The period (full stop) in line 17 is the same size as lumps which can be detected in a mammogram," explains Sheinberg.

The copy, which urged women readers to have a mammogram, concluded: "If you haven't found the lump by now, chances are, you're not going to. It was in the 17th line. The period at the end of the sentence was slightly larger than the others. So think about it, if you couldn't find it with your eyes, imagine how hard it would be to find it with your hands."

As Sheinberg says: "The only way to illustrate that concept was typography." The judges at Britain's D&AD agreed.

Levis. The famous Levis fingerprint ad demonstrates the rules of the genre. The words are straight, the picture is bent. The six words, *No two pairs are the same*, are repeated endlessly, typographically crafted into the whorls of a fingerprint. Adequate white space allows the fingerprint shape to be recognisable. The Levis logo is the only other visual element in the ad.

Hegarty reviews the concept: "Jeans are unique as a product, and Levis are the original, in that they are identified as your own by the way you wear them. They become a part of you. There are very few products that we ever own that actually have that quality, that as you wear them they become more of your personality. If you wear them at the knee more, they will show that. If you always put something in your back pocket, they will show that. The way you wear them becomes a part of you. The fingerprint was simply to say they're as individual as your fingerprint, and we thought it would be very nice to make the type work within the fingerprint as a way of pulling the two things together."

Six straight words in a bent picture. A typographical postcard from Bartle Bogle Hegarty, London.

Singapore Ministry of Health. A low-interest subject and a low budget suggested typography for a dental health message. Creative director Garry Abbott recalls: "We didn't have any money for photography, and frankly what could we show anyhow? Decayed teeth would be a turn off. Perfect teeth would make us look like a toothpaste ad."

Abbott believes typographical ads cut through against traditional ones. "We took a very simple campaign statement and simply let the key word, *teeth*, drop from the headline. It communicated instantly and, just as importantly, worked as well in Chinese as it did in English."

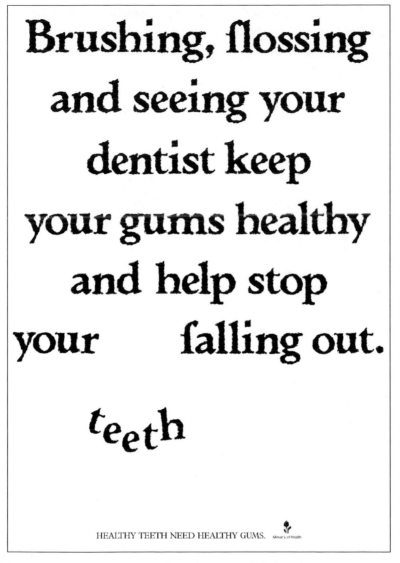

A low-interest subject on a low budget. Using a straight headline, bent typography worked by suggestion. Ketchum Advertising for the Singapore Ministry of Health.

Art director Heintje Moo and typographer Gordon Tan selected Ticonderoga as a sufficiently decayed typeface to convey the message. A Chinese typeface was modified to replicate it.

The work was selected by the Type Directors Club of New York for its Best of Ten Years Advertising Typography exhibition.

J&B Scotch Whisky. "Sometimes," says Roy Grace at Grace & Rothschild, New York, "when you're blessed, or cursed, with some horrible looking product, you make an asset of it."

With Volkswagen as his creative lodestar, Grace grappled with branding. "The typography of the J and the B was some sort of crushed Clarendon. So I had somebody create a typeface to match it, so we would have at least uniform ugliness."

The idea for a typographical campaign based on the J and B was an inspiration. In retrospect, as always, it looks so obvious.

"Sometimes you can pound your head into the wall and the most obvious solution eludes you. Some sort of electronic pulse occurs in the brain, based on assimilating as much information as you can," Grace believes. "I've always been a proponent of that old parable of the monkey sitting down at a typewriter. Given enough time, it will write every great novel. Given enough time, and enough information, you will come up with a great ad."

In fealty to Bill Bernbach, he kept the product out of the ads. Fortunately, this was one occasion when he lost the battle of the logo.

A classic typographical campaign where the product name drives the idea.
Postcards with bent pictures and straight headlines from
Grace & Rothschild, New York.

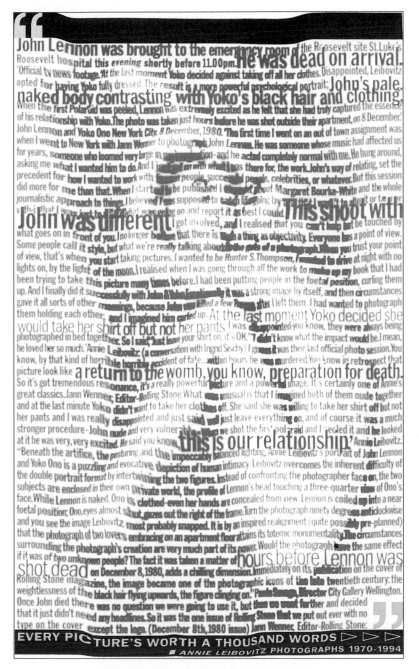

A postcard from Saatchi & Saatchi, Wellington.
A typographically bent picture with a straight headline,
turning Annie Leibovitz's words into one of her greatest photographs.

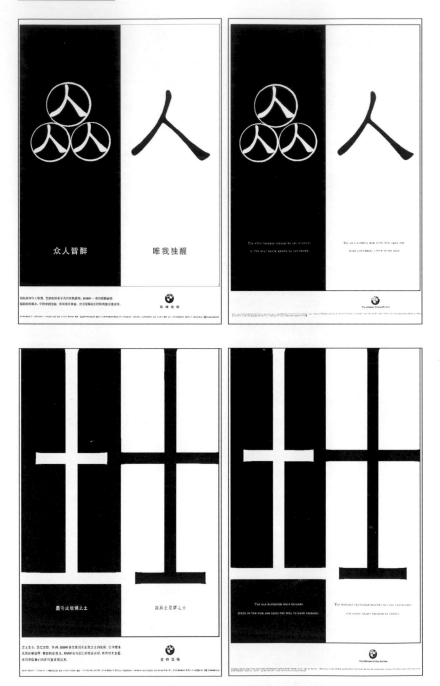

Strokes of genius from M&C Saatchi, Singapore.
Chinese, a pictographic language, is perfect for typographical ideas.

BMW. Chinese is a pictographic language. Certain combinations of strokes convey pictorial meanings. So not only can Chinese copywriters play with words, they can play with pictures within the words. Small wonder, then, that Chinese lends itself perfectly to typographical ideas.

The BMW campaign from M&C Saatchi, Singapore, broke convention by being originally conceived in Chinese. It proved so popular that an English version ran later. Usually in Singapore, campaigns are conceptualised in English first.

Typographically, it draws two contrasts: between the crowd and the individualist in one ad; between crudity and refinement in the other.

The first ad is based on the Chinese word *rén*, meaning a person. In fact, the Chinese character rather resembles a running man. The Chinese word for a crowd, *zhòng*, looks not unlike *rén* written three times. Taken together, *zhòng rén* means everybody. By contrasting a crowd, going around in circles, with the single individualist, the BMW owner is appropriately flattered. While the English subheads couch this thought in philosophical language, the Chinese original appears at first quite blunt. It reads, literally, *Everybody is befuddled; I alone am clear minded.* The Chinese subheads balance four characters on either side of the equation, a favourite linguistic gambit. But the fourth character, *zuì*, and the eighth character, *xǐng*, share the Chinese pictograph for alcohol, thereby conveying a meaning far deeper and more subtle than any two English words could ever achieve. *Zuì* expresses intoxication and stupefaction; *xǐng* implies a revival of conscious thought.

In the second ad, the character reversed out of black is *tǔ*, meaning soil or earth. Its long base stroke indicates a picture of the ground. By shortening the base stroke, and lengthening the cross stroke above, it becomes an entirely different word: *shì*, meaning a scholar or a refined, commendable person. So the reader has two choices: without the product, he is earthly bound; with the product, he will be one of the worldly elite.

The campaign was conceived and art directed by Yue Chee Guan. The Chinese copy was written by Linda Leong; the English by Paul Ruta.

City Gallery. Saatchi & Saatchi, Wellington, broke conventions when advertising an exhibition of Annie Leibovitz photographs; firstly, by choosing not to show her work in the ads, and then by choosing a typographical idea to announce the event.

The concept, *Every picture's worth a thousand words*, uses Leibovitz's own words to replicate one of the world's most famous photographic icons: her shot of a naked John Lennon in the foetal position, embracing Yoko Ono, only hours before his murder. The image of John and Yoko emerges through a sepia sea of words. Typographer Len Cheeseman, formerly of Collett Dickenson Pearce, London, magnifies certain poignant phrases: *This shoot with John was different ... a return to the womb, preparation for death ... this is our relationship.*

Typographically intricate, immensely intimate, the image confronts and demands to be read. Chris Bleakley art directed; Maggie Mouat was writer.

Choosing whether to send a postcard or a letter, whether to bend the headline or the picture, or choosing to do a typographical ad instead, will help determine whether your ideas reach the cutting edge.

What follows next is execution, perhaps the most perilous phase of all. The crafts of art direction and copywriting will determine whether everything is won or lost.

7

How to Craft Visuals

There is nothing more fragile than a great idea in the wrong hands.

"The problem is," says Bob Isherwood, "ideas have to be executed. Someone has to be able to art direct it, someone has to be able to write the copy, otherwise the idea doesn't end up looking very good. I think there is a lot missing in what are basic craft skills."

The strongest ideas in this book are the simplest. And, in every case, their art direction has kept them focused. To the unwary, the word *craft* can imply complexity; crafting an ad means complicating it, layering it with dozens of executional touches, decorating it to death.

Craft really means judgement. Craft can mean subtraction as well as addition. Craft means being appropriate. Craft means knowing when an extra detail can be added, when an extra layer of technique cannot. Craft is the watchdog of clarity.

In the same way you were asked to commit yourself to some new philosophies about advertising, brand building and generating ideas, cutting edge creativity asks you to commit yourself to a new perspective on craftwork.

"I'm not sure these days if people have the same crafting commitment," challenges Ian Batey. "We used to eliminate, eliminate, eliminate. We finessed ads right up to the time they went to press. Now I think we've lost the plot a bit. It's not important to people any more. You don't see the kind of print work that Neil French did any more, you don't see the startling stuff."

What do we see?

Roy Grace calls it high mediocrity. "Everything looks pleasant. There are so many people out there who are slick; they can make things look good. But it's sort of like cotton candy. Empty inside. What's happened, because of the present structure of the advertising business, the testing and research, the bottom of American advertising has been cut away and discarded. You don't see the real awful stuff as much. But so have the heights gone, too. You don't see that real great stuff, either. That's what's missing for me. We're too polished, we're too slick."

Grace recalls a conversation he used to have with Helmut Krone: "We used to talk about this, fifteen years ago. We were always striving for a way to articulate it. It was the need to be wrong, the need to be ugly, the need to take people off guard. Everything was so polished. There is a certain advantage in always going against the grain. We need to do stuff that's a little *raw*."

John Messum recalls Paul Arden saying a similar thing: "Paul would ask, what can we do that's *wrong*? What happens if we do it wrong?" Messum believes it can force you to break out. "You make rules for yourself. If you can break out of them, you'll find something more exciting. Doing things wrongly sometimes leads to a more surprising solution."

What Does Art Direction Have to Do?

"The number one requirement," stipulates Bill Oberlander, "is for an ad to captivate the heart and soul of the reader, and that basically comes from powerful art direction. A lot of agencies historically have presented art direction as kind of *decorative*. Art direction is considered an aesthetic that happens after the fact." Oberlander believes art direction should happen at the same time as the idea. "You have to find some kind of visual equity in the brand, and then activate it, and exponentially multiply it through all the communication levels. First and foremost is amazing art direction, relevant to the brand's emotional equity with consumers."

At Bates Dorland, creative director Jay Pond-Jones considers art direction can differentiate one brand from another. "The point is, how can the look and feel of an idea be most wholly differentiated from the competition, and from the media environment? Sometimes, with the best ads, the line is very hard to draw between art or advertising. Occasionally, you can get to communication that's like art in its originality, or naivety, or simplicity. But that's very rare."

Simplicity will be a recurring theme.

In the hands of great art directors, great ideas are never obscured. They are strengthened by minute attention to craft details, including the craft of reduction.

For example, there is no rule that says strong ideas can only work on white backgrounds. It is not formulaic. But it is commonsense. When in doubt, leave a great idea alone.

As you will see, great art direction is about judgement, moving an idea in stages through a series of crafting decisions.

When to keep it simple

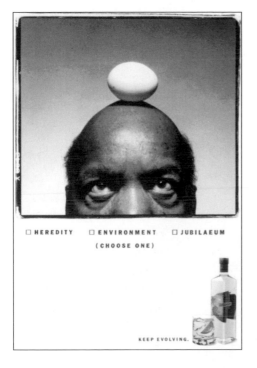

Why bury a breakthrough idea? Besides which, a white background lets the reader tick the little boxes.
Fallon McElligott, Minneapolis.

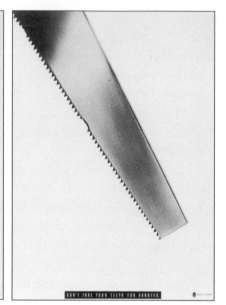

*"Nobody was going to read
a letter about teeth," says
creative director Garry Abbott.
So writer Daniel Lim and
art director Heintje Moo crafted
postcards with bent pictures and
straight headlines. The background
was not taken for granted, either.
It was left stark and clean.
Ketchum Advertising for the
Singapore Ministry of Health.*

When to add another layer

I will not drink from the toilet bowl.
I will not howl when you play the piano.
I will not mistake house guests for burglars. Or vice versa.
I will not play 'fetch' with your toothbrush.
I will not make love to your leg.

Adopt a pedigree pet from the SPCA. Call 287 5355.

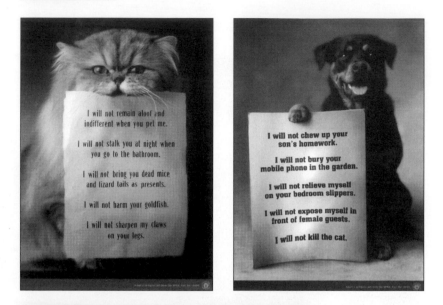

One compelling idea, flawlessly art directed by Edmund Choe. The visual elements have been reduced to two: the bent picture incorporating Jagdish Ramakrishnan's charming copy, and a straight headline at the base. Choe follows the rules of the postcard genre, letting the visual dominate 95 percent of the ad. Evidence of craft is everywhere, yet it upholds every tenet of cutting edge creativity. A Gold at Cannes was not surprising. Saatchi & Saatchi, Singapore.

When to keep layering

A postcard with a bent headline and straight picture. Adding a Filofax was appropriate at Fallon McElligott, Minneapolis.

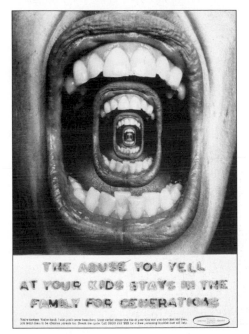

In this postcard, the bent picture is crafted to communicate abuse and tension. The straight headline is appropriately riddled with distress. Saatchi & Saatchi, Wellington.

When to craft a classic

We brake for fish.

Would you like to experience a Range Rover under optimum conditions?

Just add water.

A Range Rover can wade through depths that would immobilize a mere car.

And provide the added traction of 4-wheel drive in a downpour.

What's all the more extraordinary, though, is that a Range Rover isn't a vehicle you'll want to save for a rainy day.

Because on a dry road, it handles like a road car. And on a test track, it surges along at roughly 100 mph.

RANGE ROVER

It even surrounds you with all the comfort and luxury of a luxury car.

So why not call 1-800-FINE 4WD for the name of a dealer convenient to you?

While, at a cost somewhat above $30,000, a Range Rover is hardly inexpensive, it's well worth the price.

After all, when you buy one you're not simply buying an ordinary 4-wheel drive vehicle.

You're converting your money into a liquid asset.

When in doubt, craft a classic. A classic layout, with classic typography. A bent headline with a straight picture, from Grace & Rothschild, New York.

Is Less More?

"I'm into very minimal art direction," Neil French declares. "I think it was Chet Baker who said, 'It takes a very, very good drummer to be better than no drummer at all'. I'm inclined to think that about art direction. It takes a very, very good art director to be better than no art director at all. So what I try to do is express things as simply as possible, and hope that because it's expressed so simply, the core idea will come across. Sometimes the art direction is a bit flat, and that's my fault, and sometimes the sparsity of it actually makes it work, which is also my fault."

Gary Goldsmith echoes his sentiment. "I'm from the school that thinks people should be able to understand the ad. There was a period where it was almost like if you can read it, and if you can get it, it must not be very good. I'm all for experimental type, and doing really quirky, unusual stuff. Just because a lot of my stuff tends to be more straight, does not mean I don't like work that's more experimental. I do. But," he stipulates, "it's still got to ultimately make sense."

Dean Hanson is another minimalist. "People are more bombarded with imagery every day and if you keep it simple, like a billboard, you will win. The odds of it breaking through are multiplied exponentially." Hanson recalls judging the Clios. "The ads that cut through like crazy were from Singapore and Hong Kong. I assume the reason they're so simple is because of the language barriers they have to jump over. They have to be visual. Most of the time, if it can be done visually, it should be done visually. If you can tell the story visually, with a minimum of copy, and reduce the elements, you're so far ahead of the game. In the award shows, those are the ones that score." One exception, Hanson considers, is when you have to educate people about a totally new product. "*Then* you have to tell the story. Sometimes, long copy ads in the Neil French school are a breath of fresh air because you're just not seeing long copy any more. Long copy has really taken a hit, so when you do see it, and if it's well written, it can be very effective."

"More often than not, when you see too much flimmery and flammery," David Abbott believes, "it's camouflage for a lack of a strong central idea. The art directors I've worked with have all come from the DDB tradition. They've all been interested in what I've been interested in, which is not ornamentation, but simplicity, and clarity, and strength. So I've never had that problem, but obviously one observes it in other people, where I think people put too much into the ad and lose the strength of the idea."

Norman Alcuri opposes art direction which gets in the way of the idea. Ideas never go out of fashion, Alcuri believes; ornamentation does. "I'd be a happy man if, for the rest of my life, I could just do ads with three-quarters picture, headline underneath, three columns of type, logo bottom right, with *brilliant* ideas in them," he confesses. "Who needs art direction?"

When Bill Gallacher art directs, he thinks about the amount of time the message will have to sink in. "People aren't waiting for your ad. They're seeing thousands of visual messages every day. You have to carve a way through that by the mere thought in the ad. So your level of art direction has to hit that point. If I want someone to think longer about it, I'll add more layers."

"My things tend to be real minimalistic," admits Bob Barrie. "I see other people doing the exact opposite and being successful, but I think, generally, as a rule, simpler is better."

Some would argue that simple means simplistic, minimalist means cold and devoid of emotion. If execution can help separate brands, why opt for sparsity?

"I am a fundamental believer that it is the idea which drives things," says John Hegarty. "On my wall, I have a little blown-up quote from the dictionary and it says, 'An idea is a thought or plan formed by mental effort'. In other words, the colour blue is *not* an idea. Wonky type is *not* an idea. It's a means of making your idea more profound, or of exaggerating it. Each idea determines if it should be minimalist or more adorned. You must listen to the vibrations that the idea is sending out to you. *You* have to decide what is right." Hegarty believes the debate between different styles of art direction is nothing new. "We think it's a new debate because of technology, because of the Mac, but the Renaissance painters had the same problem. We all know the story. Christ was born of the Virgin Mary, He died on the Cross, rose from the dead after three days, and went to Heaven. The Church kept saying to them, well, paint us these pictures so that people will believe, and they had to come up with different versions of it to make people think, wow, I didn't quite see it like that."

WHEN SHOULD YOU STOP ART DIRECTING AN AD?

"You just know," says Ron Mather. "You start to feel you should leave it alone. I hate overcrafted ads. In fact, I hate overcrafted anything. Great typography or exquisite photography will never save a bad idea."

"Once you've communicated the idea in the strongest possible way, then you quit," concurs Goldsmith. "Some people build a certain fussiness into a lot of their work. Unless the idea requires that type of art direction, I don't feel the need to put artifice all over it."

"When you know that it's communicating at its clearest," maintains Andrew Clarke, "and you're pretty sure that what you've done to the ad, in terms of art direction, isn't destroying the idea, that's when you stop."

"When it touches the nerve that runs right through the middle of you," says Gallacher. "There's no logical reason, you just look at it and think, that's close to the pattern of the idea you had in your head when you thought up the idea. When the art direction reaches that imaginary point in your head, you think, right, stop there."

"When is the moment to stop? Taste tells you," Hegarty believes. "There is no absolute moment. So much of what we do is about taste. I've observed that about the people who are more successful at this craft, or at any expression of creativity. It becomes more about taste than anything else. I'm increasingly getting to the point in life when I say most things are about taste. It's like a client buying a good strategy, it's like a client understanding why one particular ad is better than another. It comes down to taste. People are attracted to taste and style; they don't actually know why they are attracted to those things, but they are."

"When the art direction gets in the way of the communication, that's when you should definitely throw it out," says Antony Redman, who describes himself as an intuitive art director. "I never had any formal training as an art director. I've always worked by myself out of necessity; the best art directors at The Ball Partnership were always occupied, working with their writers, so I was more or less *forced* to art direct my own stuff. So I can only go with my gut. I can't sit and craft for weeks. I just go with what my heart says." Redman says he art directs quickly. "I tend to play with the layouts for one or two days, until I've got something I'm happy with, then I'll work it out properly. I think you know when you're over art directing something, when you're gilding the lily, because you start thinking about it way too much, it all gets too fancy."

Barrie, a confessed minimalist, recognises a new dichotomy in art direction. "Once, my answer used to be when the ad didn't suffer by removing an element. Neil French has that wonderful talk he gives about removing all the elements from an ad and getting it down into its purest form. I still think a lot of great work is done that way. But, the world's changing, and especially young people seem to be digesting things differently," he points out. "What I've seen in focus groups is that they really get into complicated things, packed with information. They like studying all the subtle little nuances. So my answer now is, I think it varies, depending on the audience. There are probably five hundred and sixty-two extraneous elements in our Miller Lite print ads, but they work. In the case of more youth-oriented advertising, young people would get bored by simplicity. They want to dig into some meat."

Barrie's colleague at Fallon McElligott, Tom Lichtenheld, who has won some of the most substantial awards in the industry, believes in tweaking things to death. "And then some," he adds. "My motto is, anything that's worth doing, is worth *over*doing. I don't think you can stop tweaking too late. I don't mean you should overproduce it or overembellish it, I just mean paying attention to detail. Making sure every element is in the right place. It's a matter of taking things out, especially in photography, until the idea is left with nothing superfluous."

Lichtenheld talks about the joys of crafting an ad at his computer. "It's that rare kind of quiet time, with me and my pencil and piece of paper. I do my sketches on paper, but my final tweaking is on the Mac. There are always the formulae that will work, but one of the challenges is to push beyond those, even when you're comfortable with them. I see work these days which has the classic elements, a great headline and an interesting visual, and then somebody has gone beyond any format I've ever seen and brought a completely new look to it. Usually it involves more integration of those things than I've seen before. In other words, there will be *less* difference between the visual and the headline; either the type is worked into the visual, or the type is designed in conjunction with the visual so there's a completely designed unit, no part of which is just laid on top of another. I think it's a real achievement to take classic elements and bring design on top of that, to make it a thing of beauty as well as a great concept."

For Guido Heffels, crafting is a trial and error game with two players: "The left and right sides of your brain," he says. "What style, what typeface, what else can add something to the idea? The time-consuming thing is, you can't discuss it. You have to see it, at least as a simulation. And just at the moment you think you've got it, you want to check out something completely different, something you have not even dared to think about." Like Hegarty, Heffels believes you have to dare to be different. "Maybe this is what makes your ad anything but average. Maybe it won't, but then there is always a restart button."

Oberlander reviews ads by looking at them upside down. "I don't care to read them until I know the art direction is telling a story," he explains. "The way an ad looks can actually say more than the words themselves. So you push the art direction, push it and push it and push it, until you don't know where to look on the page first. Then you can develop the sense of prioritisation, where you want them to look first, second, and third. Obviously, the ad must have some kind of intellectual proposition, too, that connects the brand to the consumer, something that makes them think, that brand thinks like me, I like that brand, that brand is a friend of mine, I will take it into my life."

Goldsmith reviews ads by putting them up on a wall and looking at them from ten feet away. "I don't want to know what product the ad's for. If it's a car ad, I don't want to know it's a car ad. I want to think, maybe that's a soup ad. If it's a soup ad, I want to think, maybe that's a liquor ad. I'm looking for that element of surprise." When Goldsmith is art directing his own work, he will often list all the *cliched* visuals in the category. "If I'm doing an ad for a bank, I'll list all those things like guys in suits, a vault, handshakes, smiles, money. If I do end up using one of those visuals, I've done it *consciously.* I've chosen to use it because I'm going to defile it or something, or go against it in some way."

Clarke stands on a chair to review his own work. "If I stand a bit higher, I can see everything better. Not so much for magazine ads, but definitely for posters. If I stand eight feet away from it, I can see it in its entirety. I always believe in mapping out the ideas first on paper. But if I'm working on a Mac, believe me, I *don't* put my Mac on the floor," Clarke adds.

Typography: A Question of Controversy

If print had music, it would be typography.

Typefaces are decoded as we read. The cut of each letter will transmit dozens of signals to the brain. Typography underscores words with emotional presence, creates atmosphere, colours the way we want our messages interpreted.

But with the advent of the Mac, thousands of new faces and typographical techniques have been spawned overnight. Type is being bashed, mutilated, distorted for effect, rather than for effective communication. The tyranny of the Mac enslaves; the mouse has become the umbilical cord of creativity. Anyone who can work a Mac can be an art director or, as Alcuri calls them, a Mac hack. Even scarier is the fact that the new high-tech typographical weaponry is available to consumers at home. The mystique of print creativity is evaporating.

Two art directors have become the world's masters of typography: Neil Godfrey dominated the British industry; Neil French roamed the Asian stage. Their perspectives are sobering.

"Papert Koenig & Lois in New York, led by George Lois, one of the really all-time great designers, virtually did all their work with one typeface, Franklin Gothic," Godfrey recalls. "The discipline was that it was the ideas that counted, not the typeface. I probably haven't ever used more than about eight or ten typefaces; I tend to find the most legible ones."

Godfrey has received more coveted pencils in Britain's Design and Art Direction awards than any other art director. "You're always safe using Franklin Gothic and Gill; they don't date very much. In serif faces, one of my favourites is Plantin. Type is about colour, as much as anything else, and when you do long copy ads, you find that maybe only half a dozen typefaces give you the right greyness on the page."

Legibility should be a prime concern. "When I worked with a copywriter who spent several days of his time writing a fabulous piece of copy, the first thing I would do was make it legible." Godfrey has seen dozens of fads come and go. "I hated that period when everyone put in bags of line spacing; you could drive a bus down it. If you tried to read it, you had to make a big jump down to the next line. As soon as somebody does something slightly different, everybody else wants to do it. And yet the reason it was different in the first place was completely appropriate. It may work again in a similar idea, but *why* do similar ideas?"

Godfrey introduced many techniques which today are commonplace. "Bill Bernbach got incredibly excited when I did a campaign with David Abbott. I dropped pieces of wheat into the copy, and ran the copy around them. Then everyone started running copy around things."

Godfrey was modifying typefaces long before the computer era. "A lot of people used to accept a typeface for what it was. But what I used to do was either cut the ascenders down, or lengthen them, to give shape and balance to the page. I chose Franklin once for a raincoat campaign, but I wanted the type to look a little bit watery, to have round edges instead of sharp corners. So I brought the complete alphabet home and Leila, my wife, who was a lettering artist at Doyle Dane when it was still hot metal type, cut off all the sharp corners and rounded them. So we were inventing our own typefaces in a way."

There is always the time when a new face or technique will work, Godfrey believes, providing it is appropriate to the ad. "I've had art directors come up to me and say, I've just found a fantastic new typeface and I'm going to use it in my next campaign. My answer to that was always, hang on a bit, will the campaign *want* that kind of face? The typeface can never take over from the words. You have to be able to say, it'd be great to use that face, but this is *not* the opportunity. You have to use restraint."

Like Godfrey, French also confesses to having a limited repertoire of typefaces.

"They're the only ones I learned to trace," he explains. "I learned to trace Franklin, and Times, and Palatino for some reason, I don't know why. Perhaps in those days, there wasn't an awful lot of typefaces, and frankly I chose them because I could read them easily, and then afterwards I didn't see any reason to set anything in a typeface that would make it more difficult to read."

One of the great French legends is the fact that all his copy is first laboriously printed onto his layouts by hand, before being sent for typesetting. Rumour has it that it was a firing offence at The Ball Partnership to remove a pen from French's desk.

"It's only because I'm completely inept," he says. "I can't handle a slide rule, and I don't understand any of the new machinery, and it never looks as nice on a computer as when I do it by hand. And I don't know why that is. I think it's because computers haven't quite got the hang of kerning yet, but my eye has. I realised a long time ago that because I was completely incapable of casting off copy, as we used to call it in those days, it would be easier for me to learn something that's painstaking, rather than actually figure out mathematics. That's how much of a complete twerp I am. So I spent many, many hours with type books, tracing over type. Then I found you could get all these Japanese pens in different widths, and therefore I could do my type in light, medium or heavy, so I learned how to do that, too."

All the typesetters have to do is follow French's layouts. "I can write you a piece of copy in 10-point, or 14-point, in bold, medium or light, and in *italics* if you wish, and it will always match a good piece of typesetting. These days, it will not match a piece of typesetting from a computer, but if you then add in kerning, it will almost always fit. It frightens young art directors quite a lot. I like to see my ad full size in front of me before I send it off to be finished, and this is the only way I can do it."

Another French legend concerns his hatred of hyphenated line breaks. Books, of course, are full of them; so are newspapers, magazines, and hundreds of award-winning print ads for that matter. The human eye is perfectly able to decode a hyphen and travel to the next line. As some writers might well say, a hyphen will even help the reader read on to the next line.

"You could argue that," shrugs French, "but you'd be wrong. I want the flow of my sentence to carry you on to the next line, not a little arrow in the form of a hyphen. The flow is better achieved if you can read a word *fully*, without having to flick your eye seven centimetres to the left. Whenever I do a piece of copy, if there is a word that needs hyphenating, I change the word, or change the sentence, or change the paragraph, but I will *not* have hyphenated words at the end of lines," he insists. "Also, I am a Virgo, I am so hopelessly anal retentive and breathtakingly tidy."

With new typefaces proliferating faster than you can say "Mac", it may be surprising to learn that the world's most accomplished and awarded art directors, for the most part, shun them. It is not a question of age, but judgement.

Three young Turks first:

"The problem with the Mac is that it's a great tool, but if you don't have a clear idea of what you want, you mess with your head," says Redman. "There are so many options, so many avenues, so many ways to make something look good, you just don't know what's good any more. You still need to sit down with a pad and work out what you're trying to get across. Broken up type has its place, but you've got to know where that place is."

"Macs are only tools," confirms Messum. "I think they're vital as long as they're not abused. They open up new veins for your inspiration. Where it falls down for a lot of young people, they rely too heavily on the machine to have all the answers. I still work with a pen and a layout pad. I still truly believe in presenting an art director's rough to a client. It's too easy to pick a bit of type, stick it on a stock shot with a logo in the corner, and think you've got an ad. It's *not* an ad. Clients need to buy the idea, not what it looks like."

"The Mac can do anything you want," agrees Clarke. "I don't mind bashed up type, I've done it myself, as long as it's relevant to your idea. If it's not, what's the point of doing it?" Clarke relies on the classic faces. "I use Garamond, Helvetica, Trade Gothic, Times, Univers, Franklin, and of course, Clarendon. The classic typefaces have so many families, there's so much scope. I try to make all my work

"IT'S AN UNMITIGATED PIECE OF SHIT AND WE SHOULDN'T EVEN BE TALKING ABOUT IT!"

It was the tea-break. Outside, an excavator clawed disconsolately at the red mud.

Steve Dunn, checked shirt glowing like an inquisitor's brazier, his eyes burning with Jesuit certainty, gripped his polystyrene cup, and leant forward. His voice hissed, as steam from the fires of hell.

"And what's more, this is the most banal conversation I've ever had."

John 'Once-I-start-laughing-I-just-can't-stop' Curran eased his chair back. This was obviously not going to be an opportunity for non-stop hilarity.

"Couldn't we give it an award for lateral thinking?" Siimon Reynolds' fine, ascetic features a study in serious. His ensemble of stockbroker-striped shirt twinned with vivid lime-green Bermuda shorts belying the impression somewhat.

He switched to the smile. The sun came out. Birds sang.

Some were tempted. Not Dunn.

"That's like saying let's make a TV commercial really badly and expecting a prize for originality!" The knuckles whitened; the cup resigned itself to a non-biodegradable eternity.

Indra Sinha's Himalayan bulk was seen to shift one millimetre to the left. Totally overwhelmed, his chair leant with him. No choice. That or join the cup.

The voice, sonorous as the Ganges in flood, the eyes hawk-hooded, the face a temple mask:

"Jim..." a conciliatory rumble, "Can we give it anything at all?"

The adjudicator consulted the book of rules. Unnecessarily. "It's either in or out. Simple as that."

Silence.

The auditor, anxious, hovering like a nervous waiter. "We're ready for E22 to E30..."

"What's that?" snapped Dunn.

Siimon levitated, glowing. "English Language. Print Campaigns. Let's do it."

Like predators roaming a twilight jungle, the five figures passed softly among the serried sentinel display boards.

Tunes of Glory there were, in the background, if you listened hard. But you had to strain your ears through the cacophony of dreams crushed by the jackboot of logic. Hopes died quietly; an early night in a singles bar. Unloved. Unnoticed, even. Sad.

As much-vaunted reputations bluffed and blustered their way to the slaughter, uncaring ballpoints dispatched cherished brainchildren to cold oblivion.

Pages flicking, shuffling. The only sounds in the morgue.

Dour faces collecting the sheets.

Compiling, computing, calculating: God bless the accountants.

♦

"I think it's terrific." David Fowler's eyes shone like the stars on Sunset.

"Well I think it's shit. Would you really, seriously trust your business to a bank that so blatantly tells lies in its own advertising?" Sinha was massively, and implacably, immovable.

He blinked, it is said. Once.

Fowler's gunslinger drawl gave the lie to his bank-clerk stature. "Well, my only question is what to give it, that's all."

"I know what I'd like to do with it. I'd like to set fire to the effing thing."

It was getting late.

♦

Tense. Coiled. Steve Dunn, a snake about to strangle a chicken: "It is an insult to bald people."

"It's not. I don't find it in the least bit insulting." Fowler. No chicken, he.

"You're an expert?"

"Well, yes. I'd consider myself an expert." Fowler smiled. His eyes didn't. A blood-red ribbon restrained his flowing pony-tail . But above it, skullwise, barely a suspicion of fuzz.

"He's trying to tell you he's bald; he'd buy the damn stuff," snorted Indra.

"That's not the point at all," Dunn persisted. "The ad is a bloody insult."

As silent as a snowdrift, five men sat and contemplated their criteria.

It was late. And getting later.

♦

Indra, prowling; an intellectual bear trapped in a cave of mere advertising, chubby Buddha-fingers clutching at a clipboard, relentlessly hunting for any piece of copy Neil French hadn't written:

"We've missed something. There's a great bit, somewhere in the stuff we threw out while we were looking for something else." If Sinha's syntax was slipping, his resolve certainly wasn't.

"Dammit, we can hardly penalise the man for being good." Dunn was in danger of becoming charitable.

Sinha wasn't.

Hollow-eyed, the helpers dragged a truckload of what had so nearly been scrap cardboard back across the floor.

Were there living among those who had been presumed dead?

It was going to be a very late night.

♦

From March 9th to the 12th, 1991, Singapore advertising stood accused of complacency, incest and self-indulgence.

Five men considered their verdict.

Those who were acquitted appear in the 1991 Gong Show Annual. S$190.

No, not an account executive. Another award-winning ad.

SOME FUNNY POSITIONS YOU CAN GET YOURSELF INTO.

Account Service

Account Service people: Commonly known as The Suits, bless 'em. They are the frontline troops of the agency; the intrepid people who advise, beg, cajole, and have lunch with, clients.

The pecking order in Client Service goes: Client Service Director, then Account Director, and Account Manager, after that come the Account Executive, Assistant Account Executive, Messenger, Tea-lady, Cleaner, and Trainee Account Executive.

Regardless of whether you are a Bachelor of Business Administration, or a Professor of Dental Surgery, or merely a taxi driver right now, you'll probably start in advertising as a Trainee Account Executive: The Lowest Form of Life.

(Frankly, a degree might help. But what will help more is a love of great advertising, and a burning passion to see it run. A free tip, here: some homework will stand you in good stead. Do some.)

A lot of people (namely, clients and creative staff) tend to dismiss the humble Account Executive as a mere bag-carrier.

Which, of course, makes your job doubly difficult, or doubly challenging. The latter, we hope.

What *does* makes it so fascinating is the vast job specification.

A good account service person builds up a strong rapport between the agency and its clients, getting the work through on time, on budget, and on brief.

A *great* account service person does more. He, or she, will be able to guide the client along the prickly path of marketing and communication by pinpointing the *strategy* — the route map, if you like, to achieving the client's objectives.

He or she will then be able to brief the creative team, inspiring them with enthusiasm, not only to adhere to the single-minded strategy mapped out for them, but to excel themselves in doing so. It's a job for a master tactician.

Good account service people are able to counsel their clients, rather than just taking orders.

Great account service people are also able to perform incredible juggling feats,

harnessing all the agency's resources in order to support, execute and run the great advertising campaigns which come from great strategies.

In this way, they earn the respect of clients, creative people and agency managements.

Which is why they're as scarce as hens' teeth, frankly.

Copywriters

This, of course, does not refer to people who copy what other people write.

Nor should it refer to the poor bloke who fills up all the holes in the ads left by art directors. (Of whom, more, later.)

The copywriter is the backbone of the agency. (I'm one, after all.)

From his inspired and insecure, talented and tortured mind come the words, the ideas, the solutions. And while others may, later, craft the jewellery of a campaign, the fire in which it is born is the copywriter's domain.

Every line of this 12-page brochure was hand-printed to avoid
awkward settings and hyphenated breaks. If it didn't fit, it was rewritten.
A pleasant Sunday evening's work for Neil French.
Euro RSCG Partnership (The Ball Partnership), Singapore.

LIKE ALL GREAT ADVERTISING, IT'S SLIGHTLY INDULGENT, BRILLIANTLY PRODUCED, AND HORRIBLY EXPENSIVE.

Furthermore, it's quite possible that only half of it actually worked.

Luckily for creative people all over the world, that's not one of the criteria by which *creative* awards are bestowed. And since we've seen fit to open this particular can of snakes, we may as well strangle the buggers here and now.

Read our lips: The sine qua non of *all* advertising is its effectiveness.

If an ad doesn't work, it's a total waste of time, money, and perfectly good trees. There are no awards for doing your job right, — and neither *should* there be; that's what you're paid for. If it's *not* done right, then the client fires the agency, and both the creative people *and* the account handlers are at liberty to open little knitting-shops instead.

However many awards they've won. And quite right, too.

Creative awards are merely the end-of-term prizes handed out by our peers, for work we'd have been proud to have done ourselves.

No more than that. And no less.

Which brings us, by a somewhat tortuous process, to the matter of the Creative Circle Annual for 1989.

Remember 1989? Before it all went mad? Before Saddam Hussein, before the recession, and before the quota system? In those far-off and forgotten days, somehow it seemed the weather was nicer, food tasted nicer, in fact the entire world was suffused with niceness.

Naturally though, in the world of advertising, it was the same rat-eat-rat-smile-as-you-stab-your-best-pal-in-the-back-why-does-that-bald-old-sod-win-all-the-awards picnic that it is today.

And with an alacrity that would have put a paralytic tortoise on the winners rostrum, the Creative Circle committee has finally stumbled its way to producing the long-awaited 1989 Gong Show Annual.

It has some lovely stuff in it: The British Airways ads with the red dots; the white-space Chivas campaign of blessed memory; the wrinkly dog in the Payot ads, (sorry madam, not you); the rubbery-faced plea for a grin from yer average Singaporean . . . They're all there, reproduced in glowing colour, bound in an elegant black hard-backed cover, in a book as big and square as Gordon Tan.

It's a feast of bygone triumphs and it's all yours for the miserly sum of $160. Alright, then, $159 for cash. There is, of course, one little drawback. But isn't there always?

IT'S ALSO LATE.

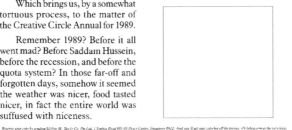

Reserve your copy by sending $159 to M. Tay & Co Pte Ltd, 1 Sophia Road #05-03 Peace Centre, Singapore 0922. And you'll get your copy hot off the presses. Or lukewarm at the very least.

Neil French at work. Every single word in these ads was originally hand-printed onto the layout, precisely replicating the font, weight and typesize. The light burning in Neil French's window at midnight became a regular landmark along Singapore's Beach Road. Small wonder. Euro RSCG Partnership (The Ball Partnership), Singapore.

"I will not have hyphenated words at the end of lines," says Neil French. Do so at your peril.

simpler, the simpler the better." When it comes to setting body copy, Clarke quips, "I'm a justified person who's open to ragged right."

Grace, asked to choose six desert island typefaces, says: "I don't think I'd have six. I got tired of choosing typefaces twenty-five years ago. I used to use a typeface that was called Standard Medium, which comes from a Swiss type, and it's now called Helvetica. I don't really use it that much any more. When I go for type at my agency, they say, oh, here he comes, here's Futura. So at the top of my list, Futura, medium or demi. Then Caslon, a really great Caslon. Bauer Bodoni would be certainly up there, as would Baskerville. Then for fun, a good, fat Goudy. I think I've been using that same typography for 90 percent of everything I've done."

"I hate gimmicky typefaces," asserts Barrie. "When I first started out in my career, there was this trend in the Southeast, that was picked up in Minneapolis, for condensing typefaces and setting everything real close. I look back at some of the ads I did in that period and I just cringe. As a result, I really tend to be like Neil French. I'm a classicist when it comes to typography. I want to be able to look at an ad in ten years' time and be able to celebrate the idea, and not get caught up in gimmicky typefaces. Right now, with the Mac, and distressed type, there's going to be a hell of a lot of ads people look back at in ten years and say, what was I thinking! The computer can be your own worst enemy simply because it allows you to do a lot more things, the majority of which are inappropriate."

Lichtenheld's love affair with typography began when he was a sign painter. "I was doing lettering that was five feet high. You really develop a nice sense for the nuances of typography when you're painting a serif that's thirty inches wide, and you know you've got to get that curve from the vertical stroke into the serif just right. In the past couple of years, though, working on BMW, I've been pretty much restricted to Helvetica." Lichtenheld's desert island typeface is Bembo. "I could work anything in all the fonts of Bembo." He encourages young art directors to study typography. "In this environment, a well done, classic piece of typography is really going to stand out. One of the things I admire a lot is when I see classic typography treated in a very current, contemporary way. That, to me, is pretty exciting because it's going to have some timelessness to it. It shows me that somebody knows the craft. When I say I admire something, it usually means I kick myself for not having done it."

Lichtenheld's priority is to make headlines less self-conscious. In that context, he believes bashed up type can make a contribution. "When it first came out, it looked like an art director had said, let's photocopy this a hundred times, then run over it with a beer truck and put it in the ad. Now I see it being used more appropriately." Citing Saatchi & Saatchi London's work for the British Army, he says: "I admire it when I see it done *invisibly*, when it doesn't feel like a technique layered onto something that didn't need it. I admire it when it's done in such a way that it works the type into the visual, so it's not type any more, it's just words, words that have an idea in them. Headlines should be part of the visual, then there are no limitations as to whether it's type, or whether you paint it on the side of a wall and photograph it. People have better and better filters for advertising these days," Lichtenheld stresses, "and you have to find techniques to get past their filters. One of them, obviously, is to make advertising that doesn't look like advertising."

"While I accept that there are some very *'interesting'* typefaces about," says French, "I've also noticed, over the years, how they come and go. I've seen two typefaces come and go in just eighteen months. One was a kind of blobby thing that looked as though it had come out of a computer. It had a very big vogue for about six months. Of course, nobody uses it now because it dated so quickly. There was another one with crosses and things all over it, it was very 'in' for a while, and I'll guarantee nobody's using it in six months' time. But everybody will always use Franklin and Palatino and Times, because they will *never* date." French lends qualified support for bashed up type. "I think it's a good thing if there's a point to it. There'd be absolutely no point doing it if it was just for the effect," he cautions. "For instance, when we did some ads about the destruction of Angkor Wat in Cambodia, it would have been crazy to have nice, tidy type. So the art director bashed it around, to make it look as though it had been destroyed, so it carried part of the message. That's perfectly acceptable; in fact, it would have been *un*acceptable not to have done so. But to muck around with a typeface, just for the sake of mucking around with it, is a waste of time. Why don't you go down to the pub instead?"

It survived a thousand monsoons, two invasions and the Khmer Rouge.

Then it came under the hammer.

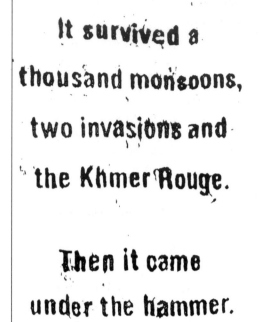

A thousand years of heat and humidity had left scarcely a blemish.

Invading armies, rampaging their way through Cambodia's temples, didn't leave so much as a scratch.

Even the Khmer Rouge, who smashed thousands of religious artefacts, had spared this sacred statue.

Then it fell to market forces.

The market for stolen antiques, to be precise. The latest and the most serious threat to Cambodia's ancient statues.

In fact, Cambodia's Ministry of Culture estimates that artefacts are being stolen from temples and monasteries at the rate of one a day. Moreover, it's happening all over the country.

The stolen sculptures are then smuggled to Bangkok, where dealers with the right connections easily obtain export licences.

After which, the now "legal" antiques can be exported in major art markets around the world.

Hardly surprising then, that Cambodian sculptures regularly come under the hammer at auction houses around the world.

We should point out that only a small minority of people in the antiques business are involved. Yet the damage they cause is enormous.

Sacred Buddhist statues are decapitated. Temple deities have their limbs torn off.

Bas-reliefs are gouged from temple walls.

All to satisfy the greed of an international art market which make enormous profits from stolen antiquities. (Indeed it's a $1 billion-a-year illicit trade, second only to drug trafficking.)

The audacity of the thieves is astounding. One statue, as tall as a man and weighing more than 100kg, was stolen from the courtyard of a palace.

It was just 200 metres from a police station.

Antique dealers are equally brazen-faced. In Thailand they have produced videos of Angkor's temples so that wealthy collectors may choose which piece of sculpture they want looted off.

As you might expect, the Cambodian government is attempting to stop the looting.

Police intercept a few of the robbers and some of the most valuable statues have been stored in a fortified warehouse.

The trouble is, the police are hopelessly undermanned, and the warehouse has already been looted twice by gangs of armed thieves.

In any event, it doesn't really matter how many policemen are put on guard duty, because the key to stopping the destruction is to reduce the overseas demand. Which means stolen antiques have to stop buying stolen antiques.

And the antique dealers have to stop selling them.

Please help. If you plan to purchase antiques from Cambodia, visit a reputable dealer who can provide an authentic provenance (history of ownership) of the piece.

Alternatively, you can buy replicas of Buddha heads, friezes and complete statues. All for a fraction of the cost of originals.

Conservationists are also trying to stop the looting of Cambodia's past.

So if you'd like to make a donation, please contact the Royal Angkor Foundation (361 141 2120).

With your help, more of these ancient works of art will remain intact, in Cambodia.

Instead of simply going to the highest bidder.

Don't let Cambodia's past become history ANGKOR FOUNDATION

Unfortunately, every piece of genuine antique sculpture from Cambodia is a rip-off.

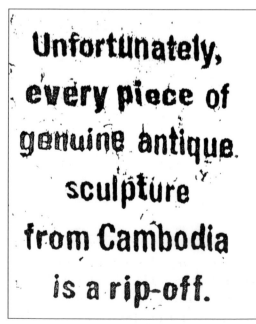

We wouldn't want to mislead you by suggesting that some antique shops are deliberately selling fakes. Because what they actually offer is much worse.

Buddha heads, hacked off sacred statues.

The hand of a Hindu deity, torn from a sculpture which had survived intact for over a thousand years.

The exquisite faces of dancers, gouged from ancient bas-reliefs which decorate temple walls.

It's not just vandalism, it's desecration. For these are religious artefacts, many of which have been worshipped by Cambodians for over a thousand years.

The motive for all these crimes is, of course, profit. The small minority of dealers involved are making huge amounts of money from stolen works of art. To give you just one example, a twelfth-century statue from Angkor, the ancient royal capital of Cambodia, can easily fetch over $100,000.

With so much money to be made, it didn't take long for organised crime to become involved. So that now, stolen antiques are being smuggled all over the world via international networks controlled by drug dealers.

The result is destruction on a massive scale.

For instance, in Angkor Wat, Cambodia's most revered temple, almost every Buddhist statue has been beheaded.

And the exquisite faces of Angkor Wat's dancing Apsaras - the temple's most famous motif - have all been chiselled off.

Worse still, this ruthless pillaging hasn't been confined to Angkor Wat. It's also happening in other places of worship all over the country.

So much so, that Cambodia's government estimates that artefacts are being stolen at the rate of one a day.

Most are smuggled into Thailand, which probably accounts for more thefts than any other country.

In Bangkok, some dealers have gone so far as to produce catalogues which are crammed with detailed photographs of Angkorian sculptures.

Collectors can then select the work of art they want and the dealer has it stolen to order.

At this point you may be wondering why the Cambodian government hasn't made an attempt to try and stop the looting.

It has. The problem is, finding enough money to improve security is extremely difficult for a poor country like Cambodia.

(For example, both the police and the temple guards are hopelessly undermanned and only intercept a few robbers.)

Similarly, the conservation workers who are trying to save Angkor also lack adequate funds.

You can help. Please contact the Royal Angkor Foundation (361 141 2120) if you'd like to make a contribution.

Another way to put a stop to the destruction is to reduce the demand for stolen works of art.

Again, you can play a part. If you're planning to purchase a Cambodian sculpture, please make sure it has an authentic provenance (its history of ownership).

If it doesn't have one, it's probably stolen.

Better still, stick to reproduction antiques. You can buy an excellent replica sculpture for a fraction of the price of an original.

And that, surely, is better than a rip-off.

Don't let Cambodia's past become history ANGKOR FOUNDATION

An acceptable occasion to bash up the type. Ogilvy & Mather, Singapore.

SHOULD HEADLINES BE SET IN CAPS
or should they be set in lower case?

"It should be whatever it has to be," acknowledges Grace. "I prefer upper and lower case, because it's the way you read books. I always believe that information should be assimilated as quickly as possible. When you read a book, it's a very comfortable process, and I think the eye is more used to it. I have used all caps, and I will use all caps again. I think the ideal is upper and lower *serif*; it's not necessarily my favourite, but I think it's the ideal."

Barrie agrees. "I prefer the understatement of upper and lower case. It's how you're used to reading."

"I don't have any criteria," says Clarke. "It's whatever feels right for the ad. I think I've used caps more often."

"I've seen great ads both ways," observes Redman. "I've also seen atrocious ads both ways. It's what works best."

While there are no rules, WAR IS DECLARED reads well as three words; but, the longer your headline is, the easier it will read in lower case.

Or, judged another way, how would you want your headline to sound if it were read aloud? If it is meant to scream, it is caps. If it is meant to be conversational, or laconic, or witty, it is lower case. (And, nudge, nudge, maybe even in brackets.)

Should Every Word In A Headline
Start With A Capital Letter?

Barrie is implacable. "Never use initial caps on words!"

"Initial caps were an affectation that started in the 1980s," observes Lichtenheld. "There is no literary or grammatical precedent for them."

Should ALL the words in a headline
be the same SIZE?

"The thing now that you see, that just defies logic, is various words in different sizes in the same headline," groans Grace. "It slows down the communication. It impacts negatively on the meaning of the headline because you're not reading it in a normal fashion; it changes the emphasis of the words. It doesn't make sense. It really is *stupid*."

"I call it the ransom note school of typography," says Lionel Hunt.

"The sooner it dies, the better. Having each word in a different size or face is a fad which I particularly loathe. It makes lines very difficult, if not impossible to read, which is the opposite to what you are trying to achieve. No copywriter should ever allow it to happen to what he or she has written."

"Keep the point size of all the characters in your headline the same," urges Barrie. "I've seen headlines that literally gave me a headache trying to read them. It was like there were thirty-two different point sizes in the line. It's something that's done because the computer allows you to do it. You paid three grand for your Mac and you want to get your money's worth."

What Should Come First: The Headline or the Picture?

As French says, people read an ad by the way it is art directed. Invariably, a bent picture will always precede a straight headline. A bent headline will always precede a straight picture. But it is not formulaic.

"If you want someone to look at the visual and wonder what it's about, and you want them to get it with the headline," advises Clarke, "then the headline goes underneath, to reveal the idea. In long copy ads, the headline goes at the top because you're leading people into the copy."

"The formula for me," says Lichtenheld, "is to determine which one is leading the idea, the headline or the visual. If the visual is a payoff to the headline, then theoretically you put the headline at the top and the visual below. If it's a visual concept, the headline is small and goes at the bottom. That said, I would always try it both ways and see which feels better."

"Rules are made to be broken," affirms Barrie. "It takes a lot for an ad to stop me. A headline, no matter how witty, is not going to suck me in. What will, is the visual look of the ad. The headline should work as an afterthought."

Should Headlines Always End With a Full Stop?

Newspaper headlines never end with a period. Editors want readers to read on.

So, of course, do art directors. Which does not explain why most advertising headlines end with a punctuation mark which signals readers to STOP.

The jury is still out.

However, one writer resolved the issue happily. David Fowler's headlines once continued, unfinished, into the first line of his body copy.

It Takes All Types

There are really only two types of typography: appropriate and inappropriate.

The inappropriate is invariably derivative and shallow; technique for technique's sake.

The appropriate is invariably the result of cutting edge judgement and taste.

Welcome to the latter.

The Village Voice. Before the *Voice* circulated free, it was sold by subscription; not an easy task, as Nick Cohen explains.

"The *Voice* has an equity that's anti-establishment, trying to cut through and present a much more honest perspective of what's going on to its readers. The dilemma was, how do you sell the corporation, the *Voice*, while you try to flog subscriptions? So we wanted to take the opposite side; the *Voice* poking fun at itself, which they do in the newspaper a lot."

By representing the opposite viewpoint, Cohen hoped they could address those people who were opposed to the *Voice*. "A lot of people think the *Voice* is a bunch of whining, moaning types, so we wanted to create a more balanced view. By being able to laugh at yourself, and question yourself, and see your own faults, you can make a connection with people. We wanted people to come away from the ads thinking, I like the *Voice*, they're just really honest people, they're not full of themselves, they understand that there are pros and cons to everything."

What developed was a classic coupon campaign, but with a difference.

"We didn't want to do anything that was slick, because that would have been the opposite to what the *Voice* is about. We didn't want to

(GULP)

You want me to commit to you for an entire year? I mean, we're talking big "S" subscription here. I don't understand why we can't just keep things the way they are. If I'm in a "Voice" mood, I pick up an issue. Why do you want to start complicating things, don't you trust me? This is a very serious step, I don't think we should just rush into it. I mean, I just got out of a really long subscription with National Geographic and it's been really hard for me. Maybe I just need a little space, a little time to myself, not tied down to any one paper. I just want what's best for both of us. Look, why don't we just stay really, really good friends?

☐ **YES,**
I WANT TO BUY A
YEAR SUBSCRIPTION
TO THE VILLAGE VOICE.

$47.95 (Just 92¢ per copy). To order, call toll-free 1-800-336-0686 (24 hours a day). Or mail this coupon to: The Village Voice Subscriptions, P.O. Box 8044, Syracuse, NY 13217.

Name_____
Address_____
City/State/Zip_____
Check enclosed_____ Bill me_____ Charge me_____
AmEx___M/C___Visa___ Card_____
Exp date_____ Signature_____

Rates and 'bill me' good in U.S. only. Canadian/foreign subscriptions $79.20/year, must have payment with order. Please allow 2-4 weeks for first issue to arrive.

VOICE

#31070

subscription holder, reporting for duty! Is that what you want, for me to become another faceless entity that you can anonymously slip your paper to? Maybe I'm an antique, but I don't mind going down to a real newsstand, paying with real money, flashing a real smile, and heck, maybe even slipping in a "Thanks, 'preciate it." What human contact do we have left? Computo-bank tellers, TV diplomas, "Personalized" bulk mail, blow-up dolls, push "1" for this - push "2" for that. How 'bout I come down there, push "3" and blow your whole operation to bits? Listen here, you... you...personality leeches, I'm a real person! I have a name. I am not, I repeat, NOT, a credit card number!

☐ **YES,** I WANT TO BUY
A ONE YEAR SUBSCRIPTION
TO THE VILLAGE VOICE.

$47.95 (92¢ per copy). To order, call 1-800-336-0686 (24 hrs/day). Or mail coupon to: The Village Voice Subscriptions, P.O. Box 8044, Syracuse, NY 13217.

Name_____
Address_____
City/State/Zip_____
Check enclosed_____ Bill me_____ Charge me_____
AmEx___M/C___Visa___ Card #_____ Exp date_____
Signature_____

Rates and 'bill me' good in U.S. only. Canadian/foreign subscriptions $79.20/year, must have payment with order. Allow 2-4 weeks for delivery.

VOICE

0 17805 66604 2

Cheap type let The Village Voice laugh at itself. Mad Dogs & Englishmen, New York.

do anything that looked like they'd spent any money on."

Commitment and dehumanisation provided fertile ground for creative concepts. "It was also about poverty," adds Cohen. "They didn't have any money, and I think the ads cost them only a few bucks to make."

Asia Watch. While walking through rural Cambodia requires a certain vigilance, a campaign calling for an unconditional ban on land mines required even more.

"We were talking to people who were in a position to do something," recalls art director Norman Alcuri. "They wouldn't be taken in by a gimmicky bit of art direction."

The subject was serious; however, there were legitimate stylistic options. There always are when dealing with futility, death and horror. "We talked about distempered type, of course. We talked about the inclusion of little graphics. We talked about different backgrounds. But we pared it all the way. I even had a black border around the ads at one point, then I got rid of it. We decided to make it more like editorial than an ad."

Alcuri allowed himself one concession with the headline type. "We asked ourselves whether we should use a stencil effect, like you might see stamped on armoury cases. We modified the type a tad, to reflect that. It's not new, I know, but I reversed the headlines out of black panels for strength." He broke convention by setting the two columns of long copy in a sans serif face, rather than a traditional serif. "You're always asking yourself, should I break the mould or not? It's what Graham Fink said, if it's been done before, should you do it again?"

Unusually for a campaign of letters, some of the visuals and headlines could have worked alone as postcards. The juxtaposition of the soldier's boot and the peasant's foot, for example, would have worked just as well without all the copy. Another ad had two identical pictures of a rice field; one was captioned *Paddy Field*, the other *Mine Field*. It would have been a classic postcard ad.

"There was a need to tell the full story, the full horror," Alcuri acknowledges. "The writer, Andrew Bruck, had gone off and done all the research. He was very passionate about it. He'd dug up all these facts, like the peasants wearing a string on their hats to stop them falling off. If their hats fell off, they used to take a step forward to pick them up. Sometimes it was the last step they ever took."

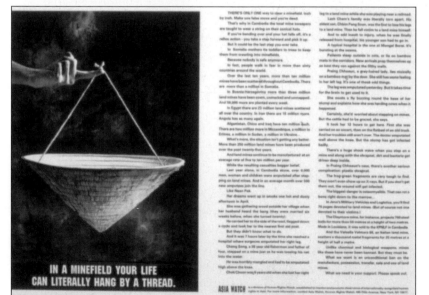

Restrained type in an editorial format. DMB&B, Singapore.

Gun Control Network. After a mad gunman massacred young children, the British government decided to ban guns with the exception of .22 handguns. Singling out the .22 did not make sense to the anti-gun lobby, nor to the creative team at Saatchi & Saatchi, London.

"The art direction had to look angry," recalls Gallacher. "Originally we just had big type, a black background, a small picture. It was very in your face. But the trouble is, a lot of people just turn away from that."

Gallacher decided to lure people in to the message instead. "We found a .22 shell, which reminds you that someone has already fired the bullet, and we thought we'd put the captions on that, like they'd been stamped into the metal."

To create a carved in look, the settings in News Gothic were degraded sufficiently, then merged with the photographic image of the shell. "Then we laid in the third visual, Kennedy and the grave, with a

Degraded type, necessary for a technical effect. Saatchi & Saatchi, London.

Outrageous type, appropriate to the idea. Mad Dogs & Englishmen, New York.

Sensual type. While people play with their ice cream, Bartle Bogle Hegarty, London, play with straight product statements.

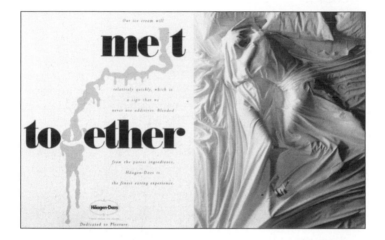

"Dedicated to pleasure" is a perfect example of what John Hegarty calls an emotional selling proposition.

In 1881, the Raffles Museum was built to improve thousands of minds.

SADLY, THE MAN BUILDING IT LOST HIS.

Diverse type, within the context of long copy. Writer Antony Redman and art director Andrew Clarke chose pastel colour backgrounds often found on Singapore's heritage architecture. Euro RSCG Partnership (The Ball Partnership), Singapore.

The statues on this temple ward off dangers and evil influences.

THEY COULDN'T WARD OFF A FIVE LANE HIGHWAY AND SIXTEEN OFFICE BLOCKS.

This was the home of Singapore's most influential architect.

IT'S NOW OCCUPIED BY GIORGIO ARMANI, COCO CHANEL AND RONALD McDONALD.

Classic type in a contemporary treatment by Len Cheeseman and Eric De Vries.
Saatchi & Saatchi, Wellington.

bit of show through. The show through makes it more like a *memory*, like your name is on the bullet. There is a certain kind of prettiness about it, to lure you in, and the message is the sting in the tail."

Gallacher believes good art direction never takes over from the idea. "At the same time, people today are used to seeing a certain kind of imagery. You have to art direct in the context of *now*, the work must look part of *now*." For Gallacher, print is not a static medium, because the thought process is not static. "When I work on print, and an idea starts to form in my head, I look at it like a piece of film. It's never flat and lifeless, it's moving, and I have to ask myself *where* do I stop the film, which frame do I take out? Should I stop it slightly earlier, or add another layer, and stop it slightly later?"

Changing Times

While young art directors worship computer typefaces, one man who designs type still works by hand. At the Type Directors Club, New York, Gerard Huerta explains why.

"It's still the basis of any creativity, the brain to the hand to what goes on paper." Huerta views the computer as a democratic assembly tool, but spends more time drawing. Huerta designs type in conjunction with logotypes. Ironically, his desert island typefaces are the standards: Helvetica, Futura, Franklin Gothic, Times Roman, Goudy Old Style for its softness, and "a nice script like Snell Roundhand", he adds.

Fellow club member and typographic designer Daniel Pelavin believes type *per se* is never illegible; the way you use it is. Young art directors, he says, should learn how to put letters together. The Internet, Pelavin believes, is driving changes in type design. "As the bandwidth increases and the paradigm advances, you'll be able to reproduce type which is finer than anything you'll ever be able to reproduce on paper."

Pelavin sees a new trend in typefaces which communicate by their movement. "Soon, every square inch of available space is going to be covered with messages," he predicts. "Eventually, every surface we put messages on will not be a static, two-dimensional one, but will have the third dimension of motion. Even the pages of magazines will be interactive and moving."

Conventional type, unconventional strategy. Fur wearers were targeted for public humiliation by what appeared to be municipal signage. Mad Dogs & Englishmen, New York.

ILLUSTRATION: WHEN SHOULD YOU USE IT?

Godfrey speaks for many art directors when he says: "I like to use something people can believe in. I rarely used illustration. Nine-tenths of the time, it just doesn't have the impact of a photograph."

Others have used it judiciously. French chose to illustrate his Martell campaign in the style of Impressionist painters. On an earlier occasion, illustration was appropriate for his Singapore Tourism work.

"Even though people are savvy to retouching, they still believe that photographs don't lie," says Lichtenheld. "I would use illustration if it was a matter of style, a retro look, or if a certain illustrator's work brought something to the ad like whimsy. But," Lichtenheld warns, "you're really relying on execution which can be dangerous, because it has to be truly unique and something people haven't seen before."

Hegarty sees illustration serving a strategic, more competitive purpose. "We have a view that when the world zigs, you should zag," he explains. "This will sound hideously pretentious, and I don't wish it to do so, but when I have an idea, I get a kind of vision in my brain. It's like a flash. And in that flash I see the ad, I see it as photography, I see it as illustration, or without either. That's how ideas have always come to me. But then I apply a point of view. If everybody's using photography, why don't we use illustration? You apply that thinking, you try to be different, you try to do something that *isn't* like everybody else. You have to ask, is this going to stop somebody? Is this going to be challenging in some way or another? People are looking for that. So that's what you must try and do. Try and find a way of capturing a difference, understanding what the idea is about, understanding what the brand is about, and do things that *belong* to that idea and that brand. You must find a way to make it more unique. And if that means daring to be different, then dare to be different."

When used appropriately, illustration becomes more than an executional option. It becomes intrinsic to the creative idea.

Sarawak Tourism. A low budget and a desire to make the Borneo rainforest less scary led to the choice of illustration for the Sarawak print campaign from Batey Ads, Singapore.

"Photography, to be any good these days, costs the earth," observes writer Malcolm Pryce. "But you can still get brilliant illustration comparatively cheaply and we had a very small budget."

Photography is the convention in the travel category. Illustration would be highly disruptive for a small, unknown advertiser. "Ian Batey has this genius for building brands. When you've got such a small budget, you need to create something which is instantly recognisable and distinctive, so it reinforces the brand every time you see it."

Illustration appealed for another reason. "Rainforests can be considered rather scary, full of dark places and frightening animals that do horrible things to you. Actually, the Borneo rainforest doesn't have the dangerous animals. It can be viewed as a botanic wonder-

Making the rainforest less scary on a low budget. Batey Ads, Singapore.

The ironies of Irish life, illustrated by Janet Woolley in a way that belongs to the brand.
Bartle Bogle Hegarty, London.

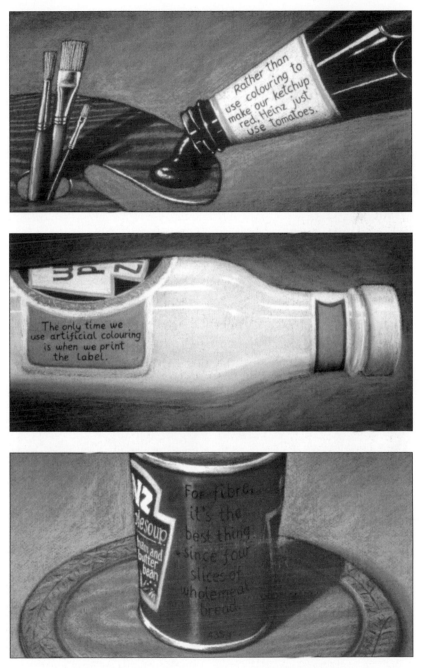

Somehow, photography would have been artificial. Robin Heighway-Bury's charming illustrations and hand-lettered captions convey the essence of Heinz natural ingredients. Bates Dorland, London.

Chaos on the streets. Theseus Chan pumps adrenaline for Nike retailer D Corner,
combining illustration, hand-lettering, typography and typewriter.
Work Advertising, Singapore.

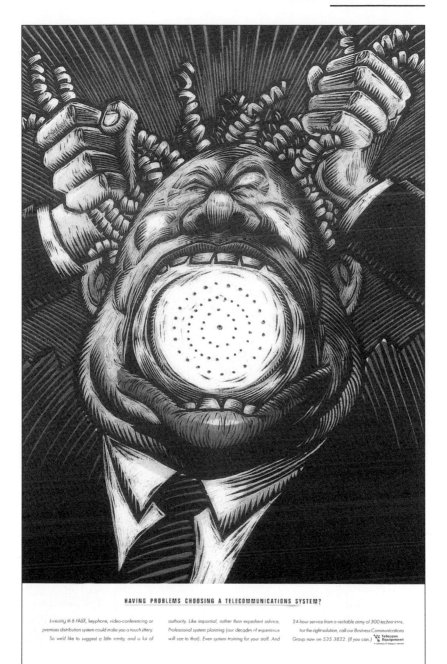

David Chin captures anger and frustration which no photograph could ever express. Euro RSCG Partnership (The Ball Partnership), Singapore.

land. We wanted to make it user friendly. We wanted people of all ages to go there, not just adventure travellers. So it had to be less threatening. We originally started off with an illustration style based on the work of a nineteenth century French painter who drew tigers in the grass and made them look quite sweet."

But Pryce and art director Tham Khai Meng felt something was missing. "The campaign had to look friendly, but there was still a sense of adventure, a cultural heritage to portray. It's always been a place where adventurers, and smugglers, and desperadoes have gone for centuries. It's always been an island of myth and mystery, most of it untrue. So we took a walk down to the Tower bookshop and we found this book which had the covers from 1950s American paperbacks."

Those quaint pulp fiction covers inspired the illustration and typography style of the campaign. Michael Lui was commissioned to illustrate a series of old-style book jackets which became posters and print ads.

From being simply a technique, illustration became inseparable from the idea and the brand.

OUT WITH INCEST

Advertising art direction is incestuous. As Godfrey says, whenever somebody does something slightly different, everybody else wants to do it. Imitating ideas in award annuals is futile; they have been done already, and the same idea, done again, is unlikely to be awarded again. The distinctive styles of Neil Godfrey, Neil French and Steve Dunn have been aped *ad nauseum*; it is flattering but equally futile. If everybody copies everybody else, art direction will cease to evolve beyond its present stage.

Technique and technology have obscured the need to be original, or as near-original as possible. For example, when was the last time somebody actually invented a layout?

Arguably, only *two* advertising layouts have ever been invented. Forty years ago, Helmut Krone invented the famous VW format at Doyle Dane Bernbach, New York. More recently, Bob Barrie at Fallon McElligott, Minneapolis, invented a format in answer to a specific creative problem. It has been imitated, universally, ever since.

"It was a period when spirits like whiskey, bourbon and vodka were losing market share to wine and beer," explains Barrie. "The campaign ran during the late 1980s when people were drinking a lot

*When you think you've hit a brick wall, use a brick wall. Visuals and headlines
integrated onto devastated buildings made the ads more harrowing,
and less like ads. Saatchi & Saatchi, Wellington.*

251

of faddish drinks. It was intended to show how people come back to their senses."

The idea was a time line which began and ended with the same object. Barrie's layout acknowledges the way an eye moves across the page.

"You'd start with white boxer shorts, and end with white boxer shorts, and show every aberration you wore in between. It reminded you that Jim Beam was a classic that you'd return to after you were through with all the fads." Modestly, Barrie admits to having seen fifteen different permutations of his Jim Beam layout. In reality, there have been many dozens.

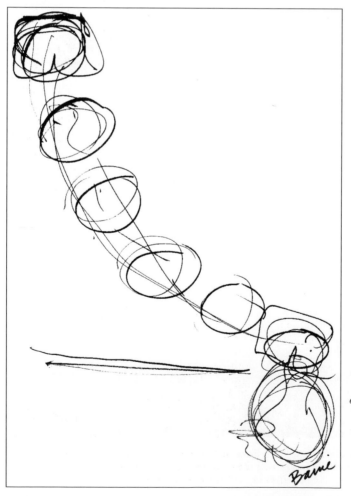

The layout invented by Bob Barrie acknowledges the way an eye travels across the page.

Typically of Barrie's work, the campaign ran for five years. Over fifty different versions were produced, from handshakes to salt and pepper shakers, from sports to jeans. However, Barrie confesses that campaign longevity is never a conscious factor in his thinking.

"You can't be thinking that far down the road. Initially, you're just trying to get a campaign out there that works. Like Hush Puppies, all

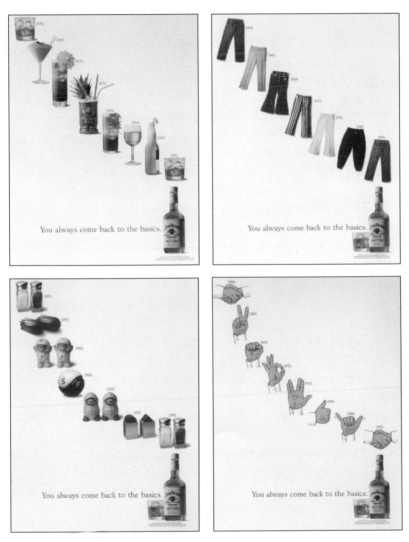

An idea strong enough to inspire 50 different executions over five years.
It's time advertising art direction got back to the basics, too.
Fallon McElligott, Minneapolis.

we wanted originally was to get five ads running in the spaces that the client had booked. We thought that was going to be it, so we tried to make them the best that they could be." Barrie believes longevity is inherent. "If a campaign strikes a chord with people, then it's usually the type of campaign that can be extended. *Time* was very extendable because it was playing off yesterday's news. Jim Beam was extendable because each year new things kept coming back into style, like penny loafers and Smiley buttons and all those classic things, so we could just play off culture and keep it fresh and relevant."

Inventing a new layout is not always possible, or even necessary. However, it is *always* possible to introduce something which gives the work an outstanding point of relevant difference.

New Zealand Red Cross. "Our Red Cross work started with a more traditional look," reports Kim Thorp, executive creative director of Saatchi & Saatchi, Wellington. "The concepts and headlines were strong, so we always knew they would be good ads. But it was our typographer, Len Cheeseman, who pushed their visual power."

Cheeseman worked closely with the creative team, Ken Double and Steve Cooper, to create a startling new look.

"The idea was to make the whole campaign look more representative of the war-torn countries in which the Red Cross operates," says Thorp. "We selected several locations around Wellington where buildings were either about to be demolished, or were located in the seedier parts of town. We then erected scaffolding and our in-house illustrator, Evan Purdie, literally spent his summer holidays painting the headlines and graphics onto walls with house paint. Some of the sites were very large. It took an enormous amount of work and time."

The walls were the ads. Each was photographed and ran as the dominant element of an ad, above a small strip of red copy. By integrating visuals and headlines onto ravaged surfaces, the campaign became more evocative of the Red Cross and less like advertising.

British Army. Alexandra Taylor, at Saatchi & Saatchi, London, is one of Britain's foremost cutting edge art directors.

Rather than apply technique to rescue weak ideas, she deploys it to make strong ideas resonate. The agency's British Army work demonstrates how conventional headlines, copy and logos can be integrated into visuals. More organic pages are the result.

In advertising, incest is a very public crime. Crafting art direction leaves the art director alone on the page.

"I like feeling alone," volunteers Lichtenheld. "It's that rare opportunity to get back to the craft of myself and the writer, and the blank page. Whenever I'm three-quarters into a TV shoot, I start to wish I was back in my office crafting a print ad. I wouldn't have thirty people around me, I'd have much more control, not as many variables." Lichtenheld, a realist, talks about the frustrations of executing ideas. "From the point I have the idea to the time it's done, it's downhill all the way. When you first imagine an ad, you see it as great as it can possibly be. From there on, it's a process of trying to keep it great and accepting the disappointments that come along the way."

Alexandra Taylor framed shots of devastation in the windows of passing cars. More like a commentary, less like a commercial communication. Saatchi & Saatchi, London.

More British Army work from Saatchi & Saatchi, London, where technique integrates visuals and headlines, making strong ideas look less like ads.

Lichtenheld gets his ideas when he is swimming. "I write headlines, too. It's fun because writing headlines is something I know I don't have to do, so it's easier. I have a beginner's mind when I write. I don't know what the bad ideas are."

Lichtenheld suggests one way to sidestep incestuous art direction. See the page beyond the terms of an advertising layout, he urges. "The page is a blank canvas and *anything* can be a layout, especially now that designers and art directors are working together more. If the brand is covered in some other way, the logo can be dispensed with. If the visual is the concept, you don't need a headline. So all of a sudden, you have just one visual that *is* the ad. That said," he puzzles, "we always seem to gravitate back to the elements, the same elements: the visual that gets across the concept; the headline; and then you usually need a few words of body copy, and the logo, and the phone number, and the slogan." Slogans, says Lichtenheld, are little security blankets. "They're okay if they relate to something in the reader, but mostly they're meaningless within people's lives."

Colleague Hanson says homework is the best defence against incest. "It's so tempting when you're doing an ad, and you're against the gun, to open a CA or a D&AD and just say, okay, I'm going to rip that one." Hanson stores a treasure trove of typefaces, reference material, cuttings, videos and ideas in big metal files. If something strikes him, he squirrels it away. "You're the audience as much as anybody else," he believes. "I've got all kinds of things. When I hit a wall, I go and dig in there. I'm constantly refreshing my memory about what's in the files." It sounds an extremely complicated way to work, but Hanson swears by it. "It's not a question of whether I *have* to do it, I *want* to do it. If you want to do good work, you have to look at the world around you, at the stuff that stimulates you, and you have to write down ideas all the time, then you file it. Once I was watching Discovery Channel, and there was a Jacques Cousteau special on the Andaman Islands, and I saw this swimming elephant. I held on to that tape for three years, and then Coke came up." Hanson's swimming elephant commercial for Coca-Cola was lavished with recognition. "Everybody should have those gems stored away. Trouble is, there's nothing more devastating than if you turn on the television and someone else has got there before you."

Hanson says there is nothing more magical than to hold a magazine and see your ad run for the first time. "There's something that happens when you pick up a magazine and fold it over. It's never going to go away." For Hanson, great print ads are the ones which are fresh in a well-worn category. "Anyone can do a condom ad. I like to see a great bank ad, because everyone has done bad ones. It means someone has persevered and *beaten* the category. Those are the ones I really love, that make me envious."

Gallacher believes self-confidence can overcome incest. "You've got to learn to trust your own beliefs and your own self. Bring *yourself* to the industry, not what other people have done in the past." Gallacher maintains that advertising is not a sprint to the finish. "It's a marathon, and the more you learn, the better you become. You have to be able to art direct according to the product, and the copywriter's tone of voice, and the target audience, so you *can't* have just one style." Gallacher seeks his inspiration everywhere. "I go down to Zwemmers photographic book shop. I sit and watch TV. I watch how they do the programme titles. I soak it in like a sponge. All that award books can do is show you how to make things simple. You have to learn to use your own emotions."

Barrie often seeks his inspiration from editorial design, not advertising award annuals. "I once did a campaign for Continental Bank, long copy ads, and I chose an editorial look because there was a lot to say."

Simplicity is Barrie's answer to incest. "Usually, I'll start with the idea in its purest form, and from there I'll create a look for it that's unique to the product or the campaign. I'll keep it simple enough so it doesn't get in the way of the idea. And if the idea is strong enough to begin with, it will remain strong if you don't complicate the layout."

Godfrey has a similar view. "Every ad has its own way of being put together," he observes. "One of the most successful agencies has been Abbott Mead Vickers, and strangely enough they've rarely moved off the beaten track of what we call the old DDB way of doing it. The *Economist* campaign is just a straightforward line on a sheet of red paper. It's a perfect layout, based on the masthead of the magazine, and you do not have to move out of that."

Let's say the foot is your company,
the banana is a change in interest rates,
and the floor is extremely hard.

Continental Bank

A lot of people are uninformed about
the latest developments in business banking.
(Unfortunately, many of them are bankers.)

Continental Bank

*Bob Barrie seeking
inspiration from
editorial design.
Fallon McElligott,
Minneapolis.*

Hegarty sees originality in terms of freshness. "We often have ideas, and we've seen that idea before," he explains. "But have you expressed it in a way that's different and fresh? I always like to use the word *fresh*, rather than the word *original*. I think *original* is an overused word and a dangerous word. When you sit on award shows and people say, we're only going to give awards to original ideas, I think, well, that's it, we might as well go home. God was the last person who had any original ideas. The rest of us are just imitators."

Hegarty talks about how freshness can be achieved. "The style with which you put something down adds to the freshness. It's the *voice* of the ad. Think about it in those terms. Should the voice be quiet? Does it need to shout? Does it need to reverberate with a thousand other voices behind it? There are so many ways of speaking to people. As somebody once said, you can give six people the same joke. One person makes it very funny, and the other five don't. Well, that's because that person has the technique. It's the same with art direction. You have to decide how best to tell the story."

8

HOW TO CRAFT COPY

"To all those people who say that the word is dead," Indra Sinha challenges, "I say, if you take the words off your ads, what are you left with?"

"Generally in advertising," David Abbott reminds us, "I think it's the words you remember."

"Words actually get deeper into the psyche than pictures," Neil French insists. "And they got in deeper even when I set them in that almost unreadable Germanic typeface for XO, because in research, people were able to parrot them perfectly. If something looks interesting, people will make the effort to read it."

Someone once asked Carl Ally if he thought people read ads. Ally's immortal reply: "People read what they *want* to read."

If Ally is right, the issue is not about whether the word is dead, but rather about supply and demand. If we can assume that the demand is still out there, *what* are we supplying to satisfy it?

"Writing, in certain markets, is stagnant," Tim Delaney observes. "If you look to some of the writing in America, which invented the whole vernacular, the whole fast talking, off-the-cuff remark, the classic New York one-liner which a lot of copy is based on because it's very clipped and quite raunchy, I think they can still write brilliantly. You don't see a lot of it, I might add, but when they *do* do it, they do it really well. In the British market, I think it's almost non-existent. You've got the influence of those agencies which say copy is dead, the fact that people can't be bothered to write it, and when they do write it, it's not very well written."

Sinha agrees. "We're told nobody wants to read, therefore nobody wants to write. Kids who come out of art schools flip coins to see which one has the terrible task of being the copywriter. I wonder why they bother? Why call themselves copywriters? They should just call themselves ad creators, and share the horror of having to actually put words on a page."

Nor does it help when aspiring copywriters buy textbooks containing such spurious advice as, "Copywriting relies on the heavy use of *cliches*", and "*Cliches* provide impact and stimulate action". Lines like "For goodness sake" are upheld as shining examples of the copywriter's craft in food ads.

As we prepare to write cutting edge copy, none of these issues should really concern us. Instead, remember that the myths and lies about how advertising works are receding, brand building is changing fundamentally, and in the bigger context, words are an inseparable part of all that. Whether the copywriter has to write fifteen words for a postcard, or a letter of fifteen hundred words, the demands of the craft remain.

And they begin with style and the writing process itself.

How Should Copywriters Develop Their Own Styles?

It may sound pretentious to suggest that advertising copywriters have anything in common with authors and poets. They do, of course. Words are their tools of trade. Words are their only means of expression and persuasion. Copywriters should never pretend otherwise.

In Oakley Hall's *The Art & Craft of Novel Writing*, Jorge Luis Borges describes symptoms familiar to all young copywriters: "At the beginning of their careers many writers have a need to overwrite, to impress. By the excesses of their language, these young men and women try to hide their sense of inexperience. With maturity the writer becomes more secure in his ideas. He finds his real tone and develops a simple and effective style."

The argument can be made that the best style is one that appears to be no style at all, contends Hall. Perhaps the writer's true style begins to emerge when he makes no deliberate effort to produce one. As Ernest Hemingway said, "Prose is architecture, not interior decoration."

"I'm not a writer, I write copy, I write a kind of language that I understand is right for advertising," maintains Tim Delaney. Yet Delaney's style is one of the most imitated in the industry.

"A writer's style is more than his diction – word choice – or his rhetoric – his intention to persuade," explains Hall. "It is his use of sentence rhythms, short, long, simple, complex, or of compound sentences connected by *ands* that suggest the diction of the King James Bible. Style is reflected in the use and originality of metaphors, the form of the conditional, or the use of the present tense instead of the more conventional past; in differences of punctuation, the use of dashes, parentheses, and exclamation marks; in the use of dashes rather than quotation marks to set off dialogue; in the use of italics, the upper case, even semicolons; in fact, style emerges from all the author's quirks and mannerisms, weaknesses and strengths."

"I don't have a *conscious* style," says Abbott. "I suppose we all have a style, just in the way that we talk or shrug. I think I write like I am, whatever that means. It's not a very studied procedure. People tell me that they can recognise a piece of my copy, but it's not a game I can play." Abbott illustrates a specific example of his style. "We were doing a pitch for a holidays company. We'd found this great photograph of a couple on a balcony in Paris looking over the roof-scapes, a very moody photograph. We were selling cheap weekends and city breaks, and I think the headline was *How can you possibly declare your love without a balcony?* In the body copy it said something like, 'You can have a weekend in Paris for £119'. I wrote the small print and it said, 'That's for two people, sharing a room'; then I added brackets and said, '(That shouldn't be a problem, should it?)'. I use brackets a lot, as it were, in conversation." Perhaps, then, he writes as he speaks? "I suspect that's true, but it's not something you can judge for yourself."

French believes style cannot be forced. "I wasn't aware that I had a style, until people told me I'd got one. It wasn't conscious. I think I probably write like I talk. I tend to put *ums* and *ahs* and dots and things like that in, because that's how I speak. When you're reading something, if you can hear the man's voice, it's far more appealing, if not more convincing. And I think everybody does that to an extent; Indra certainly speaks *exactly* the way he writes. But it's not the kind of thing you can give advice on. As soon as you tell a copywriter to write like he talks, he's going to think, how do I talk, how do I talk! Because it's unconscious, and the worst thing you can do is force anything. The best way of writing is to write, just sit down and keep churning it out, because the more bored you get with trying to force syntax, the less forcing you'll actually do. Just get it down on paper."

French suggests writing long letters and keeping a diary. "I used to when I went on holiday. I used to take a little book and write two or three pages every day. You can't keep putting 'Sat on beach, drank', 'Sat on beach, drank', 'Sat on beach, drank'; God, this is boring! In the end, you've *got* to write something else, so you just fill in. And then when you get home and you pick it up and read it, it is actually like you're talking to yourself because it's not important, it's just waffle. If you waffle interestingly, people will read it. And if you waffle boringly, like this, *nobody* will read it."

Antony Redman questions whether a writer can superimpose the same style across everything. "I think style is dictated by the subject or product. Sometimes you might want to write the twisty, turny stuff, other times not. What's more important to me, especially if I'm writing a long copy ad, is to have facts which *I* find interesting. It's the same if you're telling a story, if you're a novelist or a film maker. If something moves *you*, and you put that into an ad, or a novel, or a film, then it's going to move *other* people. If you're doing a serious ad, particularly a public service ad, you've got to make it sound reasonable to people. If you write long copy that sounds unreasonable, people are going to switch off. You can have anger in it, but it's got to be a quiet anger. Some people get angry and bang the table, whereas someone who's angry but speaks quietly, with some knowledge of the topic, you'd actually fear them more."

Rather than construct walls between themselves and their readers, Sinha argues that great copywriters allow their own personalities to come through in their work: "The difference between a great advertising writer and a good one is that the great one breaks through, his personality expresses itself. I'm not talking about just serious ads, it could be a frivolous thing. When someone's personal experience shines through, in the words, in the way they're used, it will always communicate in a more lively way, like one person talking to another, *instead of a set of ideas talking to a theoretical person*. Tony Brignull wrote an ad about Parker Pens, where he talked about the nib moving over the paper, 'leaving a trail of wet, shiny words'. Only someone who loved using a pen, and knew what it was like, could have written that. It immediately communicated the joy of writing with that instrument far more than clever phrases, or puns or wordplays about its balance or value. Tony is the greatest advertising copywriter that Britain has ever produced, and always in his ads you had his personal passion breaking through. That's what made his ads great."

Hugh Mackay concurs. The transmission of the writer's passion makes the reading experience potentially more intense than the viewing experience. "It's the magic, the power, the passion of the creative act in the words. And it sounds paradoxical; they're just words, they're just ink on paper, they're not a complex audio-visual experience. But the really creative, passionate writer does something with those words that the reader finds peculiarly engaging. John Bevins is fond of saying, if you enjoy writing the copy, the consumer will enjoy reading it. When there's real passion and intensity in the writing, there's likely to be the same intensity in the *reader*."

How *Shouldn't* Copy Be Written?

For generations, advertising copywriters have been taught that the most powerful words in the English language, or any language for that matter, are "new" and "you".

Sinha takes exception to "you". "I think I'm at odds with most of the advertising world on this. I actually don't like the way advertising is done. I think it's done in a way that's manipulative, which works against itself in the long run. More enlightened self-interest might be to stop being so obviously manipulative, and start trying to communicate," he suggests. "Copywriters always talk of 'we', and will always talk to 'you', and I question whether this is necessary. It's one of those conventions. *Who* are 'we'? 'We' becomes a faceless corporation. 'We' are always benevolent and wise, and have 'your' best interests at heart. There are three places where the second person, talking directly to '*you*', is commonly used. One is advertising. Another is a certain sort of pornographic sexual fantasy where 'you' are in a room with a beautiful blonde, blah, blah, blah. And the third is multi-user reality in cyberspace where you are constantly told 'you' are standing on the corner of a road, or 'you' are this, or 'you' are that. These are the three sleazy uses of the word 'you'." Sinha believes copywriters should break the mould. "By saying 'we' all the time, it just encourages the writer to feel part of a community of copywriters. No one actually feels as though they're writing on behalf of the client. What they're really doing is saying, 'we', me and my fellow copywriters, and the 'you', half the time, are the award jury judges. It's a very incestuous kind of world in which ads are often written just to win awards."

"Writers should see themselves as not the client's representative, but the reader's representative." John Bevins never writes copy from a first person plural perspective. His work is addressed to "you", talking about "*them*". "I think 'we' worked for a while when writers first started using it. It looked like the advertiser was talking. But it's become such a *cliche*."

Good writers wage a daily battle against *cliches* and formulaic copy. Of greater danger, however, are their own *unconscious writing habits*, the little affectations which are often mistaken for style. They can take the form of favourite linking phrases, or (wait for it) the use of bracketed phrases in the middle of sentences, or the use of capitalised letters to Really Make A Point, or sentences starting with "Time was when ..." and "Truth is ..."

"You have to beat those affectations out of yourself," warns Bevins. "You have to be constantly vigilant. They can very quickly become a habit, and you read back over your copy and really cringe."

"Writers definitely slip into an easy groove," agrees Bruce Bildsten. "More so in the United States, where young people's books all look the same. There's a certain attitude, a kind of smart aleck attitude. There aren't enough different styles, and different ways of coming at it."

The conventional agency environment does not help. Copywriting becomes a very commercial process, a very *conscious* process. The writer's real emotions are suppressed. The work becomes very external, restricted, lacking warmth and wholeness. The text is thin, not textured, not layered. There is no emotional resonance.

According to Hall, the conscious mind must be persuaded or tricked into getting out of the act. The creative mind must be rescued from the "dead hand of the conscious". Hall quotes John Hersey's description of the Censor of the Mind. The censor, near the surface of the mind, selects and filters and gives form. It is the arbiter of taste. But it is also an interrupter, an inhibitor, conservative and repressive. If we can paralyse our censors during the writing process, we will have free access to the "rich deep-brain source of primary feelings". Once we have trawled our subconscious, the sensor can handle the verification process later.

Advertising copywriters are well aware of those feelings when something wants to come out and do something completely different from the conventional. Some stifle those urges, either through self-consciousness or shame, and resort to the familiar and formulaic. It is safer.

Sinha says: "Just let what comes out, come out. There's this little critical thing that sits on your shoulder and says, no, that adjective isn't good enough, or don't use adjectives at all, and if you listen to it too much, it's going to stop you from getting very far in. Superficially, when the critic tells you that you haven't said something well enough, you've got to say, shut up, you can start judging when I've actually got out the content I want."

Sinha goes on to talk about the times when the right words do not come. "You can sometimes feel unable to do something. You're trying to achieve an effect, or write something very powerfully, but it won't become powerful. You can throw all the words you like at it, and they all mill around, and none of them adds up to this powerful effect. Now many people think when they hit a brick wall, that it's bad news. But I would say, no, it's not, it's actually good news, because if it's this hard to break through, the victory is going to be that special. It's like your own inner deep judgement, not a superficial thing that sits on your shoulder like a critic, but a deep judgement saying, not yet, not yet, not yet. You're restless, you're fidgeting, you're depressed, you find all kinds of interruptions and excuses not to write, and then you start to feel very guilty about it. Nine times out of ten, it's that subconscious aspect of yourself saying, not yet, not yet, it hasn't happened inside, because the actual creativity does seem to happen at some deep level of the mind without the conscious being involved, and when it's ready it will come out and then words *aren't* a problem."

"I think I must have been trepanned at an early age," declares French. "I don't think I've got a little censor. I never consciously go around any feelings that I shouldn't do something. The basic principle that I have about writing is that you've got to be interesting, and by its nature that usually means being a bit controversial. So I always start off by thinking, how am I going to make somebody go, good Lord, how did he get away with that? Then, I just write it."

What Should You Know About Writing?

William Wordsworth described the task of writing as "emotion recollected in tranquillity".

Cutting edge copywriters write alone, in one uninterrupted burst of concentrated thought. Abbott writes it as it comes out. Delaney writes in a flurry of scratches and scrawls. French's light burns till midnight.

You should trust your subconscious, but still make conscious preparations.

Great writers know that adverbs are the enemies of verbs, adjectives are the enemies of nouns. Hemingway learned to distrust adjectives as he "would later learn to distrust certain people". In *The Railway Man*, Eric Lomax conveys his grief in sober prose:

> The passion for trains and railways is, I have been told, incurable. I have also learned that there is no cure for torture. These two afflictions have been intimately linked in the course of my life, and yet through some chance combination of luck and grace I have survived them both.

Lomax, a boy who loved trains, became a prisoner of the Japanese on the Burma Death Railway. Despite his suffering, he can describe torture with sparsity:

> Torture, after all, is inconspicuous; all it needs is water, a piece of wood and a loud voice.

After several attempts, Raymond Chandler found these words to describe footsteps:

> After a while they got faint, then they got silent.

Rudyard Kipling brought his sombre description of a First World War battlefield to a powerful climax; he told of the British soldiers who would

> wear their red way through every yard of it.

Like art direction, writing is a craft of reduction. Rely on alliteration and assonance; the labial explosives of big-bellied *B*s; an accumulation of soft, subtle *S*s. Revisit *Under Milk Wood* for imagery and musicality; you might just hear Richard Burton reading:

> To begin at the beginning:
> It is spring, moonless night in the small town, starless and bible-black, the cobblestreets silent and the hunched, courters'-and-rabbits' wood limping invisible down to the sloeblack, slow, black, crowblack, fishingboat-bobbing sea. The houses are blind as moles (though moles see fine tonight in the snouting, velvet dingles) or blind as Captain Cat there in the muffled middle by the pump and the town clock, the shops in mourning, the Welfare Hall in widows' weeds. And all the people of the lulled and dumbfound town are sleeping now.
>
> Hush, the babies are sleeping, the farmers, the fishers, the tradesmen and pensioners, cobbler, schoolteacher, postman and publican, the undertaker and the fancy woman, drunkard, dressmaker, preacher, policeman, the webfoot cocklewomen and the tidy wives. Young girls lie bedded soft or glide in their dreams, with rings and trousseaux, bridesmaided by glow-worms down the aisles of the organplaying wood. The boys are dreaming wicked or of the bucking ranches of the night and the jollyrodgered sea. And the anthracite statues of the horses sleep in the fields, and the cows in the byres, and the dogs in the wetnosed yards; and the cats nap in the slant corners or lope sly, streaking and needling, on the one cloud of the roofs.

Listen. It is night in the chill, squat chapel, hymning in bonnet and brooch and bombazine black, butterfly choker and bootlace bow, coughing like nannygoats, sucking mintoes, fortywinking hallelujah; night in the four-ale, quiet as a domino; in Ocky Milkman's lofts like a mouse with gloves ...

"Bible-black", "muffled middle", "dumbfound town", "bedded soft", "wetnosed yards", "slant corners" and "lope sly" are profound craft examples from Dylan Thomas. If you want to write like that, Jack Kerouac suggests you should "be crazy dumbsaint of the mind" and "remove literary, grammatical and syntactical inhibition".

The minimal use of adjectives and adverbs makes Richard Foster's copy stronger. Go on, count them. Abbott Mead Vickers, London.

Great writers can teach us about writer's block, too. Hemingway said, "Always leave some water in the well". Deliberately stop writing at a point where you know what will come next, so tomorrow you'll have a place to start.

To stimulate better writing, one aspiring young copywriter retyped dozens of award-winning ads so he could experience great copy emerging onto a page beneath his own fingers.

How Should Headlines Be Written?

"I don't think I have a set approach," muses Abbott. "I sit down, and I surprise myself by starting a sentence, but I'm not conscious of what the end will be. Somehow it works out. Sometimes it's quite neat and I think, I wonder where that came from."

Abbott is a quick, disciplined writer. "I try to find something that's going to be persuasive and insightful, and that pleases me in a craft sense because I've chosen the right words and it's concise. I find myself writing them very quickly, and then looking again at them the next day, and changing bits and pieces. I've always been quite quick," he regrets, "and I think there's a danger that it's easy to settle for kind of 'good enough', because you have a facility which gets you to 'good enough' quite quickly. You think, well, I've done that, let's get on to the next thing. I think I might have been a better writer if I hadn't found it so easy."

Delaney looks for intelligence in headlines. "There is a kind of familiarity about the construction of headlines which is dubious. Everybody gets a bit bored with it. I want the *thought* in the headline to be an interesting thought, which is relevant to the proposition." Delaney identifies the strengths of great headlines: "Intelligence in the thought, a degree of intelligence in the construction, and some kind of originality, which sounds a bit difficult to achieve, but a way of combining the thought with the construction to create an original way of doing it."

Sometimes, as was the case with his Timberland Red Indian ad, headlines come out of body copy. "You might say that's a pretty nice thought, and you just keep it back." Choosing headlines has become intuitive. "Not because I'm brilliant, but because I've had experience at it. Someone will come in with twenty ads, they might be for Harrods or Porsche, and I've got to pick two. I will know instantly."

Being both creator and critic is an intuitive skill which all great copywriters possess. As Indra Sinha admits: "I would normally write a headline first. Sometimes, it's very hard to find a headline which will do justice to the subject, particularly if you're working in the field which I was for many years, which was human rights. You're writing about some very brutal things that have happened to people. Sometimes there just aren't words to describe what has happened, so one tends to let them emerge somehow. You can't be glib or clever about them," cautions Sinha. "Well, you can be, but it would be very inappropriate." He cites one example. "There was an ad with a headline which said *Kids, you can never find them when you want them*. When you learned the subject was actually about children who had been seized and kidnapped and murdered, then you saw that attempt to be clever was a rather desperate one. It was very superficial."

Substance, not superficiality, should be the copywriter's priority. "David Abbott's *The board and I have decided we don't like the colour of your eyes* was a wonderful headline. Also one of Tony Brignull's, a very subtle one, *The life of a designer at Dunne & Co. is one of continual self-restraint*, was a very dry, very lovely line. They are lines with some substance to them."

Sometimes, Bevins writes headlines after he has finished the copy. "In a sense, there are two kinds of copy. There's the kind of copy that supports the headline, or expands on the line. Then there's the kind of copy that's more like a story, that in itself is supported by the headline, and the headline may not be written until after you've written the story. There are lots of people who write books without knowing what the title of the book is going to be. Once you've written the story, the challenge then is to find the best way to get people into it." Very often, Bevins finds his headlines are inspired by what people say. "I was at a Banker's Trust seminar and one of the speakers was describing the share market. He said, 'A rising tide lifts all boats, but a falling tide lets you see who's been swimming naked'."

"There's always the old style of copywriting," Ben Hunt reminds us. "You sit there and write twenty headlines. The best one becomes the headline, and the other nineteen appear in the body copy."

*A straight line sets off
a bent line,
by Malcolm Duffy.
Collett Dickenson Pearce,
London.*

*A straight line and a
bent question,
by Tony Brignull.
Abbott Mead Vickers,
London.*

This whippet is a victim of recession. It used to be a labrador.

When this picture was taken Sally weighed 26lbs.

The normal weight for a one year old labrador is about 60lbs.

The RSPCA inspector who rescued her found that every one of her ribs was visible and estimated that she had not been fed by her owner for over three weeks.

There is no excuse for this behaviour, but there is an explanation.

The owner in question had been made redundant and could not afford to feed the animal.

We were able to bring a successful prosecution banning him from owning a pet for five years.

But it was a long, expensive process, and only one of many we have to deal with every week.

Which is why we desperately need your help.

Our business is booming in this recession. Our uniformed inspectors are constantly being called upon to cope with its effects on animals.

Animals locked inside repossessed houses with no food or water.

Animals abandoned in remote lay-bys. Animals in pain whose owners cannot afford to pay vets' fees.

Our policy is never to refuse a call for help. But it's a policy that costs money.

We receive no aid from the Government and depend entirely on donations from the public.

Ironically, at a time when people have less money to spare, our need for it has massively increased.

Please send us whatever you can.

If you cannot help us, please don't hinder us by taking on a pet you cannot afford or giving an animal as a Christmas present.

And then, perhaps, the RSPCA will be starved of cases like this one.

Please tick the box if you are already a supporter.
Please use my donation to fight animal cruelty.

£100   £50   £25   £10   other £

I wish to give via
Visa/Access No:

Signature _____ Expiry _____

Name _____ Date _____

Address _____

To: RSPCA, Dept LTDT, Freepost,
Bristol BS3 3YY.

RSPCA

Headlines by Peter Souter, using horrific juxtapositions.
Abbott Mead Vickers, London.

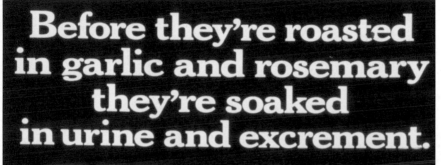

Before they're roasted in garlic and rosemary they're soaked in urine and excrement.

The trucks that carry livestock across Europe hold up to 800 sheep at a time.

The journeys can last over twenty-four hours, but the animals' bladders cannot. They begin to urinate and excrete inside the lorry.

One sheep produces around a litre of urine and 700 grammes of faeces a day.

And so do the other 799.

Since they are trapped in such a confined space their fleeces quickly become coated in droppings.

For the rest of the trip they're wet, cold and some even suffer skin burns.

Eventually the urinating stops, but only because the animals are given no water in transit.

The size of Continental trucks means that unfamiliar flocks are often mixed together (an unsettling experience for any animal).

In the crush the weaker sheep lose their footing, fall to the floor and are trampled by the others.

Some die.

And all this happens so European meat traders can squeeze a little more profit from their livestock.

The sheep could be slaughtered close to their farms, refrigerated and then transported (a method favoured by many farmers).

But offal and hides fetch a slightly higher price abroad and freshly killed meat is also at a premium, so the practice continues.

At least until the law is changed.

EC agriculture ministers are about to meet to discuss livestock transportation regulations.

The RSPCA want to see an eight hour limit on the transportation of live animals for slaughter enforced immediately across the European Community.

Britain's representative at the negotiations is Gillian Shephard and there's still time to let her know your views on the crucial issue of maximum journey time.

Which is why we need your help.

Please phone the number below for a free RSPCA information pack and to find out what further action you can take.

Perhaps we can then persuade Mrs Shephard RSPCA to look after our sheep.

STOP THE NEEDLESS TRANSPORTATION OF ANIMALS.

A familiar phrase, taken out of context by John Bevins Advertising, Sydney.

Are there any formulae for headline writing? As you will see, some headlines play one sentence off another, or one fact off another. And, as a rule of thumb, the longer the copy, the shorter the headline.

*Long copy,
short bent headline,
straight picture.
Antony Redman,
Euro RSCG Partnership
(The Ball Partnership),
Singapore.*

How Should the Copy Begin?

Classic book openings tell us everything we need to know.

> It was the best of times, it was the worst of times.

> I first remember being sexually abused by my father when I was about 3. It may have happened before, I don't know.

> Last night I dreamt I went to Manderley again. It seemed to me I stood by the iron gate leading to the drive, and for a while I could not enter, for the way was barred to me.

The first lines of a book are the most important. They communicate the flavour of what is to follow. Authors know they have only one chance to capture your imagination, or leave you cold, in which case you will not bother to read further and you will not buy the book.

In the first quote, Charles Dickens began *A Tale of Two Cities* with a cryptic observation of the times.

In the third, Daphne du Maurier's compelling narrative portends events in *Rebecca*.

The second quote is actually from an ad, a chilling account of child abuse written by Mike Boles at Saatchi & Saatchi, London, for the NSPCC. Boles, like other great copywriters, knew he had only one chance to hook his readers.

All well and good, some copywriters might argue, but shouldn't the selling proposition appear early in the copy? John the Evangelist thought so. The first sentence of "copy" in his Gospel puts the "product" into context immediately:

> Before the world was created, the Word already existed; he was with God, and he was the same as God.

Four sentences later, John advances his selling proposition:

> The light shines in the darkness, and the darkness has never put it out.

Text that stark and powerful, free of adjectives and adverbs, is worthy of emulation, but not easy to achieve.

"I've spent an extremely long time on openings," recalls Sinha, "usually two or three hours working on two or three sentences, just writing them over and over again with different word orders. What I've found is, when I've needed to do that, I've then thrown them away, because it's obvious that anything that needs to be written that many times is no good."

"Just write off the headline, or off the thought, and you'll find out whether it's good or not by the fact that it can sustain the argument or the creative platform," advises Delaney. "It was a kind of myth of copywriting that you write the ad, then take out the first paragraph, or the first five. I've never done that. I've always liked my first paragraphs." Not that it was always so easy, as Delaney readily admits. "When I was trying to become a copywriter years ago, and not very confident at it, I used to share a room with this old buffer. In the morning he used to come in and sit down, put a bit of paper in the typewriter, and just type all day and go home. And he used to do it all day, just type and smoke. He'd come and have a talk with me, and he saw I was stuck one day, and he said, what's the matter? And I said, I can't do it. And he said, just keep writing. What he taught me was absolutely true, which is what you do when you can't write, or even can't start, is *start anyway*. So I started. I used to literally sit down and say something which related to the headline and the story. I'd just write it down. Could be a question, rhetorical, ever wondered why this thing happens; or, there's a time when etcetera, etcetera. And I'd just write on. And I'd keep going, as though I didn't want anyone to interrupt me, I'd write it by hand, write, write, write, write, write."

Abbott wants to get into the argument that flows from the headline as quickly as possible. "I don't sit down and say, I've got to write the first great *War and Peace* opening line. I'm not conscious of that."

French advocates a "little bit of a slide in" from the headline. "It doesn't have to be the next expected line, but some relevance to the headline would be really nice. The whole point is, to get someone to read the copy, *you have to be interesting all the time*. So if your headline is interesting enough to get them in, don't blow your advantage in your first paragraph."

"I very much believe in that," says Sinha. "You have a duty *not* to bore the reader. Therefore you must start with something that will capture the imagination immediately, and often it may appear to have no connection with the headline. It doesn't matter, so long as the proposition that you've advanced in the headline is done justice to somewhere in the ad; preferably, don't leave it too long before you

What's it like to be raped as a 3 year old? A victim explains.

I FIRST remember being sexually abused by my father when I was about 3. It may have happened before, I don't know.

I can see it now, me lying in bed, with that big face coming towards me. He'd kiss me good-night, but he didn't stop at kissing.

He used to tell me it was our secret. And if I ever told anyone about it I'd be sent away.

But even as a child I knew something wasn't right. It was those words, "I'll protect you". How could he be protecting me? He was bloody hurting me.

It's strange really, he was my enemy, but at the same time my only friend in the world. He made me depend on him. He controlled me. My body was his toy for more than 9 years.

At school I found it hard to mix. I felt different. I'd never let anyone get close to me. In the changing rooms after P.E. I hated people seeing my naked body. I was so ashamed, thought they might be able to tell what had been happening to me and call me a poofter.

Even when I managed to find a girlfriend I still wasn't sure if I was heterosexual. I was terribly rough with her. I suppose I wanted to be in control of someone, like my father was with me.

Sex terrified me. Having an orgasm just made me think of what my father did inside of me. And that big smiling face.

I met someone else eventually. We got married. After 2 years she left me. She said I was cold and didn't understand her.

But that's how I was. I just wasn't aware of causing or feeling mental or physical pain. Some-thing inside me had been switched

off long ago. There were times when I could actually cut myself with a knife and not feel a thing.

After the divorce, I turned to drink. It was a way of escaping. But I still suffered deep depressions.

Last year, my father finally died. I think that's what made me contact the NSPCC. I was 53 years old, and it was the first time I'd ever told anyone about my childhood.

Once a week for 6 months a Child Protection Officer worked with me. He got me to tell him everything about my experience. Talking about it was very painful. For over 40 years I guess I'd been trying not to think about it.

Eventually though, it started to work. He made me realise that what happened wasn't my fault.

For the first time I can ever remember I actually began to feel good about myself. It was just like being let out of a dark and lonely cell.

I'll never forget what happened to me. But at least I can start to live my life.

For further information on the work of the NSPCC, or to make a donation, please write to: NSPCC, 67 Saffron Hill, London, EC1N 8RS or call 071 242 1626.

To report a suspected case of child abuse, call the NSPCC Child Protection Helpline on 0800 800 500

NSPCC
Act Now For Children.

A compelling first-person narrative by Mike Boles. Saatchi & Saatchi, London.

Leading with a question, Andrew Bruck catalogues the horrors. DMB&B, Singapore.

*A gripping yarn
from the trenches by
Antony Redman.
Euro RSCG Partnership
(The Ball Partnership),
Singapore.*

pick up the thread. Often if you find you've been working very hard on a piece of copy and you cut away the opening you've been working on until you come to the part where the real story starts, that's where your powerful opening is."

"I think the headline *is* your first paragraph." Redman draws an analogy with books. "When somebody reads a book, they don't have the advantage of reading a headline. So some of the great lines, like *Lolita*, they're the headlines that start off the book. So because the headline has dragged people kicking and screaming into the story, I think you need intriguing ways to keep them reading. Novelists do it as well; they mess with the chronology of the plot, so they will have one scene, which was ten years ago, jump to thirty years hence. It keeps the reader involved. And that's an interesting factor: you're playing with them, and if you do it right, they *enjoy* the fact that you're playing with them. It's the same with an ad. If you've said it in the headline, and you've got people interested with the headline, there's no reason then to have your first sentence repeat the same thought. I've seen that a lot in ads, and it's tedious. And what I've learned is once someone's written the copy, a lot of the time the first two or three paragraphs can be chopped."

It is far better for the writer to be ruthless with the copy, than the reader.

How Should the Copy Continue?

"This is a kind of heresy," admits Delaney, "but I believe you write ads by sitting down to write them. You don't start knowing what an ad should be until you write it. *It's a voyage of discovery.* I think you embark with some information you have trust in, and you sit down, and then you start writing, and you simply do not know which way you're going. It's not to say you're going to wander off strategy, because that's part of what you sit down with; but it's only when you start writing, and thinking, and doodling, that you get to the point of what an ad should be. It isn't ever in the brief."

Delaney writes by hand. "That's the way I've always done it. I'm not a typing copywriter. My thoughts go faster than I can type. I want to scratch them out. I just want a ruled pad and a Pentel, and I can write really quickly then. I tear through it. Nothing interrupts me. I don't have to look at the screen. It's all just absolutely concentrated. It's a scrawl, I can hardly read it myself. It's all about hand extension of brain, not about how it looks, not about how many paragraphs, or anything like that."

Long copy is relatively easy to write if you enjoy doing it, Delaney believes. "But I think a lot of people can't do it, therefore they don't enjoy it. Steve Dunn always used to say to me, here's how much copy you need to write, and I'd go and write it. I can always write it to the length; if someone says, do me this much, I can write it almost without looking at it. What happens is, I go through it all, re-read it as I'm going, and then keep going. Then I go back and fix this bit, cut that bit, or whatever. It doesn't take me long."

Delaney's job, as he sees it, is to tell a story. "If it's about Porsche engines, it's about linking. You've got all the facts arrayed in front of you that you want to impart, and you just lay them out in front of the reader the best way you can. What I'm doing is assuming interest, which is presumptuous, but you *have* to do that because if you worry about interest, you'll think, my God, they'll never read it. So you have to tell the story in an entertaining way, use all the powers you've got as a writer to keep them entertained and feed them information they'll find relevant, and keep building, and then come to some kind of conclusion."

Samuel Goldwyn said a story should start with an earthquake and work its way up to a climax. Bevins takes the point. "If you've given them a great headline, you have to keep giving, and giving, and giving. It's a constant process of handing out small gifts, whether you're giving them something to make them laugh, or information they can *truly* use, not trite, shallow information. At the end of the read, there mustn't be a sense of disappointment." Bevins says ads have the same potential as movies, books and even jokes to either enrich or impoverish their audience. Something in the ad should touch the reader's spirit. "I once did an ad for Microsoft Word, back in the early days, about 1984, and it was trying to get writers to use word processors and show them what a word processing programme could do. I'd found this list of words which Shakespeare had actually invented. I'd had no idea that words like suspicious, critical, distrustful, were originally created by him. So the headline was something like, *Suspicious, critical, distrustful of people who invent words?* And it went on to say that every word in the ad in *italics* was a word invented by Shakespeare. When they got to the coupon, the word *Hurry* was also in italics; yes, he invented that, too. At the end of it, people could say, I'm glad I read that, because I've really got something out of it beyond what it is I'm meant to get out of it, which is I should throw away my typewriter and use it as an anchor for my dinghy."

What distinguishes great long copy? More than anything else, its readability.

"For me, the transmission of the idea is the job," states John Salmon. "The form of it is less important than the content. I'm not given to puns or verbal constructs. I write in the tone of voice of the target audience in *easily transmitted language.*"

"The most important thing for me is to craft every paragraph and the point you're making in that paragraph," says Redman. "Some long copy ads might take a day to write, others a week before they read well."

"The difference between good copy and bad copy for me," Hunt says, "is that good copy will have a flow in it. It will sound like it's not lecturing you; it will speak to you as a person."

"The copy has to flow," confirms Bildsten. "If you want people to read something continuously, it must flow as a continuous piece of writing. If it feels like you're just cobbling things together, then you're going to lose people."

How does Sinha make his copy flow?

"I *don't* do it by one of the ways which is quite common, which is to link the end of one sentence to the beginning of another with a little bit of wordplay, or a little piece of irony. If it's done in a very accomplished way, I suppose you don't notice it so much, but when it's not done very well, which is mostly the case, it's clunky, and almost obscene and insulting. In fact, I don't think you would read on because it's patronising to have these heavy-handed links made for you. The way I'd keep a person reading on is I'd vary the *rhythms*, I'd look at the *musicality* of the words, I'd try and make the language *interesting*. More than anything else, I'd make sure there was an idea in every single bit of every paragraph, so the reader was propelled onwards by a flow of ideas, and if you don't have ideas, you're writing empty words and you won't keep anyone's attention." Sinha's advice is to read your copy aloud. "If you have an ear for language, you hear rhythms of sentences, the way they flow onwards from one another. It's instinct. The very good trick actually is to read out aloud what you've written, and if it doesn't read well, if it sounds awkward or embarrassing, then you know you've got a problem. It's the best acid test of all. Read it aloud, and listen to it, and everything sorts itself out, because the words want to tumble out in a way that's attractive."

Abbott agrees. "I read my copy aloud, which is the old piece of advice. I've always done that. You spot the *false notes*, and you also check the flow, and you can hear when it doesn't flow, and that's the point of copy, to impart information in the most effortless way possible for the readers because they're not buying the magazine or newspaper for your contribution. It's very silly not to make it an easy diversion, an easy, rewarding one." Abbott still writes by hand. "I don't really think very much about how I write, I just do it. Usually I'm quick. Nine hundred to a thousand words, you work a bit harder on that. It's usually written as it comes out. I'm always a bit suspicious of copy that I have to rework."

French writes by hand, too, but directly onto the layout. He selects a pen which lets him replicate the font and type size of the finished setting. "I write to fit the ad, and I develop my argument as I go on, and when I see the final bit of the last column looming up, I wrap it up and get off," he laughs, "or switch to a finer nib and continue in 6-point."

French hardly ever rewrites an ad. "Although," he admits, "I have got to a point where I've done an ad and finished up a column short, and I can't waffle any more, so then I throw away the lot and do it again in bigger letters."

French writes and art directs his own work. His methodology is a fusion of both disciplines. Like Delaney and Abbott, he writes the entire piece in one sitting, but with the added advantage of being able to assess the reading experience during the writing experience.

"Generally speaking, I have a rough idea of what the thing should look like, and I know the type size it ought to be to make it look as though I've got something interesting to say. You can't do an ad in

24-point and hope that anybody will mistake it for an interesting ad. But if you do something in 12- or 18-point, people go, gosh, they've got a lot to say, and there's a complete difference. *Double the amount of words can sometimes look far more interesting.*"

The copy as visual, and the copy as copy, are French's dual preoccupations. "I always start off thinking, well, it's going to be somewhere between 12- and 18-point, and then, just on the basis of the look of the ad, I'll decide how many words it's going to be. Then, I'll start in the top left corner and carry on until I get to the bottom right corner, and work around the logo, if there is one." As he writes, French is acutely aware of his target audience and their sensibilities: blue rinses or football hooligans or bankers. Holding their interest may call for an occasional icon, or some visual respite from words, although French's work is usually without artifice. "If ever you see a large logo on any of my ads," he quips, "it's because I couldn't think of enough to write."

If flow is the greater priority in copy, content comes a close second. Communicating dozens of facts in a continuous piece of writing can be either a dull regurgitation or a vibrant reading experience. As Bildsten warned, the facts cannot be just cobbled together.

"I refuse to allow myself just to write the bald fact down," says Sinha. "I have to think, what does the fact signify? If you ask yourself what the fact signifies to you, the writer, that's one thing. But ask yourself, what does it signify to the reader? After all, you're telling the reader for a purpose. You have to turn facts, and numbers, into people's personal experiences."

When Frank Sinatra died, the media reported that millions of Americans were mourning his death. However, one correspondent reported that probably half the American population had been conceived while their parents were listening to a Frank Sinatra record.

"A perfect example of how to take what is otherwise a fairly sterile fact, and turn it into something which adds a whole dimension to what Sinatra was about," Sinha maintains. "A perfect example of how to present a fact."

But first, the facts have to be found. "I was doing research for our Save Water campaign, and I stumbled across the fact that some strange speakers had been invented which emulated the sound of

TED BUNDY. JEFFREY DAHMER. THE BOSTON STRANGLER. HOW DO YOU THINK THEY GOT THEIR START?

From psychopaths and murderers to child abusers and wife beaters, almost all violent criminals have a history of animal abuse.

Ted Bundy's first victims weren't pretty, dark-haired co-eds. They were cats and dogs.

The Milwaukee Cannibal, Jeffrey Dahmer, was suspected of killing and eating over 17 people. But his murderous career actually began with the killing and torturing of animals.

Albert De Salvo, the Boston Strangler, didn't become a strangler overnight either. As a young man, he experimented with puppies and kittens. He trapped them in orange crates and shot arrows through the boxes.

Ed Kemper, David Berkowitz, James Oliver Huberty – even the teenager who brutally murdered two children in Kobe, Japan, this year was no exception – all of them graduated from abusing animals.

The FBI and law enforcement agencies in many countries recognise this connection.

In fact, the FBI's Behavioural Science Unit uses animal cruelty as one of the factors in assessing the 'threat potential' of dangerous criminals.

Sociologists, psychologists and people who counsel battered women recognise it too.

So why do violent people pick on animals?

Research shows that animal abusers usually grow up in troubled and violent families. Ironically, they may themselves be victims of abuse.

For some, the animals are merely scapegoats. Their anger is really directed against parents, neighbours or society as a whole.

For others, the violence is a means to get attention, to shock people or to terrorize them into submission. By strangling a cat, an abuser demonstrates his power. "This is what I can do. And there's nothing you can do to stop me."

It's also a way of saying "you're next." It is a warning.

But a warning that is frequently ignored by the only people who can help – the witnesses.

Tragically, almost 7 out of 10 cases of animal abuse go unreported. Neighbours look the other way and passers-by quicken their steps.

It is only when we hear of women being attacked on the streets or children murdered on the way home from school, that we begin to take notice. "Who could do such a terrible thing?" we wonder.

If you witness any act of animal cruelty, please call the SPCA or the police. Please remember that the animal may not be the only one in need of help.

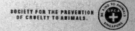

SOCIETY FOR THE PREVENTION OF CRUELTY TO ANIMALS.

Jagdish Ramakrishnan establishes a connection between animal abuse and human violence. Saatchi & Saatchi, Singapore.

PEOPLE WHO ABUSE ANIMALS ARE CAUGHT SOONER OR LATER.
BUT NOT NECESSARILY FOR ABUSING ANIMALS.

What is the difference between a boy who kicks a dog and a man who beats his wife?

Apparently, just a matter of time.

Studies conducted over the last three decades show that people who abuse animals invariably go on to abuse humans.

When the FBI analysed the lives of violent criminals and serial killers on death row, they found that almost all of them had tortured cats and dogs when they were young.

Other research shows consistent patterns of animal cruelty among people who commit child abuse or spouse abuse.

A survey of fifty-seven families under treatment for child abuse revealed that in 88% of the families, at least one person had abused animals.

People who counsel battered women report that up to 70% of the women with pets have had their dogs and cats beaten, choked, mutilated, tortured, dismembered, hanged or shot by their husbands.

What does an abuser gain by attacking helpless animals?

He gets revenge. He gets a feeling of power and control. And when he discovers he can get away with it, he gains the confidence to start attacking people.

And the violence doesn't just progress from animals to humans.

It is also passed on from generation to generation.

An abused child, in turn, becomes an abusive child. He vents his anger and frustration on dogs, cats and smaller children at school.

When he grows up, he becomes an abusive husband and an abusive parent. In the process, he produces another generation of violent children.

How do you stop this vicious cycle?

Organisations like the Humane Society International stress the importance of correcting abusers early. Cruelty to animals, whether by a child or an adult, should never be ignored. It is a warning sign.

Not only is it a sign of a mentally disturbed individual, it is also a sign of a troubled family where child and spouse abuse may already be happening.

If you witness any act of animal cruelty, please call the SPCA or the police. Please remember that animals are never the only victims of animal abuse.

SOCIETY FOR THE PREVENTION OF CRUELTY TO ANIMALS.

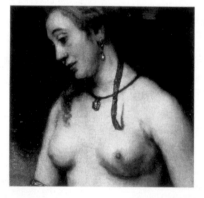

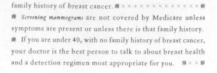
John Bevins invites us to detect cancer in a classic painting.
John Bevins Advertising, Sydney.

READ ON TO FIND OUT WHAT JAPANESE WOMEN DO IN THE TOILET.

A polite Japanese lady will cover her mouth when she giggles.

She will bow her head to hide her eyes when embarrassed.

One could only imagine the crisis this creature faces inside the ladies' room.

She enters the cubicle, closes the door, pulls the latch and sits. Soon, the crowded washroom reverberates with the sound of her urine splashing into the water at the bottom of the toilet bowl.

An unavoidable nuisance of modern life you may say. A source of deep humiliation if you happen to be a Japanese woman.

Her solution for years has been to conceal the noise. Not by a well-timed cough.

But by flushing the toilet whilst relieving herself. The familiar commotion created by the gurgling cistern drowns out her business.

But by flushing the toilet whilst relieving herself. The familiar commotion created by the gurgling cistern drowns out her business.

Depending on the length of her stay, the toilet may be flushed up to three or four times.

And she may walk out quietly, without anyone knowing of the noise she has made.

Her face saved.

Unfortunately, the water is not. With each flush, 10 litres of water disappears into the sewerage. That's 30 litres a visit. And over 100 litres daily.

Now multiply that by the number of women in all of Japan.

A self-conscious avoidance of shame results in a shameful loss of pure drinking water.

And water is now one of the most precious commodities in the East.

Over 70% of India's water supplies are contaminated. In New Delhi, the Yzmuna River is deluged with 50 million gallons of untreated sewerage, 5 million gallons of industrial effluent and 125 thousand gallons of DDT. Not in a year. But each hopeless day.

The mighty Ganges swallows the raw human waste of no less than 114 crowded cities.

Shanghai spends millions piping clean water to its vast urban sprawl from over 900 miles away.

So too does Singapore and Bangkok. The Philippines and Indonesia inexplicably lose over one third of all water pumped to their thirsty cities.

Saudi Arabia's supply will be exhausted early next century. The next war in the Middle East won't be over crude black oil, but crystal clear water.

India and Pakistan are almost certain to find themselves in a similar position as they attempt to resolve the competition for the thick murk that flows through the Hindus River basin.

Hong Kong has the pleasure of possessing more Rolls Royce automobiles per capita than any other country. Yet you risk your life by drinking from the tap there.

Ironic then, that the source of life brings death. Bubbling with disease, fouled water robs the lives of 25 thousand Asians daily. 10 million a year.

The majority of them small children too frail to fight.

The World Bank estimates it will cost at least $128 billion in the next 10 years to simply meet the basic drinking and sanitation needs of Asia.

The World Bank estimates it will cost at least $128 billion in the next 10 years to simply meet the basic drinking and sanitation needs of Asia.

An amount almost beyond comprehension.

The crisis is real. It will not go away.

It calls for us all to re-evaluate how we use the clean water that is available.

And for the more ingenious ones amongst us to find solutions.

In Japan, electronic gadgets are now installed in the ladies' rooms. Attached to these gadgets are speakers. They emulate the sound of a flushing toilet.

Now there is no need for the timid women to flush any more than is necessary.

The Fuji Bank has installed this system and already reports a $70,000 saving on water bills each year.

How can you begin to change things? The battle begins in your home.

Everytime you turn on a tap, look at that stream. You wouldn't last three days without it.

More than food, or love, or wealth, you need water to survive.

(TREAT WATER WITH RESPECT)

Antony Redman discovers a bizarre connection between modesty and water conservation. Batey Ads, Singapore.

287

flushing toilets." Redman turned it into a long copy ad, *Read on to find out what Japanese women do in the toilet.* "Which is something that has always interested me. If you read it, you don't think it's a water ad, which is the first rule. Then the copy goes on to describe their source of embarrassment." From this bizarre and seemingly trivial beginning, Redman had to steadily shift the reader into the serious consequences of wasting water. "If you just string facts together, it reads like a list; people will switch off. The best jokes don't tell you the punchline at the start. You have to link the facts in a way that's talking to a person, telling them things they never knew, twists of fate like water, the source of life, is bringing death. And you have to do it very reasonably, and ask for the reader's help, in this case, to treat water with respect." The ad took over a week for Redman to write.

Sinha can relate to that. "Unlike Neil French, I'll rarely get it right first time. I tend to rely on many drafts. I'll throw words at the computer screen and revise and revise. What's quite useful, having struggled with the material for a long time, is to put aside everything I've been doing on it, and then just write a draft straight off, off the top of the head, and it usually flows because by then I'm *desperate* to say all the things I need to say and I'm not concerned with all the trying-to-be-clevers and curlicues and what-have-you's."

How Long Should the Copy Be?

"The great writers like Richard Foster seem always to write to the right length," Abbott reflects. "They seem to know when the job is done." Abbott instinctively knows when to end his own copy. "I suppose when it begins to bore me. Then I go back and cut another third out of it."

"What a lot of people refer to as long copy is, in fact, a paltry flea-bite of copy," argues Sinha. "What I call long copy is thousands of words. That's when you're really into it. I've begun lately, out of sheer bloody-mindedness, to say, look, you are just going to have to read three thousand words or whatever. And I'm not going to do that usual paragraphing trick any more! I'm going to write it like proper joined-up stuff. I'm afraid you are going to have to read ten-sentence paragraphs sometimes."

"I'm never afraid of long copy being used," confirms Mackay. "If

Bankers Trust ads are deliberately crafted to look daunting by John Bevins, Sydney.

someone is in a magazine or newspaper, they are there to read. And readers, generally speaking, love the word. They love print. They love the reading."

Mackay cites a successful long copy campaign in Australia for Bankers Trust. The ads are dense with copy.

"They're intentionally made to look difficult to read," explains their writer, Bevins, "so there's actually a sense of achievement in the readers when they've finished reading. I've never necessarily subscribed to the view that copy has to be broken up by subheads. I've never believed that every paragraph has to be one sentence. The

"You are just going to have to read it," says Indra Sinha.
Collett Dickenson Pearce, London.

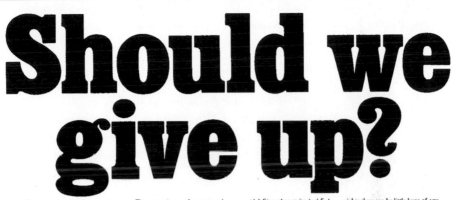

Should we give up?

The pictures on the other page are upsetting.

Normally, we wouldn't publish them. Our advertisements purposely stay away from violent and horrific pictures.

When we publicised the murders of street urchins by Brazilian and Guatemalan police, we spared you the sight of children with their tongues ripped out and eyes burned from their sockets.

When we wrote about Iraq's use of chemical weapons against Kurdish civilians, we deliberately did not use the photographs that made our volunteers cry.

We at Amnesty have no choice but to look at these pictures. And hear the stories that go with them.

The story of Agostinho Neto.

The African doctor's waiting room was full of people when the Portuguese secret police arrived.

They dragged him out of his surgery, past his terrified patients. Ignoring the screams of his wife, they began methodically to flog him in front of her and his young children.

Later, he was flung in jail. There were no charges. There would never be a trial.

The case of Dr Agostinho Neto was one of six which, in 1961, prompted a British lawyer, Peter Benenson to write an article in the Observer.

'Open your newspaper any day of the week and you will find a report from somewhere in the world of someone being imprisoned, tortured or executed because his opinions or religion are unacceptable to his government. There are several million such people in prison – and their numbers are growing. The newspaper reader feels a sickening sense of impotence. Yet if those feelings of disgust all over the world could be united into common action, something effective could be done.'

With these words, he founded Amnesty.

A passion for human rights.

Amnesty began as a small group of lawyers, writers and publishers who shared a passionate commitment to human rights.

From a small office in London, they started gathering information about people who were in prison for their political or religious beliefs.

They wrote letters of support and comfort to prisoners, and of protest to their jailers.

Out of this early work grew the Amnesty reports, the letter-writing groups and the urgent action network, which can muster thousands of protest telegrams within hours of a prisoner's arrest.

For three decades Amnesty has campaigned against the terrible things to which the pictures opposite bear witness.

We've tried to show that turning a blind eye to a government's human rights crimes is both immoral and foolish. (It took the Gulf War to demonstrate this – but we'd been issuing warnings about Saddam Hussein every year since 1980.)

During the last thirty years, we have examined the human rights record of every nation on earth and, regrettably, have had cause to criticise most.

(Each end of the political spectrum thinks we're biased towards the other. In fact we're non-partisan. We speak out for the rights of individuals, whatever their views, and against those who abuse them, whatever theirs.)

In the last thirty years, we have been able to close the files of more than 97% of the cases we had taken up.

No-one can deny that it's an outstanding achievement for a small, chronically underfunded, organisation.

Except that it's not enough.

A million failures.

Among the files we closed was that of Agostinho Neto, the Angolan doctor who was one of Amnesty's first 'prisoners of conscience.'

In 1975, when Angola won its independence from Portugal, Dr Neto became his country's first president.

Sadly, during his Presidency, his government was accused of imprisoning without trial, torturing and unlawfully killing many of its political opponents. How could such things happen under the rule of someone who had himself suffered so much?

Were we naive to imagine we could make a difference? In the last thirty years, things have not got better, but worse.

In 1961 we believed, didn't we, that the world would never tolerate another

genocide? Since then we've had Suharto, Pol Pot, Idi Amin and Saddam Hussein.

We've had Emperor Bokassa who stocked his fridge with human heads.

For every prisoner freed, thousands are still in prison. For every person plucked from the torturers, thousands suffer agonies beyond our imagining. For every life saved, hundreds of thousands have been lost.

Between them, Suharto, Pol Pot, Idi Amin and Saddam Hussein have executed and tortured to death more than a million people.

For Amnesty that's a million failures.

All we've done in the last thirty years is bale a few buckets from a sea of human misery.

Should we give up?

So we come to the crucial question. Should we give up?

Please think carefully before you answer. While you make up your mind, here's a poem by Agostinho Neto.

Next door
someone groans
his fingers edged with blood streaming
from nails broken by the palamatoria

He is thinking of victory
and no sleep comes to his prison days
or dreams to fill his solitude

There are minutes when the world
is summed up in the torture chamber

Oh! Who will sleep
when he hears his best friend go mad
there in the next cell
his spirit is killed by torture?

"Who will sleep?" asks Neto. Dare any of us?

Left to themselves, governments will go on imprisoning, torturing and killing, and other governments will go on turning a blind eye.

Until they start respecting human

rights there can be little hope of any real political, social or environmental progress.

How can we persuade certain Latin American governments to stop the killing of trees in the rainforest if we can't persuade them to stop the killing of their own street children?

Name a single nation that took positive action when Saddam Hussein gassed 5,000 Kurdish civilians with chemical weapons *three years before the Gulf War.*

War and famine are still, in 1991, devastating the Horn of Africa where, in the past two decades, millions of people have become refugees or have died because of repressive regimes with scant regard for human rights.

So long as such regimes are allowed to rule unchallenged, there will be poverty and disease and famine and war.

Only one power can stop it.

Only one power is strong enough to say to the world's governments 'I will no longer allow this to happen.'

That power brought democracy to Eastern Europe.

That power won women the vote.

Western governments did not lift a finger to save the Kurdish people from slaughter until that power forced them to intervene.

That power is public opinion.

'Pressure of opinion a hundred years ago brought about the emancipation of the slaves. It is now for man to insist upon the same freedom for his mind as he has won for his body.'

(Peter Benenson, The Observer, 28th May 1961)

Think twice before saying to us 'No, don't give up.' You cannot ask us to continue, yet do nothing yourself to help.

The strongest voice on earth belongs to you. Use it. Join us.

I wish to be a member of Amnesty International. I enclose £15 Individual ☐ £20 Family ☐ £6 OAP ☐ £6 Student, Under 18, Claimant ☐ I wish to donate £250 ☐ £100 ☐ £50 ☐ £25 ☐ £10 ☐ Other ☐ I enter my Access, Visa, Mastercard No. ☐☐☐☐☐☐☐☐☐☐☐☐☐☐☐☐ Card expiry date ☐☐☐☐
Signed _____ If paying by credit card you should give the address where you receive your credit card bill.
Mr/Ms. _____
Address _____
_____ Postcode _____
To Amnesty International British Section, FREEPOST, London EC1B 1HE.

AMNESTY INTERNATIONAL

reader should be seduced from the start." In fact, the reader has to contribute as well, Bevins says. "It's like telling a joke. It's not just given to somebody, they have to get it. The audience has to complete the circle."

Bevins advises writers to show people their work and gauge their response. "My team will always tell me when to stop."

Bildsten suggests an alternative to the traditional long copy presentation. "Instead of writing it as a continuous piece, you can give *bursts of information*, bites of copy." He quotes Chiat/Day's Nissan Pathfinder campaign. "You visually tease people to read the copy bites."

SHOULD THE LAST LINE REPRISE THE HEADLINE?

Conventional wisdom says the copy should always end by reprising or reflecting back to the headline. One popular device is to express that reflection with a pun or a wordplay. If we accept the fact that copy should avoid insincerity, isn't this little trick too trite, too precious? Doesn't it smack too much of technique?

"I'm in two minds about it," debates French. "When I started to learn how to write copy, I was an account executive, the lowest form of life next to an amoeba, and I realised, luckily, that I didn't know anything, which was probably what set me aside from most account executives. So I went out and bought all the award books. If you read all the award books then, all the copy ended up with a reflection, in some way, of where it started. The copy made a nice, neat circle, and so I believed that was what you had to do. I copied it, slavishly. For more years than I care to admit, I ground out copy and reprised it at the last minute, so the damn stuff would have some relevance to the headline. It's only been in the last decade or so that I actually realised this was time wasted really, that Joe Consumer didn't give a toss, and the fact you'd led him in with one idea didn't mean you had to leave him with the same idea. In fact," French concludes, "leaving him with an entirely *different* idea suddenly struck me as a far more adventurous and rebellious use of copy. It was like leading them in with 'Come and see the naked lady', and turning them out wanting to buy the Encyclopaedia Britannica."

Abbott is more concerned with the way the argument is rounded off, rather than whether it reflects back to the headline. "There is a right way to conclude an argument," he advises. "It's not necessary to refer back to the headline. Once you had to end with the great pun or the great little twist. I still don't disbelieve in that, although I believe a lot less in puns."

"It depends whether you've formed an argument that's kept in contact with the headline," says Delaney. "There is a kind of formula which is found in lots of advertising copy, and I've followed it myself, which is to wrap with a kind of reference back, because they always did it on Volkswagen. It's like the last chapter of a book; it's got to reflect something of the premise of the book. But if you've moved on from the premise of the headline, and found a different thing to talk about, then just finish naturally."

"I think *every* paragraph should reflect the headline." If it does not, warns Mike Lescarbeau, the ending will stand out very awkwardly if it has to reach all the way back to the headline. The entire ad should be a continual amplification of the premise. "The end line should just be the end of a clever piece of copy."

Bevins believes it is instinctive to wrap with a reflection. "But I don't think it's a rule."

Redman is sceptical. "I think writers only do it to show how clever they are. It looks tricky. If you can do it brilliantly and make people go, wow, you're the best writer in the world, give it a shot. But if you're writing about a serious subject, your cleverness might just ruin the effect you've had on the reader. Sometimes it's best just to end soberly, and sincerely."

"It's conventional, and usually it rounds off the copy quite nicely." However, Sinha does not consider it mandatory. "There are times when it's quite appropriate *not* to do it. There's a very fine murder story by a Hindi writer and the last sentence of it has got nothing to do with the story at all. It's about riding in a car after the event, a description of the way the countryside was passing by the window. And yet, because it has no apparent connection, it gains a kind of surreal power. That apparently irrelevant ending casts the whole story into stark relief. If you study the work of great writers, if you can learn something from them about how to open and end things, you can apply those lessons, even though there is a world of difference between a literary short story and an ad."

While opinions differ, one rule is mandatory. Whether or not it reflects the headline, the last line should ask the reader to *do* something: either to buy the product, or boycott the bullfight, or save water, or send money.

"What makes you get your cheque book out isn't how loud they speak, but how well they speak." Abbott discusses the discipline of public service advertising and why young copywriters should adopt what he calls *rationality with passion.* "I think when you're young, there's more blood coursing through your veins at a faster rate, and you get angry. You get angry in print and you use exclamation marks. But it's like when you meet an angry person. Usually, they don't actually persuade you, whereas somebody who may be passionate about something, but speaks in a quieter voice, and bungs in some reasons, some rationality with passion, is usually more persuasive, and you get your cheque book out. They've said something which either makes you feel guilty, or sad, or happy, or nostalgic, or whimsical, or giving, and you want to bloody *do* this thing. Part of the process of making people respond to cause advertising is not just to tell them there's a problem, but suggest to them that if *they* do something, there's a good chance that the thing could be solved, and that they will have played a part, and that their money isn't going to go into some central administration fund. It isn't just giving for giving's sake, because there's a great deal of cynicism about charities."

SHOULD COPYWRITERS BE INVOLVED IN THE ART DIRECTION?

How their words appear on the page is a fundamental issue for copywriters, stresses Delaney. "I'm usually given a word count to write to, then from a word count I move to a letter count. I usually spend time down on the Mac with the guy putting it together, and we'll move letters and words and everything around to make it all fit. The fitting part of copy is a fundamental part of what you do for a living. Every sentence has to fit. That's what crafting is."

Salmon was once a typographer. "I made it my business to find out what was legible and what wasn't. There is so much rubbish talked." Salmon believes there is an inherent conflict of interest between copywriters and art directors. "Some are more concerned with the copy's appearance as texture or design, rather than with its trans-

WITHOUT A NEW HEART

**SARAH DIES
IN TEN DAYS TIME.**

THAT WAS TEN DAYS AGO.

Thump, thump, Thump, thump, Thump, thump.

Imagine knowing your heart could stop beating at any moment.

Thump, Thump.

Imagine not knowing when.

Thump, thump.

Imagine knowing that.

Thump.

Sarah Moore has never had to.

She's lived with that fear all of her life.

So have her parents, for eight sleepless years.

She's still alive. Just.

Her heart kept beating by a tangled mess of wires and machines, she calls 'The Spider'.

She suffers from congenital heart disease.

She hasn't eaten too much fat.

She's never smoked.

She's never even had a chance to exercise.

She was born with it.

If she's lucky she'll find a donor. About nine children a year do.

If she's not, she'll die.

Just like the thirty-five per cent of heart diseased children who die every year.

Simply waiting.

At the Variety Clubs of Australia, we help 'Sarahs'.

In 1997, we donated over five million dollars to sick, disadvantaged children and their families.

We supply medical equipment for use in the childrens' homes while they await their operations.

If a piece of vital equipment is needed, so the operation can take place, we'll pay for that.

And we even provide transport to both child and parents, before and after the operation.

Such support continues long after the stress of the first incision.

As long as it is needed in fact.

For, if all goes well, recovery usually takes three to four months.

Followed by constant medical supervision to fight off what Sarah's parents shiver at, the 'R' word. Rejection of the new organ.

It's a big ask.

But for years we've answered it.

Sarah, Bobby, Jane, Susan or James.

They're all the same name to us.

Which is why we constantly raise funds.

Variety Club Bashes, McHappy Day and many local initiatives help.

The Gold Heart Appeal helps a lot.

It only costs two dollars to buy a Gold Heart Badge.

It's a silly little thing. But it really does mean a great deal.

If we sell five hundred thousand we can help many more 'Sarahs'.

That's a huge amount. Afterall, Australia's population is only eighteen and a half million strong.

But we never get discouraged when the weak are concerned.

Thump, thump.

This Febuary is Gold Heart month.

Thump, thump.

Please don't forget to buy one.

Thump...

It might just keep

Thu...

a heart

Th...

beating.

Thump, thump Thump, thump. Thump, thump.

VARIETY CLUBS OF AUSTRALIA
the children's charity

*Typography invests a visual dimension to Jay Furby's copy.
Saatchi & Saatchi, Sydney.*

mission as language. Helmut Krone, who was probably the greatest art director of all time, would make sure that the copy was broken up into short paragraphs, with lots of widows, lots of broken lines. It would look like it'd be *nothing* to read it. Whereas George Lois, another great art director, would be inclined to have wide measures and treat the type as a patch of texture."

Writers, and their art directors, should learn basic editorial techniques, not only to keep readers reading, but so their ads slip into the editorial texture. Subheads work like signposts, promising more rewards in the text ahead. Indented paragraphs make the reading experience more familiar; so do justified copy settings. Judicious widows let air into the text. Quotations set in italics signal fresh surprises. Icons help pace the read, segmenting the argument; French once used a chilli and a shamrock, Andrew Clarke used a burning match. In his Metropolitan Police campaign, Neil Godfrey even ran editorial-style introductions in a larger type size across two columns. It is not mandatory to use these techniques, but it makes sense to know what they are.

"Because people aren't predisposed to read advertisements, because they've got no particular reason to want to do so, you've got to catch them." Sinha discusses the benefits of one-sentence paragraphs. "They break up what otherwise might be quite dense text and make it look typographically attractive on the page. They also give a sense that there's a lot to say. By writing like that, you can take a relatively short number of words, two or three hundred, which in editorial terms is nothing, but when you lay them out like that in a nice, large type size with lots of easy, relaxed leading, you can fill a page and it looks like long copy."

Redman has reservations. "I've spent many a day sitting in front of a computer, trying to rewrite lines so they fit into the column, so there are no widows, no big holes left in it. But then you look at some of the best copy that's written, and it's got widows, and it's got holes, and it's not justified, so I think it can be a little bit fussy when you start worrying about that too much because it also can destroy the flow of the ad. I've seen type set ragged, I've seen it set across the entire width of the page rather than broken into two or three columns, and it still works. The *major* priority is to select a typeface and a type size that makes it readable."

HAS COPYWRITING CEASED TO EVOLVE?

One who makes traditions absolute runs the risk of making them obsolete.

And so it is with copywriting. The craft is riddled with convention. Construction is predictable. Tonality rarely changes. Puns, twists, techniques are staples. Experimentation is discouraged.

"We have fallen into a mould," charges Sinha. "What idiot says that because it's a paid for space, it has to be written in a paid for way, with a potato in the mouth, talking down to '*you*'? You can put absolutely *anything* you like in that space. You can write journalism. Neil Godfrey and I did a campaign for the Metropolitan Police. One of those was a skinhead spitting at a policeman. It won a lot of awards, but it wouldn't have, had it been left to one of the people on the jury who is a very famous English art director, well known for being a dumb blonde, who said, this isn't advertising, this is journalism. To which I say, thank you very much, that's the best compliment that you could have paid me, it's far better than that Pencil you gave me."

Unlike art direction, where visuals are being pushed to extreme limits, copywriting has failed to evolve. It is all too easy to blame the audience; to argue that they are a visual not verbal generation. Yet more books are being sold than ever before. More people are reading than ever before. Audiences are better educated, more sophisticated, more inclined to enjoy great copy. The truth is more painful. The genre has largely self-destructed. Over the years, writers have failed to reward the readers.

"One of the reasons the craft has wallowed over the years, why it's dying out, is because copywriters just picked up styles from other copywriters," argues Bevins. "I think they should be inventing their own styles. It's one of the really interesting opportunities in copywriting. There are things we haven't tried, we don't experiment enough, and that's one of the offences of long copy."

Hunt agrees. "Copywriter is probably a good word because you copy other writers when you start. When I came to Asia, I was working with Neil French. He was an influence on me. And it's not just advertising writers. If you're reading Hemingway, you suddenly find your sentences are getting shorter." Hunt believes the hardest thing is *not* to copy. "Anybody can sit down, and with a bit of practice, write like somebody else. It's like singers. A lot of singers can sound like Ella Fitzgerald, but there's still only one Ella Fitzgerald. Hopefully, as the years go by, you grow out of it. You develop your own voice. Your writing starts to sound different, but it's not immediately obvious."

French can view the issue from both a writing and art perspective. "If you look at something that Indra writes, it's classic, and it could have been written by Hemingway or Scott Fitzgerald. If you look at the kind of drivel that I churn out, it's some guy talking, which is why it's full of my own 1950's-learned throwaways. We never grow out of what we learn when we discover language. I'm still Old Bean'ing people like an old fighter pilot, and that in itself has a credibility because they think, well, this guy's for real, nobody would write like that on purpose. The music and nuances of language change with the times, but they don't necessarily outdate themselves. The visual part of life changes from year to year; we don't wear drainpipes, but we still talk very much the same as we did in the 1960s."

If art directors dare to be different, why don't copywriters? As Delaney observes: "Advertising is very conservative, incredibly conservative, given that its role is to represent commerce, and commerce is moving, being pushed by consumers. Nike have done pioneering work with all kinds of communication. They've hired intelligent writers. They've done things which once I didn't like very much, but which I've come to admire them for, after writing for sports products myself. You're talking to a young audience where it's not a matter of writing and sounding cool, because that's really corny, but where you look for new ways to express yourself which aren't the conventional advertising structures or prose structures. It's a matter of adopting certain styles, a certain conviction, looking to other writers, from other areas." But if it feels self-conscious, Delaney warns, it will fail.

Perhaps writers, by nature, are even more conservative than the industry they serve. Could it be that the desire to produce something which is new, different and good is outweighed by the fear it will be new, different and bad?

"This may sound indulgent," cautions Hunt, "but new, different and good, and new, different and bad, it doesn't matter; as long as it's new and different. I try to do a spectrum of work, the classic work, and some esoteric work, just to try to push back the boundaries. I've just written some stuff that I thought was over the top. When I was writing it I thought, I can't present this, it's off the wall, but the client just bought it. An eight hundred-word stream of consciousness ad, for an ice cream."

"I think that genuinely new work wins through in the end," affirms Sinha, "but it seems to be the case that it may not catch on for the first couple of years of its life." The Benson & Hedges surrealistic work, he says, which was very innovative when it first came out, was not taken seriously for awards until it became acceptable to do so.

"If you had a moratorium on awards for ten years," suggests Sinha, "if you said there will be no awards for the next ten years, and said that after those ten years there will be awards for the most new and original things that had emerged, then you might find that within those years all the new ways of expressing ourselves will just come out, because there would no longer be any compulsion to impress juries who are steeped in the old, conventional ways."

9

THE GLOBAL VIEW

The final challenge for cutting edge creativity is the global campaign. Advertising on a global level, we are told, cannot hope to speak with a cutting edge voice.

Usually, the argument is that one culture's creativity cannot be imposed on another. Cutting edge work is far too clever; it would not be understood outside sophisticated Western markets.

Oddly enough, comprehension is not the issue. True cutting edge advertising is all about clarity, simplicity and imagination. Brands which have adopted it have become the new international icons.

As always, resistance to cutting edge work resides in a mix of fear and vested interests.

CAN THE SAME IDEA WORK UNIVERSALLY?

"It strikes me as odd," observes John Hegarty, "that if Hollywood manages to do it, music manages to do it, and Picasso managed to do it, yet advertising can't. And yet advertising is the one industry which is supposed to be able to bring people together. Physical borders are put up by people. The skill of great advertising is to come up with an idea that does cross borders. If you accept all the problems that that has, then you would never produce something great. You should look for the things that *unite* us, not divide us. Then you can create advertising that crosses borders."

Simon Sherwood continues: "If you start out by looking for the differences between people, be they political, ethnic, or religious, you'll find them. They're there. There are differences between the French and the Germans, between the Vietnamese and the Thais, but there are also some similarities. Our view has always been that when it comes to consumer behaviour, when it comes to consumer response to brand messages and what they want out of brands, those similarities are *stronger* than people up until now have believed."

Sherwood asserts that global agency networks have been structured around the differences rather than the similarities. "The way agencies have built their networks reflects the belief that different markets are different from each other. They all argue, oh, but that wouldn't work here. So the conventional agency network is there to recognise the differences, and what we've tried to do is look at it from the other end of the telescope."

At Leo Burnett, Singapore, chairman Linda Locke believes universal ideas will work if the product itself is universal. "If you're selling Levis jeans, you're selling that same American lifestyle. Ads written for the British market have also worked in our market. But when people design ads with the global village in mind, that's when it seems to come unstuck. It's better when you stay *true* to what the brand is all about."

Ian Batey discusses one such brand: Singapore Airlines. "We've been heavily involved in the brand for twenty-five years. It is a brand that is the same wherever it goes around the world. It flies with the same equipment, it flies with the same people, and it provides the same consistent service, so we can run the same ads everywhere. Now one could argue that your appeal varies in different markets and societies; that you are different things to different people. And it's a fair enough argument. But my view is, you are what you are what you are. If what you offer is not something that appeals in certain markets, rather than change your offer, rather than try to change who you are, you just stop going into those markets."

What concerns Batey is the need to remain consistent in a shrinking world. "We all know the world is shrinking by the hour in terms of our communication abilities, it's shrinking by the hour in the views we have on life, the world is shrinking in so many areas that I think you *can* spread the gospel according to what you feel is right globally, and it will work. The people who have found this extremely hard to bite on are the Japanese. Outside of Japan, they didn't really know what to do with their global brands. Therefore, they decided in America to do it the American way, in Europe to do it the European way. As we all know, that has been partly successful; but in the medium to long term, I think you need a *consistent* voice, so that wherever you are, whoever you talk to, there is a consistent personality and a consistent voice. You've just got to make sure that you get it right to begin with."

Write down the ten most important things in your life.

1 _____
2 _____
3 _____
4 _____
5 _____
6 _____
7 _____
8 _____
9 _____
10 _____

We've got friendly neighbours. We've got strong allies. We've got good defence. And, frankly when we look around, there are no visible threats to our country.

But if we're honest, we'd have to ask: What has luck got to do with it?

In truth, nothing.

Because, since 1967, our freedom has been guaranteed by our citizens' armed forces.

Imagine if the people of Kuwait had been asked that question, twenty-four hours before the Iraqi invasion.

Probably, their answers would have been much the same as yours.

But, twenty-four hours later, how many of the things they valued would still have been in existence?

It's a fact of life in today's world, a fact that's been repeated continually in history, that people never really know what they've got until it's gone.

Perhaps, in Singapore, we're luckier.

And today, it's by no means a matter of luck that the Singapore Armed Forces safeguards our economy, our jobs, and our way of life.

The fact we've survived and prospered all these years is the result of people sharing the responsibility for their own independence.

And making an occasional sacrifice.

People who recognise that the effort is worth it. Because if they don't make it, no one else will.

Singapore. We can't take it for granted.

写下你生命中最重要的十件事

1 _____
2 _____
3 _____
4 _____
5 _____
6 _____
7 _____
8 _____
9 _____
10 _____

或许我们是幸运的。我们的邻国友善、盟友强大、国防牢靠；环顾四方，似乎没有什么内忧外患。

但让我们扪心自问：难道这一切都是偶然的吗？

绝对不是。

因为自1967年开始，我们的人民武装部队就一直担起了保家卫国的重任。

今天，新加坡武装部队坚持确保我们经济繁荣、工作稳定、生活安逸，丝毫不容松懈。这，也绝不是偶然的。

而我们之所以能生存到今天，甚至享受骄人成果，靠的不是别的，正是人们坚守国家独立、人民自由的信念与责任。

还有偶尔必须作出的一些牺牲。

因为只有你们，才让每个新加坡人深信：这一切都是值得的。只有你们继续努力，我们才有今天，更有明天。

新加坡，我们岂能掉以轻心。

试想想，倘若科威特人民在伊拉克攻战他们的前二十四小时内有机会回答同样的问题，他们的答案会是什么？

也许跟你的一样。

但是，二十四小时之后，他们所珍视的一切，又仅存多少？

事实上，在不断重演的历史中，人们往往对所拥有的一切不加珍惜；直到有一天失去了，才懊悔企图追回，一切却已经太迟。

When concepts are based on human issues, not wordplays, the same ad – with the same layout – can work in different languages. The argument in the copy was universally logical, and presented with the same tonality in each language.
Euro RSCG Partnership (The Ball Partnership), Singapore.

WHAT SORT OF IDEAS WORK UNIVERSALLY?

Food, shelter and income are basic universal needs. But every year, in newly developing nations, millions of consumers are progressing beyond them. They are acquiring new wealth and new, higher expectations. But when wealth ceases to coexist with sophistication, how should brand values be communicated?

According to conventional wisdom, newly rich consumers in newly developing markets can hardly be expected to understand advertising concepts beyond their personal fields of reference.

In Batey's view, it is horses for courses. "If you go into Bangladesh, with a population of forty to fifty million, and you're advertising high ticket brands like expensive cars or air travel, you always automatically know that all you're talking to is five hundred thousand people. And you don't change your tune to them because they're highly educated, very international, very urbane people. Even with mass consumption brands, you're selling a dream. You can reach out and connect with people, no matter how low on the scale of education or income they might be." Batey distrusts conventional consumer focus groups. "Marketers have to learn to say, let's blow people's minds out. The new Asian is grabbing onto all the things he can get from the West with an extraordinary amount of appetite. He sees them as symbols of success, and he wants to exhibit his success. He's jumping in like Flynn. Whatever we think is successful in the West, I'll bet you by and large will be successful in the East."

Sherwood is convinced that advertising has to lead people. "When advertising just recognises that people aren't very sophisticated, it becomes rather crude and simplistic. Really effective communication is about giving people a point of view. It's not about holding up the mirror, it's about getting in front of people, and leading them. Great advertising should present *a vision that people want to share.*"

"What was outside people's radar in China five years ago, no longer is," asserts Andrew Bell of Leo Burnett, Hong Kong. Major cities like Beijing and Shanghai are increasingly more sophisticated. "Chinese consumers are hungry for information, they're driven to discover new information, especially in the provinces. They read the ads as part of the paper." Bell cites a long copy print campaign which his agency produced for Carlsberg. "The ads were about the brewery, how the beer is made. Consumers read every word. China is a nation of new consumers. They even read every word on the packaging. If something is new to them, they want to know what it will do for them."

Yet conventional global advertising has steered towards the lowest common denominator. The myth has always been that cutting edge work would *not* work.

"Our market has been very exposed to a lot of cutting edge Western stuff," explains David Guerrero of BBDO/Guerrero Ortega, Manila. "MTV gets most of its Asian viewership from the Philippines. People here are much more sophisticated than marketers give them credit for."

Guerrero describes the opportunities for cutting edge print. "There's a touching faith in advertising here that's long gone in the West. Newspapers are incredibly densely packed with copy. One editor of the leading newspaper told me that his job is actually to *expand* the stories his writers send in, rather than cut them down. People read an enormous amount. In fact, this is one of the few markets where English long copy ads will still be read and succeed." The print medium, says Guerrero, is very diverse and free. Newspapers liberally pull down cabinet ministers and celebrities with glee. "Despite the fact that Tagalog is the language of the streets, most people find it a real pain to read. The lingua franca is now a thing called Taglish, which is a mixture of Tagalog and English, and it's a lot easier to get to grips with."

The lowest common denominator has always been the problem in advertising, Hegarty observes. "How do you create something that has integrity to it, and has drama to it, yet talks to as many people as possible? That's what makes the job so challenging and so difficult." Hegarty believes people are able to accept much more than agencies and advertisers give them credit for. "There are always going to be cultural differences, and Heaven forbid, there should always be. But people are able to operate on a global basis as well as on a local basis. It's not a case of giving up one for the sake of the other."

How the Cutting Edge Cuts Through

By seeking similarities in their global target audiences, marketers can liberate themselves from the lowest common denominator in advertising.

Sherwood tells how. "If you go all around the world, which we've done, and talk to 15- to 19-year-olds, Levis' core target market, you'll find that while they're hugely different in some ways, they're remarkably the same in others. And I'm not talking about lowest common denominator similarities. For example, they share the same anxieties about growing up. They're concerned about the same issues. Their relationships with their parents. How they relate with schools, with authority. If you can find messages that touch those areas, you can talk to a much broader group, globally, in ways that you might not have thought possible."

Visual narratives, like the agency's work for Levis, Sherwood suggests, offer the most potent opportunities for cutting edge global print and television.

"When mankind passes down its history from one generation to the next," he explains, "very often words have not been the medium to do it." From simple cave paintings to ornate works of art, the human condition has been preserved visually. "One of the things that we've developed is the visual narrative, coming up with ideas that have a powerful visual presence, that tell a story visually."

"If you want to aim for superior global advertising," says Locke, "it's got to be something on a *human* level, with human insights." Locke describes a telecommunications commercial shot by Leo Burnett, Thailand. "It was about a father on the phone in an airport lounge, enacting a bedtime story for his daughter. When the camera tracked around, you saw he was actually using a videophone. That emotional connection could be shown anywhere on the planet, and every father and mother in the world would get exactly the same thing out of it. Something which *touches the emotions*, something with the use of *humour*, will start to separate you from the competition, and the more rational work will probably become a thing of the past."

Much global advertising is still rational. But, as brand building itself changes, so will communications. Rather than trying to

Ihr guter Stern auf allen

▶ Eine herkömmliche Lawine reicht oft schon aus, um ein herkömmliches Auto aus dem Tritt zu bringen. Für die G-Klasse fängt dann der Spaß erst richtig an: 54 % Schräglage, 60 cm Wassertiefe oder 80 % Steigung – überhaupt kein Problem. Dank ihrem permanenten Allradantrieb und den drei Differentialsperren macht die G-Klasse an den Steilhängen des Piz Palüs ein genauso gutes Bild wie in den Straßenschluchten von Paris. ▶ Der Vorwärtsdrang dieses Mercedes wird eigentlich nur vom serienmäßigen ABS (für Geländefahrten abschaltbar) gestoppt. Der Fahrer selbst entspannt sich während der Fahrt zwischen Leder (Sonderausstattung) und Edelholz. Nicht umsonst haben die Leser von auto motor und sport die G-Klasse mittlerweile schon zum sechsten mal in Folge zum besten Geländewagen überhaupt gewählt.

Mercedes-Benz
Ihr guter Stern auf allen Straßen.

Unser meistgebrauchtes Ersatzteil.

▶ Wie gut, daß wir unser Geld nicht mit dem Verkauf von Ersatzteilen verdienen müssen.

Denn bei der sprichwörtlichen Langlebigkeit von Mercedes-Bauteilen läuft der Absatz von Ersatzteilen erfreulich schleppend. Und wir tun alles, damit er in Zukunft noch schleppender läuft: Während eine Auspuffanlage vor ein paar Jahren üblicherweise alle 40.000 km ausgetauscht werden mußte, ist das Doppelte heute die Norm. Ein Keilriemen muß bei einem Mercedes in der Regel überhaupt nicht mehr erneuert werden. Jedes Jahr lassen sich unsere Ingenieure wieder eine Menge Neues einfallen, was sich erfreulich bremsend auf unsere Ersatzteilverkäufe auswirkt. Schließlich wollen wir nicht der größte Ersatzteillieferant der Welt werden, sondern das beste Auto der Welt bauen. Für dieses Ziel forschen bei uns mehr Ingenieure als bei jedem anderen Automobilhersteller der Welt. Trotz hochmoderner Fertigungsmethoden mit Robotern und Computern kommt bei uns nach guter Mercedes-Tradition immer noch auf 10 Autowerker ein Mann, der nur für die Qualitätskontrolle zuständig ist. ▶ An einem Bauteil sind unsere Bemühungen um Langlebigkeit jedoch spurlos vorbeigegangen: am Mercedes-Stern. Obwohl wir ihn genauso sorgfältig herstellen wie alles, wird er öfter verlangt als jedes andere Ersatzteil. Das sagt viel über die Lebensdauer dieser Ersatzteile, aber auch viel über unser Markenzeichen. Manche hängen an ihm mit solcher Inbrunst, daß sie es als Souvenir mitnehmen. Deshalb mußten wir den Mercedes-Stern allein in den letzten zwei Jahren 1.480.521mal erneuern. Womit er tatsächlich unser meistgebrauchtes Ersatzteil ist. ▶ Gegen die Beliebtheit des Mercedes-Sterns können wir nichts tun. Wir möchten aber alle seine Liebhaber darauf hinweisen, daß man den Stern auch ohne größeren Kraftaufwand bei jedem Mercedes-Händler erwerben kann.

Dort finden Sie auch das, was diesen Stern so berühmt gemacht hat – den Mercedes.

Mercedes-Benz
Ihr guter Stern auf allen Straßen.

One of the world's most recognised brands maintains tonality, encourages flexibility.
Springer & Jacoby, Hamburg.

transmit fixed, dogmatic brand characteristics around the world, brands will offer relationships.

The way those relationships are offered by global advertisers will also change. Flexible control has replaced rigid, centralised control. Mercedes-Benz has long practised this policy; tonality and certain layout specifics are carefully engendered globally, while individual markets generate and share ideas. The brand can speak with consistency and flexibility.

Locke cites the experience of British Airways. "In order for people to understand the new vision at British Airways, they had to have centralised control. When better work came out of the local offices, it was allowed to run." Locke believes that advertisers with organised global marketing structures and a commonly understood vision can gain more by allowing local markets to "explore a bit". However, she adds, "If they're very unstructured, with different advertising saying different things all over the world for a brand which is universally recognised, they'd probably need to go the other way, and put in some tight controls until everyone understood what the brand was all about."

THE UNIVERSAL TRUTHS

Disrupting conventions and achieving creative breakthroughs are possible in every market and in every language. There are no exceptions. Conventions exist everywhere. Creativity exists everywhere. The Greatest Lies are still The Greatest Lies, wherever they are told. The step-by-step path to cutting edge creativity applies universally.

In terms of execution, global cutting edge print should be more visual than verbal.

As Neil French advises: "If you base something on a line, especially an *idiom*, then you are definitely going to lose its power in other parts of the world. It is very difficult for an idiom, which makes so much sense to one country, to be translated or bent in some way to the thoughts of another country. Suddenly, it loses all its power. But if you base your campaign on a thought, or an attitude, then it doesn't necessarily lose its power and its life. Attitude travels, words don't necessarily travel."

Sometimes, simple English words like *Always* or *Just do it* can be used in non-English speaking markets, but, as French warns, there is no guarantee that they will be fully comprehended. Even the simplest English phrases such as *Just do it* cannot be translated literally into languages like Chinese. The abstract use of *it* in English has no word-for-word Chinese equivalent.

Humour probably is the most exportable commodity. When America's One Show staged an exhibition in Taipei, Little Caesar's TV commercials had the predominantly non-English speaking audience in stitches. When the Japanese entered their famous Nissin Cup Noodle *Hungry?* campaign at Cannes, it won the Best of Show. Every year, humorous print and television work from all over the world wins major prizes at the London International Advertising Awards and the New York Festivals.

In their home markets, humorous print ads usually represent the cutting edge.

Singapore Ministry of Health. According to conventional wisdom, Chinese advertising should not be funny. Concepts should be based on superstition, good luck and prosperity. By applying some lateral thinking and humour, a dental hygiene campaign broke that convention.

Chinese readers opened their newspapers to find a rather incongruous message. At first glance, it did not appear to have any connection with dental health, or anything else for that matter. Translated line by line, the large Chinese characters read "14 is 14, 40 is 40, 14 is not 40, 40 is not 14", which is quite meaningless. However, as any student of Mandarin knows, it is a Chinese tongue twister when read aloud:

"Shí sì shì shí sì,

"Sì shí shì sì shí,

"Shí sì bù shi sì shí,

"Sì shí bù shi shí sì."

The tagline in small print reads: *Try saying that without your real teeth.* Chinese readers loved it; it was the only ad in the paper that gave them a chuckle. In the local advertising awards, it won Best of Show for Chinese-language print.

Breaking conventions with Chinese humour. Ketchum Advertising, Singapore.

Simplicity should be another tenet of cutting edge global print, Guido Heffels stresses. "Focus on the major content. You can't throw five different balls at a consumer in every ad." Heffels votes for visual communications. "Why take the long way round?"

Bob Isherwood believes the power of a single-minded idea communicates with people everywhere. "With more local markets accepting global ads, agencies have to acknowledge that it's not good enough to compete with the guy down the street. They actually have to compete with the guys across the ocean. Which means there's only one standard, a world class standard."

If Isherwood is right, what does it take to become a world class communicator?

"If you want to talk to millions of people," says Hegarty, "you must know how to talk to *one* person. And when you can talk to one person, then you can talk to millions of people."

As usual, the client has the last word. New York-based Robert Gibralter, Vice President for Global Advertising at Avon Products, Inc., describes his development of a global cutting edge campaign.

"Avon is over one hundred years old, a universally recognised brand all over the world, with immeasurable latent goodwill. We are looking for cutting edge advertising to launch our new growth trajectory into the next century."

Gibralter's enthusiasm is underscored by what he sees as a "fascinating time in the history of women, global brands and commercial creativity". Avon, he says, is a company which lives and breathes values. Not only do Avon products have an important place in the psyches of consumers, but working for Avon affects the lives of its sales representatives, especially women in such developing economies as Mexico and Poland. Gibralter is tapping local markets to help create a corporate image that is unified yet diverse enough to appeal to consumers all over the world.

Does he favour any particular strategic planning model? "I like the Brand Balance concept, to help understand the rational and emotional sides of a brand, and to lay the architecture for creative minds from around the world." But Gibralter is pragmatic. "Everyone seems to have a proprietary model. However, in the scheme of things, the model is merely a diving board for great creatives to soar, a brush in the hands of painters. None of these models can endure forever. They can post-rationalise great work, and promise to inspire new work. Ultimately," Gibralter observes, "each of the great creative masters has the edge within themselves and actually smash their own models to deliver truly outstanding work."

10

THE CUTTING EDGE AGENDA

W hat does it take to be a cutting edge print communicator? Certainly not comfort. Comfort equals oblivion.

Being in the right agency will help. As Dean Hanson recalls: "I started in a very bad agency, which was a very good thing. You can gain an appreciation. It's healthy to be frustrated a little bit, as long as it doesn't crush you. I know so many people in this business who are really good, but they've never been given a shot."

Having great clients helps. "Love your clients to death" was Michael Ball's edict at The Ball Partnership. When you find clients who appreciate and approve your work, treasure them. Neil French used to send the clients and suits to pick up the awards. Without their trust and support, the work would never have happened.

Having talent helps. New York headhunter Judy Wald says: "Execution can be learned; concepts are what you have to have, cutting edge concepts."

Above all, resilience. John Bevins wrote his first ads in school for surfboards. He is still writing. Antony Redman could not get in to see creative directors with his book; but when he posed as a court official, armed with a fake summons, all doors opened.

Not everyone succeeds. The great English

actor Sir Alec Guinness left advertising after working "in a very minor capacity" for thirty shillings a week.

Those who have succeeded tell us how.

HEROES AND HERESIES

Roy Grace. Roy Grace joined as an art director and left twenty-three years later as executive creative director of DDB Worldwide and chairman of the American company. In that time, he contributed twenty-five spots to "The Hundred Best Commercials of All Time" and four of the seventeen commercials enshrined in the Museum of Modern Art's permanent collection. His Volkswagen *Funeral*, Alka-Seltzer *Spicy Meatball* and American Tourister *Gorilla* are American legends. He is chairman of Grace & Rothschild, New York.

Roy Grace joined the Hall of the Gods, and became one of them. DDB, New York.

"I have been doing this since I was seventeen-years-old. I'm having trouble with the math because I don't want to believe it. Forty-four years, too goddamn long. My first agency job was at Benton & Bowles for a year, then Grey Advertising for a year, and then twenty-three years at Doyle Dane Bernbach. Before I went to DDB, I'd had twenty-five different jobs in advertising, promotion, graphics, publishing, always as an art director. I'd never felt I was able to do the kind of work that really satisfied me until I went to DDB. It was like coming home. I was free to do my best because the agency was so disorganised at the time. You were pretty much an individual who would succeed or fail on your own merits. Very little politics. It was chaotic. I had a supervisor, but I never showed him any work. He was too busy doing his own work, he didn't care. You'd do your work, sometimes you'd show it to Bernbach, sometimes not. It was just a wonderful place to work at the time."

Bill Bernbach's quotes still echo along creative corridors in every country of the world. "I don't know if he ever said anything profound in my presence other than 'I like it' or 'I don't like it'. Before he got into advertising, he wrote speeches for one of the New York governors, that's where his eloquence came from. He was an excellent speaker. He was a man who was dedicated to doing the best, provocative, graphically exciting advertising. He did it not as a necessity, but because of love and enthusiasm. And it was just a delight to work for him. What Bill was, was a great judge of advertising, and a great leader in advertising. He never was a great creator of advertising. The couple of times I worked on ads with Bill, he would come up with the most God awful ideas. He was very, very strong in his opinions and beliefs. He was a tough man. He would say, 'Fire that guy', and make sure he was out on the day it happened. He was not a pussycat."

Bernbach was already a legend when Grace joined. He had already changed the face of American advertising, but did he have any sense of his own importance? "Oh, he sure did. Later on, significantly so. It was a fascinating place to work, not only because of Bernbach. It was the level of talent in all the people around you. It was extraordinary. The level of competition was very strong, good, clean, open and honest. We needed Bernbach as a legend, as an icon.

We not only perpetuated Bernbach's genius, we enlarged it. He was our battering ram against clients, against the threshold of creativity, and we used him in ways I don't think he could have fulfilled because he was only a human being, trying to run a business. We were always disappointed that when a client didn't buy an ad, Bernbach wouldn't resign the account on the spot, because that was *our* legend."

Art director Helmut Krone was another towering figure at DDB. "A very complicated man. I loved Helmut. But after working with Helmut for about fifteen years, I finally understood how Helmut's mind worked. Helmut could always be expected to say and do the opposite of what you'd expect. This was true in his work and in his life. Once you understood that about Helmut, you could deal with him. I don't think there's ever been anyone like him for print art direction. I don't think there'll ever be anyone like him again. A fierce dedication, absolute passion for excellence."

According to legend, Krone invented layouts, including the famous Volkswagen layout. "He didn't invent them, he rediscovered them at the appropriate time. Helmut would say things like, 'Everything I do I stole from somebody'. He was a great researcher. I believe that everything that exists existed at one time or another before in another form. Helmut would unearth forgotten devices at the appropriate time, and I learned that from him. It was okay not to steal, but to be *influenced*. He just had a unique mind and a unique way of working. It was hell for writers to work for him. You could sit in a room with Helmut for days and he'd never say a word. No matter what you said to him, he wouldn't answer you. Why? I think two things. Helmut was a difficult person, and I think Helmut was *trying* to be difficult. He was trying to feed his own legend and reputation, and he did a very good job of doing it. It took a long time for me to get to know Helmut well, to be able to go out to lunch with him and have a normal conversation with him. He was a very shy, introverted, very bright person."

There were other giants, too. "I remember David Abbott. He was in the early, filthy dirty, stinking offices at DDB. You could see then he was talented. He was very young, and he was in a foreign country, and he was in the Hall of the Gods, but he was good and it was a shame he didn't stay. David Abbott in one office, Mary Wells in another, great, great people."

Looking at the industry, Grace is critical of conventional agency structures. "There is too much bureaucratic nonsense. The more a bureaucracy attains size, the more negative its impact becomes. A lot of these large agencies aren't advertising agencies in my sense of the word; they produce commodities. The people doing the work are overly supervised. They get terrible guidance. But I'm a fond believer in the genius of Man, in water always seeking the path of least resistance. Whenever you have something that reaches a level of mediocrity, another way pops up that's better."

Grace talks about sustaining a career in advertising. "There's an internal editorial process that you must have. You must be brutally honest, brutally objective, to maintain a certain level of quality, because it's always easy to say, *this* ad is not important. I wanted so desperately to be good at advertising. I think it was not so much fear of failure, but fear of not succeeding. I wanted to be bulletproof in what I did, so I became the worst critic I could imagine. It's the need to be absolutely certain that you're right and to ask the questions before the client asks them, to ask the questions before the marketplace asks them, about your premises and your execution. I have always believed you work for somebody. The great thing about working for DDB, I had finally found that somebody – Bill Bernbach. Long after Bernbach died, I was still working for him. I would say, what would Bill think? Would Bill like it? Now I'm still working for somebody, and it's taken a long time, and it's me."

David Abbott. "When you see young people coming into advertising now, they all seem to me much better prepared than we were. Most of us arrived via other jobs. I came via university, via running my father's shops when he died. I had no idea about ads or advertising, I'd never really written an ad, whereas now the kids seem absolutely passionate and bright. I had to be in advertising to discover that there was a different sort of advertising over in America. I lapped it up. I knew the body copy by heart. Somehow the rhythms of Volkswagen ads were in my head like a tune, so when I got the chance to write on it, I knew it. I knew how many lines there were in a column, I knew what the cadences were, I knew what the tone of voice was, because I literally read those ads every day. Now the people joining us from art colleges and copywriting courses do the same."

Before joining DDB, David Abbott worked at Mather & Crowther. "The writers and art directors were on different floors. I sat in an office full of copywriters and we fed out our paper which went into the art directors in the studio. I wrote my first commercial, which won an award, but I had nothing to do with it once the script left the copy office."

Neil Godfrey was the first person to be sent to DDB's New York office. Abbott followed. "We were real guinea pigs. Doyle Dane was the first agency where I worked in the art director-writer partnership. I was working with an art director on Volkswagen. I'd done some reasonable jobs, and my first ever Volkswagen TV commercial was for the square-backed sedan, about an eloping couple in the middle of the night, and I thought we were doing pretty well. One Monday morning I came in and my partner said, 'I've been in to see Roy Grace and told him I can't work with you any more, we're not cracking it'. Then Roy called me in and said I'd be going back to London soon, and he moved me on to something else. I thought I'd failed."

Abbott admits that he was permanently terrified. "I had arrived on a Friday and started work on the Monday. My wife was seven and a half months pregnant. It was July, it was stinking hot. We were living in a hotel for seven weeks. At the end of the day I used to get the *New York Times* and try to find a sublet. Whatever impression I gave of being assured, I was trembling inside. I used to cheat. I used to go home at night and stay up until four o'clock writing lines, then I'd go in and pretend they were impromptu. I'd say things like, 'I don't know what you think of this, maybe it just needs a bit more work', and I'd been polishing it for about four hours. Until I got one ad through, it was nerve-racking. But I was absolutely thrilled to be there, totally overawed. There were thirteen hundred people, seventy creative teams, at the office party in Christmas, 1966. All the corridors were full of heroes. They asked me to stay on. I was tempted, but I wanted to get back to England. I had by that time three little children."

Despite an outwardly gentle manner, Abbott recognises a restless, competitive streak. "If we're doing a pitch, I still tense up. I still don't want to get beaten. I think we are now quite a hard agency to beat. I think we've got used to winning our fair share of things. There's a kind of history of standards which you don't want to betray, which we do betray of course, I betray them all the time, but by and large you don't want to stop trying. This is a very dissatisfied agency, and I think that stems from a part of me. I'm much more conscious of all the things that *aren't* right than the things that are right. It's the things we *don't* do well that preoccupy me more than the things that we do do well."

If Abbott's first experience working with an art director had left him unnerved, a few years later he would commence the longest creative partnership in British advertising. "When we started this company, I had never worked with Ron Brown. He was at Young & Rubicam and I rang him up. He'd worked at Doyle Dane, but after I'd left. We had a chat, and I didn't know whether we'd get on or not, but anyway he agreed to come. And he's been prepared over the years to work my way of working, which is quite difficult for an art director because I've been doing lots of other things as well as writing ads. We don't sit down all day across the table with each other. It's grabbing moments, or it's me coming in, I'm afraid, with bits of paper and saying, 'Do you think this will work, Ron?' And if he'd been a different personality, he might have said, this is not a true partnership. In fact, it *has* been a true partnership because he's made an enormous contribution, and he's written lines, and he's just grown up about what I've had to do, and he's been prepared to put up with it. I wouldn't have been able to do what I've done without an art director like Ron. I suspect I probably would have stopped doing ads. My aim has always been to go on doing ads, so it was luck that we could work together and there was no jealousy or resentment. He's a very even-tempered man. He's also a great craftsman, which I've always admired, and I don't think I could work with an art director who wasn't meticulous, and didn't care a lot about the details, and be quietly passionate about the craft."

Neil Godfrey. "I came straight out of the Royal College of Art as a painter, so I really was very naive in the ways of how advertising worked. I saw the page as the equivalent of a painting, as a space to put shapes and textures in. I'd been working for a few months at Doyle Dane in London, then they sent me to New York. The people who I thought would be the stroppiest and strongest were exactly the opposite."

Godfrey's immediate supervisor was Krone. "Everyone was in awe of Helmut because of his great Volkswagen and Avis campaigns. I was just amazed whenever he asked my opinions on things. I was surprised that Helmut could be a bit unsure. He'd been working on one particular job for a year. He'd tied a piece of washing up soap to a scented toilet soap with string, and by strapping them together he was saying the new product had the right combination of both of them. The agency had just hired a new, young account guy. He knocked on the door and went into Helmut's office which was very Bauhaus, severe white with tubular furniture. He said, 'Look, Mr. Krone, you've been working on this for long enough now, the client has been asking for this job, so can I give him a date?' Apparently Helmut stood up, put on his jacket, and went home. A week later he called up and said, 'Is that man out of my office yet? If he is, I'll come back'."

Godfrey describes how DDB created an inspiring atmosphere. "Instead of people pitting themselves against each other, and being rather petty and jealous, everybody was interested in what the other person was doing, just to see the great ideas that were coming out, and to want to do better through admiration rather than through jealousy. I remember walking past Roy Grace's office one day and he showed me this Volkswagen ad he'd done. It was a pencil line drawing of the top of a Volkswagen and the caption was *How much longer can we hand you this line?* And he said to me, 'I'm not sure about it, is it too simple?' I said I thought it was terrific, and he said, 'Okay, well maybe I'll think about doing it'. And it turned out to be one of the classic Volkswagen ads."

Client relationships were different, too. "What was particularly great about DDB and Colletts, in the 1960s and 1970s, was that clients couldn't wait to meet the creative people. I went out to dinner many times with clients and their wives. We used to do it because they thought we were geniuses. There's a slightly different attitude now. The clients all have Camcorders and think that they're movie producers. That film that used to be a bit of magic, you can't give them that any more. But there's still an opportunity in print to work the magic for them."

Tim Delaney. "I'm fifty-two and I started in the mailroom of an agency just off Park Lane when I was fifteen. I've been writing ads for thirty-four of those years and it's weird in the sense that I still really enjoy it. It's really strange."

Tim Delaney travels light. "I don't keep any of my ads at all. I don't regard them once I've done them. I don't give them any value. I don't have a reel, I've never had one. I don't see it as something which is about the best or worst, I kind of see it as a job, but it's a job I really enjoy. I like the work other people do as well. I don't see the work as some kind of testimony to me, or some kind of legacy to other people. I don't see it in any other terms than what's in *front* of me, and maybe that's why I enjoy it."

Delancy still signs off every brief in the agency. He questions them if they aren't right. He expects his people to be demanding of themselves. "Creative people often don't work hard enough. They go to lunch, whinge, and go home. They should be more prolific. Our agency did forty-five television commercials last year. If people want to write, they have to write and write and write. Creative people should take greater interest in not just the business of advertising, but the business of *business*. Go to clients, to boardrooms, learn the culture of clients, earn the respect of clients, not just in the advertising sense, but the business sense. It won't turn you into a suit, or make you less creative; it will make you a more perceptive, better connected creative."

How can creative people sustain a career in advertising? "It's not a lot different from sustaining a career in other areas. Fundamentally, you've got to *like* what you do, and if you're lucky in life, you can like what you do. I suspect that only about 5 percent of the people employed like what they do. So if you like advertising, that will sustain you. If you're in an area of advertising that you like, and one of the things about copywriting or creating ads is that it's very stimulating, you are constantly finding means of expression, that will sustain you. If you're good at it, then you'll get people to buy your ads, because they'll like them and they'll run them, and that will sustain you. If you're bad at it, they won't, and that'll make you very unhappy and then you should leave. If you've got a talent, you should find a place where that talent is appreciated by the agency, and *used* by the agency, and appreciated and used by their clients. That will make you happy because it means you're not doing something which is completely futile, so that should sustain you. Finally, you can be sustained by the fact that that is a relatively rare thing, and therefore you'll get paid handsomely, and therefore that will give you a lifestyle which you may not get if you become a milkman."

Neil French. "I never had any training to do anything except be a rent collector and a bullfighter. I never had any training to be a bouncer. I never had any training to be an advertising man. I left school when I was fifteen, I had no 'A' level English. I didn't go to art school, didn't go to art college, don't know nothing about nothing. But, I understand people. I understand people *very well*."

As a student of human nature, Neil French qualified with honours. "In a long and varied career, I've mixed with so many different types of people of different educational levels, and of different financial levels, that I'm able to actually put myself in the position of talking to one of those people every time I do an ad. I can almost picture the person I'm talking to. And I find that an ad is a bit like a conversation, or telling a joke, if you like, or telling a story. You *vary* the way you tell it according to the audience, and it's those little variations that make the thing work for that particular audience. I learned those things especially when I was a singer; you'd look out at the audience, and you'd see the blue rinses, and you'd do a completely different delivery than you would if the place was full of football supporters. Although the material would be the same, the way you delivered it would vary. And so that's the same with an advertising campaign. I try and look at who I'm talking to, like the poor bald men; of course, in their case, I not only know how they think, I am one."

One group of people, French admits, have escaped his radar. "I think less and less these days I'm capable of talking to young people, because I don't have any kids, and I don't know anybody much under twenty-five, so I probably wouldn't be any good these days, selling young stuff. I'm not sure I ever was. I think I probably missed out being young at some point. I think I went straight from being a schoolboy to being an adult."

French reflects on young creative people entering advertising. "Knowledge of the consumer is the most important thing, and it's one of the sad things that you see these days. Kids come out of art college with a lot of knowledge about computers, and *no* knowledge at all about the people to whom they're going to be speaking."

Gary Goldsmith. "I started off in the business as a writer. I couldn't think visually at first. It seemed like every ad in my first student book was a big line and a little product shot. I worked in a not-very-good agency, and all the art directors were ruining my ads, not that they were that good to begin with, so I decided to become an art director. For me, it was really a process of having to *force* myself to think visually. Even to this day I have to force myself to think outside of words. I think a lot of us tend to think in terms of words. Actually, it's much harder to think visually, at least for me it is."

Over the years, Gary Goldsmith has developed a theory that people should do work outside what their tendency is. "I tend not to use people in my advertising. And I thought about why I never did, and it's because of the ads I've seen that I have this predisposition that they're all corny and hokey and contrived, and the people are all very artificial looking and not like anybody we ever knew. I always resented the idea of an ad trying to tell me what I looked like, or what I should be dressed like, or how I should behave. A client once asked me, 'How come there are no people in this ad? We need people in there, so people can relate to them', and I told him, well, there *is* somebody in the ad, and the somebody in the ad is the reader, *that's* the person that's in the ad, because we're creating a situation where they're putting themselves in it, as opposed to having to see a mirror image of something that's not them. But I have forced myself a few times to use people. I've said, how can I use people in a campaign that's not like the conventional way? Sometimes you have to do an exercise with yourself where you say, okay, these are my tendencies, these are the things I typically do, and I'm not allowed to do any of those things on this assignment, I'm going to have to go against those things. If you generally use small, tasteful type, then use big, ugly type, and somehow make that work. And that's what I did with myself about using people. I'm going to do some campaigns with people if it's the last thing I do, and do it in a way that's my *own* way. And it was good because it forced me to do something I wouldn't have done, and it forced me to deal with a different side of solving the problem."

Gary Goldsmith, working outside his tendency. Lowe & Partners, New York.

Goldsmith believes young people joining the business often lack resilience. "The schools are preparing them in such a way that they're actually *more* prepared than we were when we got out of school. They're doing ads that look like finished ads when they're in school. Their expectations are very high. They think they're going to get out, get a job, and everything is going to proceed very smoothly. A very talented kid came to see me with a nice portfolio, came out of art school, showed me his work, and his main concern was that he might go to an agency that would try to change his style. I asked him how many campaigns he'd produced, real campaigns, real ads, and he said, 'None'. And I said, well, you don't have a style then. After you've been in the business ten years, and you have twenty campaigns, then you'll have a style. You have to go into it open minded, try to learn from everyone you can, do work without thinking about your style, just think about solving each problem and let your style become what it will become. But if you're twenty-two, and your style is set after only working on your book, you've got the wrong attitude. My advice would be, *be patient and impatient at the same time*. Always be fighting to try to do more work, good work, but cut yourself a break. Don't expect that you're going to get out and be the world's best writer or art director in the first year. Give yourself a chance. Be resilient. People get discouraged way too early now. Just go in every day and try to do something good."

Bob Isherwood. "I left school at thirteen and a half, and I was an apprentice motor mechanic for two years. I was the worst motor mechanic that Ford had ever seen. I didn't have many skills, except I used to like to draw. I knew someone who had just finished art school and become an animator. He said I should go to art school, too, and I was so desperate to get out of being a motor mechanic, I thought, yeah, that's what I should do, and I got into art school, and that changed my life completely. After four years in art school I worked for a year, then I left Australia. I went straight to London, and I just looked up anything that had advertising in its name in the phone book. The first place didn't give me a job, but the next one did, Advertising Design Associates, and I worked there doing pharmaceutical advertising design. But my first real job in advertising was at Young & Rubicam. I think I had work in the second volume of D&AD, but that was as a graphic designer."

Bob Isherwood, Saatchi & Saatchi's worldwide creative director, is actually based in the Sydney office. "We feel very much that a company doesn't have boundaries, and that includes geographical ones. I have always worked on the basis of getting people who are better than you are, regardless of where they happen to be. Don't just get someone because they happen to be down the street and easy."

David Droga. Recruited by Isherwood, David Droga was twenty-seven when he was appointed Saatchi & Saatchi's regional creative director for Asia. Within a matter of months, his Singapore office was named International Agency of the Year by *Advertising Age*. He is now executive creative director of the London agency.

"I don't think talent itself is the key to success. It's a competitive nature, having a real drive, wanting to compete on a global basis, not just with the agency down the road. I inherited a competitive spirit, I'm the youngest of five boys. My four older brothers all got scholarships to Cambridge. The way I'd describe myself is that I have an immense ego, but also immense insecurities, and that's the combination that drives you along. When I sit down to do an ad, I'm always thinking, how can I do something great? And in the back of my mind, I'm thinking, but what if you *don't*? That's what pushes you to work the midnight hours, trying to surprise yourself. I've always been a selfish writer, I've always wanted to do the ideas myself."

As a loner, Droga is wary of the traditional creative pairing. "It is a dangerous scenario. Nothing can outdo a great team, but sometimes similar personalities clash, sometimes somebody won't want to voice an opinion because it might sound foolish. If you're stuck with the wrong partner, it can be an awkward situation, especially if the teaming has been thrust on you. At OMON, the writers did the ideas, the art directors art directed them. When I came to Singapore, I experimented with the teams, I shuffled them. We do what Fallons do, different people work with each other, so they experience new people, new things."

Droga keeps fresh by setting his goals higher and higher. "I had a lot of goals when I first got into the business at OMON. I wanted to be the best at the agency, then I wanted to be the best in Sydney, then the best in Australia. Then I looked for a bigger canvas, which is Asia. There are some agencies that have done good stuff in Asia, but it's still a new market, relatively unexplored. And I keep surrounding myself with new, young people, to keep the pressure on myself, having people push you as much as you push them. You've got to be cynical about advertising, but you've also got to respect it. It's also not taking yourself too seriously. Some people just want to get to the top because they're very competitive."

Can young creatives expect resistance from older, more entrenched creatives? "To a degree. But I was sheltered at OMON because we were all young, all arrogant, going against the grain. There are certain older people who believe you have to pay your dues and have the battle scars to warrant certain positions. My argument is, well, bringing freshness and naivety to the table is where you get new perspectives. I don't think you should ever carry too much luggage with you."

Nick Cohen. "I think that it's really important to understand that everyone is only as good as the *next* bit of work they're going to do. Our business is one where people do some good work, and then they feed and live off that for the rest of their careers. If you look inside yourself, you realise it's a young person's business. What you did a few years ago is irrelevant to what's going on now. If you really are good and you want to prove yourself, you have to do something that's vital now. Maybe if people shelved their egos and had a bit more humility."

Tom Lichtenheld. "You've got to find what you love and let it kill you. It's tough, getting tougher, and schools are turning out students who are ready to start doing ads. I couldn't get into this business now with the book I had when I started."

Tom Lichtenheld values humility. "Judging an award show is very humbling. It makes you feel most of your own work is mediocre. It makes you think, I could have done a better idea, I could have executed it better, I could have stuck to my guns better, I wasn't tenacious enough to talk to the print production person about that gutter space, there were too many gaps between those words."

Norman Alcuri. "You should break thinking rules, not art direction rules. Art direction is about communicating, because we're still salesmen, and also about appetite appeal. There's a German saying, the eye eats along. I think you should absorb everything around you: movies, CD covers, editorial designs. I still look through award books, even though those guys have always had more time and money than me, and they're better."

Norman Alcuri shares one of his golden rules. "It took me a long time to learn this, and somebody should have told me, years ago, but if ever you have any doubt about what typeface to use, or what styling to use, just look at the pack or the logo. Make a link between the ad and the pack. Use a background colour, or a border colour, that matches the colour of the pack or the logo. Somebody has spent thousands on designing that pack, and the logo, which has a typeface attached to it."

Bruce Bildsten. Bruce Bildsten has spent most of his career at Fallon McElligott since graduating from college in 1981. An award-winning copywriter, he is now a creative director. "You have to make sure you're not judging work on what clients think is good, especially when you have as much contact with clients as I do. You have to look at things from their perspective, but be careful not to do that too much. I'm around them so much, the biggest trap I can get into is to start to think like them, or become a filter for them internally."

Bildsten seeks his inspiration from design. "I like to look at design annuals instead of ad annuals, to be quite honest, because I like to think more visually. I find them more inspiring and less of a trap than looking in ad annuals. It's also more helpful to look at foreign work than American work."

What sacrifices will lie ahead for cutting edge communicators? "*Sacrifices* is a good word. A lot of young people go to schools where they think they've learned everything. They think it will be easy, that opportunities will be handed to them on a platter. The number of opportunities available to people here at Fallon now, versus when I started, is just astronomical. Everyone has got opportunities with huge TV budgets within a few months of landing here, and they can be right out of school. The most successful people here stay humble and they really work hard. You can get so sucked up into the world of production, for example, and be so conscious of the hotel you're staying at, the places you're going, and the directors you're working with, in the end you can just end up with nothing. Generally, and maybe this is just the old curmudgeon in me, I don't think people are as willing to work as hard as we were, not willing to go through as much as we were. They don't generate as many ideas to begin with. There's the belief that it's easier than it really is. There are art directors now who cannot draw a thing, period. It worries me because when they come to me as a creative director, I can't even begin to judge their ideas unless they take them another step further. Sometimes the ideas might be so utterly brilliant that I can overlook that, but generally there's so much that's missing, and sometimes they may get it right in the end, but sometimes they may not."

Indra Sinha. "I think that it's tempting if you do one sort of thing very well, to always do it. I'm accused a lot of writing extremely long copy ads when maybe it's not necessary. I believe in the power of the word, and therefore I actually want to write. It's not a conscious decision that I have done successful ads for one campaign, therefore I'll do it the same way again. Probably, I'm best known in the industry for doing things like the Metropolitan Police ads, and Amnesty ads, but actually they're not the things that are closest to my heart. The closest ads to my heart were some silly little ads I wrote for an Indian bookshop, which were written in the first person in an Indian dialect, full of things like, 'He speaks English like a native'. They were character sketches of my friend who ran the bookshop. We used to do six or eight a year. They were very scurrilous, they made fun of people. One year, I put three of them into D&AD, and they all got in."

Bill Oberlander. "My advice to art directors is to go back to school and study design. There are too many poseurs, too many fake art directors in this business, too many copywriters with a set of markers or some Mac skills who don't understand how graphic tension on a page can really change the way people feel. I'm training designers to be art directors, and I'm having art directors think more like designers."

Bill Oberlander's advice to creative directors and agency heads? "Recruit younger people who keep you young. Recruit the right kind of clients who keep you believing that it's possible. If you recruit the wrong clients time and time again, you're going to get more cynical, more bitter, more jaded, and more dispirited, and then you just give up."

How Others See Us

Editor Anthony Vagnoni of *Advertising Age* writes about nothing else but people who make ads. "The best people do not, repeat, do not take themselves too seriously. They have healthy, grounded egos. They live in the real world. They don't live and breathe advertising."

Vagnoni believes too many young creatives are so obsessed by advertising that they have become desensitised to life. "The best work doesn't breed off itself. It's fresh. You've got to find insights in the real world and apply them to products. You've got to have a healthy sense of yourself; you're not finding a cure for cancer, you're not Francis Ford Coppola." He suggests two role models. "Jeff Goodby, because he's not from the self-referential school of advertising. Cliff Freeman, because he has had consistent success throughout his career, not just one great campaign."

In London, Gee Thomson at *Shots* thinks advertising must move forward rapidly. "People see the machinery of advertising too easily. It's been very clumsy in the past. Images like sex and fast cars have worn thin. They are too blatant and not acceptable to the new, young people of today. Advertising needs to come from unexpected angles."

Thomson believes the people who stand out in advertising are usually very individual. "Advertising has absorbed difficult people, off the wall people. Above all else, they are truly original thinkers. They have themes in their heads which they pursue."

Michael Lynch, publisher of Australia's *Campaign Brief*, identifies the qualities of great advertising people: "If you take a local example, Lionel Hunt and the Campaign Palace, it's about not compromising. Not taking every client there is. Putting everything into your ads and letting the money come later. Talent helps, which is found early in life; a hack usually never becomes anything more."

Lynch says doing ads self-sustains. "The great names still do ads. It's like doing it for the first time, every time. If I was young and wanted a career in advertising, I'd beg, I'd starve, until I got into the right agency. Don't do the middle stuff, the drivel." Lynch cites Droga as a role model. "He's only been in advertising ten years. He was only at OMON for the ads, not the money. Now he's let loose at Saatchi's." Lynch advocates going to Cannes. "Not for a job, but to see the tricks, pick the trends." Great suits, Lynch believes, learn what great ads are by reading creative books, watching *Shots* reels, developing instincts for breakthrough ideas.

At Hong Kong's *Media & Marketing*, publisher Ken McKenzie argues that the most successful creative people have inquiring minds, a down-to-earth manner that unlocks doors everywhere, and the quiet confidence to stand by the right idea. "They realise that every task, no matter how mundane or distasteful, is a building block in their career. They don't go round saying how passionate they are, they don't have begrudging scowls, and they don't trash hotel rooms."

McKenzie calls for the return of the creative superstar. "The new messiahs are sorely needed, because there is an industry waiting to follow. They'll not only need strong personal intuition and creative mystique, but leadership abilities and the techniques of trial lawyers to bring clients into line."

OVER TO YOU

Hundreds of great writers, art directors, account service people, planners and clients have defined the cutting edge for you. Now the industry needs your contribution.

If success comes easily, in a "baptism of caresses" as Will Self called it, be wary. Be wary of imitating your own success.

Lee Strasberg's advice for actors holds true for creative people everywhere: "Neither life nor talent stands still. Standing still leads inevitably to retrogression. The actor does things that he has done before, perhaps more easily, but without the electrifying spark that usually arises in young people when they do their first productions. We then see the terrifying struggle that almost always begins with success, when the actor begins to repeat and to imitate, if not someone else, what is even worse, to imitate himself and thus pay a terrible price in his most important commodity, the very thing that singled him out at the beginning, his talent."

If creativity is a destructive process, if it means tearing down what has gone before and rebuilding afresh, what better place to start than with ourselves?

BIBLIOGRAPHY

Bond, Jonathan, and Richard Kirshenbaum. *Under the Radar: Talking to Today's Cynical Consumer*. John Wiley & Sons, 1998.

Dru, Jean-Marie. *Disruption: Overturning Conventions and Shaking Up the Marketplace*. John Wiley & Sons, 1996.

Ehrenberg, A. S. C. Repetitive Advertising and the Consumer. *Journal of Advertising Research*, April 1979.

Festinger, Leon. *A Theory of Cognitive Dissonance*. Row, Peterson, 1957.

Hall, Oakley. *The Art & Craft of Novel Writing*. Story Press, 1989.

Krugman, Herbert E. The Impact of Television Advertising: Learning without Involvement. *Public Opinion Quarterly*, Vol. XXIX, No. 3, Fall 1965.

Mackay, Hugh. *The Good Listener*. Pan Macmillan Australia, 1998.

INDEX

ABOUT THE AUTHOR

Jim Aitchison, an Australian, was former creative director of
Singapore's legendary Ball Partnership and Batey Ads. He has won
hundreds of awards (many for Chinese ads which he wrote), and
judged some of the world's top shows. After twenty years in
advertising, he is now an author and divides his time between
Singapore and New York.